Biblical Figures in the Islamic Faith

Biblical Figures in the Islamic Faith

STEPHEN J. VICCHIO

WIPF & STOCK · Eugene, Oregon

BIBLICAL FIGURES IN THE ISLAMIC FAITH

Wipf & Stock
A Division of Wipf and Stock Publishers
199 W. 8th Ave., Suite 3
Eugene, OR 97401

www.wipfandstock.com

ISBN 13: 978-1-55635-304-8

Cataloging-in-publication data:

Vicchio, Stephen.
    Biblical figures in the Islam faith / Stephen J. Vicchio; with a foreword by Bruce C. Birch.

    xxxii + 266 p. ; 23 cm. Includes glossary and indexes.

    ISBN 13: 978-1-55635-304-8

    1. Bible—Islamic interpretations. 2. Koran—Relation to the Bible. 3. Jesus—Islamic interpretations. I. Birch, Bruce C. II. Title.

BP134.B4 V53 2008

Manufactured in the U.S.A.

For Tom and Mary Lee,
with gratitude for all they have done in the past six years
in helping to keep my family together.
And for Reed who is loved and sorely missed.

Contents

Foreword

Few would question the need for greater understanding between Christians and Muslims in the troubled times we are now experiencing. This did not begin with the tragic destruction of the World Trade Center towers in New York. Relationships between predominantly Muslim countries and the western nations have been deteriorating over a period of decades. It has broken out in overt conflicts and has expressed itself in a rise of terrorist activities directed against European and American targets. Even Russia fought a protracted and largely futile war in Afghanistan, and at this writing the United States and its allies are mired in a war in Iraq with no end in sight.

The public discussion of these events has been filled with misconceptions and half truths. In general, Americans have discovered that we know very little about Islam or the world of its adherents. Events are reported and discussed as matters of politics and policy, and Islam is often treated, not as one of the great and enduring world religions, but as a political ideology. Muslims living in the United States are treated with suspicion, as if a religious commitment automatically carries with it a set of loyalties to other nations and their interests. We do not understand the varieties of religious traditions within the larger frame of Islam, e.g., Sunni, Shi'ite, Sufi, Wahabi. The average American looks at the world of Islam as utterly alien and possessed of little in common with Christians and Jews.

It is into this context of ignorance, misunderstanding, and suspicion that Stephen Vicchio offers his book. His goal is modest. He wants us to know that Islam's scripture, the Qur'an, and the revered writings of Muslim teachers and scholars who came after the time of Muhammed, contain numerous references to the important biblical figures of Christian and Jewish scripture. Indeed, these men and women are also regarded as holy and revered figures in Islam. Vicchio believes that by understanding how much Muslim tradition overlaps with the biblical traditions of Judaism

ix

and Christianity, we might begin to expose a wedge of common ground on which understanding and respect might begin to be built.

Vicchio begins with a brief introduction sketching some fundamentals of Muslim history and culture, and clearing away some common misconceptions. His main goal, however, is to give us a detailed look at the treatment of Biblical figures in the literature of Islam. The broad range of this research and presentation is startling. He begins with the Qur'an but continues on to the collected writing of the roughly two hundred years after Muhammed (Hadith, Sunnah, Akhbar) that came to be regarded as authoritative in the various traditions that developed in early Islam. He then traces the interest in these biblical figures on into modern treatments of the role of these figures in Muslim scholarship and how these figures are understood and used in the traditions of Islam yet today.

The result of Vicchio's scholarship and presentation will be a revelation to most Christian and Jewish readers. It has become somewhat commonplace to refer to Judaism, Christianity, and Islam as the three Abrahamic faiths. This shows a beginning awareness of the beginnings of each of these three great religions, birthed in the Middle East, in a common ancestor, Abraham (Ibrahim). Abraham's faithfulness and his closeness to God make his a revered figure in each of these three great faiths, and for each Abraham is a beginning of the story of the particular relationship between God and the people of each of these religions.

The surprise to most readers will be the extent of common ancestors. Virtually all of the major figures of Jewish and Christian scripture make an appearance in Muslim holy writings. Moses (Musa) is a major figure in the Qur'an and later Muslim writings as he is in the Torah of Jewish/ Christian scripture. But many lesser figures are given prominent attention in the sacred literature of Islam: Adam, Enoch (Idris), Noah (Nuh), Lot (Lut), Haggar (Hejirah), Ishmael (Ismail), Isaac (Ishaq), Jacob (Yaqub), Joseph (Yusuf), and Job (Ayyub). Vicchio treats each of these figures from the Hebrew Bible as they appear in Islam and the list could be longer. From the New Testament, he gives major treatment to the role and perception of Jesus (Isa) in Muslim tradition. Mary (Maryam), the mother of Jesus, is also a revered figure in the Qur'an and later Muslim tradition. Also given treatment are John the Baptist (Yah Yah), Joseph, Satan (Iblis), and the Dajjal (the Anti-Christ).

Vicchio's detailed treatment of these biblical figures as they appear and play their role in the sacred traditions of Islam opens up a world that westerners barely know exists. In the present situation of tensions and hostilities with parts of the Islamic world, it is easier to believe that Muslims are entirely "other," alien and without common meeting ground as religious people. Vicchio will not let us rest with that misconception. The Qur'an and early Islam drew heavily on Jewish and Christian traditions and practices.

One of the delights to be discovered in this volume is the richness of Muslim treatment of these Biblical figures. There are many stories and traditions related to these beloved characters that are not in the pages of Jewish and Christian Bibles. In Jewish tradition there will be a kind of familiarity with such material, for the additional stories and insights into Biblical characters in the Qur'an and early Muslim texts is very much like the traditions of midrash in Judaism. The teachers of the rabbis and the collected texts of midrashim and Talmud contain materials that expand on the stories of Biblical characters in a very similar fashion to what we find in the Qur'an and the Hadith. Christians, particularly Protestants, have been less exposed to these fuller tellings of Biblical stories or additional traditions about Biblical characters. They will be more likely to see such traditions as undermining the authority of scripture text. But an effort to open the liveliness of the traditions of our Biblical ancestors will be amply rewarded for the nature of the stories found in the Qur'an and other Muslim writings is reverential and focused on enhancing the significance of these figures for the devout life.

Although this volume will surely expand the sense of common ground we share with Islam, it will also expose some genuine differences. What is needed in true interfaith dialogue and understanding is not simply a search for points in common but a knowledge and appreciation of the places we genuinely differ, even in our appropriation of traditions about the same Biblical ancestor. The places in the volume where Vicchio helps us to see these differences are many, but we can illustrate this exposure of divergence with two illustrates examples.

In a divergence that will be especially important to Jews, but significant as well to Christians, Abraham comes close to sacrificing his son Ishmael out of obedience to God and not his son Isaac. Ishmael is the son through whom Muhammed and Arab peoples in general trace their ancestry to Abraham. Although the Qur'an itself is somewhat vague on the identity of the son, early Muslim tradition is very clear that Ishmael was the son in question and much is made of this. This reading, of course, totally alters the role of Isaac in the story and this reading of the story emerges as an important difference that must be acknowledged in any interfaith dialogue.

For Christians, of course, the Muslim treatment of Jesus is the place of great divergence. Although Jesus is a greatly honored prophet with a central role to play in Muslim tradition, he is not considered the son of God or in any way divine. Perhaps even more troubling for Christians is the dominant view in Islam that Jesus was not actually crucified, but some other person died in his place. Vicchio treats the various theories put forward to explain his, but Muslim views on this subject will remain a stumbling block for many in interfaith conversation. Nevertheless, understanding of where traditions share common stories and where those stories diverge are extremely important for religious traditions to develop understanding and respect one for the other.

What Vicchio has done is to provide us with an invaluable resource for understanding the extent of our common ground with Islam while also making us aware of areas of genuine difference. As I was writing this preface a concrete example of the important doors this could open came to my attention.

Frank Burch Brown, a faculty member in the arts and world religions at Christian Theological Seminary in Indianapolis, was asked in 2005 to compose a choral piece for performance by the Indianapolis Symphonic Choir for its annual Festival of Carols. The repertoire of the Symphonic Choir had often included Jewish choral words, and its conductor had wanted to extend the chorus group's range to include more segments of the community. Brown knew the Muslim tradition revered Mary as the mother of Jesus and included many emotions of her, both in the Qur'an and later writings. He began to wonder if he could find a text that expressed a common affirmation of Mary and her honored role as the expectant mother of a holy child that both Christians and Muslims could affirm. He found that text in a saying from Abu al-Qasim ibn 'Asakir (1175 CE) which expresses Mary's experience of hearing Jesus praise God from within her womb.

> Mary said, "In the days I was pregnant with Jesus, whenever there was someone in my house speaking with me, I would hear Jesus praising God inside me. Whenever I was alone and there was no

one with me, I would converse with him and he with me, while he was still in my womb.[1]

Brown's musical setting for this text, borrowing on idioms from Middle Eastern and Andalusian music, was performed by the Indianapolis Symphonic Choir on December 3, 2005, and has been released as a recording in October 2006.[2] One of the reported results has been a remarkable expression of appreciation from the Muslim community and openings for interfaith conversations that might not have been possible otherwise. It was a discovery of common ground.

Readers of this volume by Stephen Vicchio will find such common ground here. Its assumption is not that Judaism, Christianity, and Islam are somehow the same, but that in spite of genuine differences that is a shared inheritance and a mutual influencing that can provide opportunity for widened respect and deeper understanding in a world that desperately needs a reaffirmation of common humanity in the midst of our differences.

—Bruce C. Birch, Dean
Wesley Theological Seminary
Washington, DC

1. Tarif Khalidi, editor and translator, *The Muslim Jesus: Sayings and Stories in Islamic Literature* (Cambridge, Mass: Harvard University Press, 2001) 195.

2. Frank Burch Brown, "Mary with Jesus," in *From East to West: A Festival of Carols with the Indianapolis Symphonic Choir*, Eric Stark, artistic director. Indianapolis Symphonic Choir, 2006.

Acknowledgments

THE WRITING OF THIS book, like most books, has incurred many debts. Several friends, students, and family members have assisted greatly in the preparation of this volume. Among those are my colleagues at the College of Notre Dame, particularly President Mary Pat Seurkamp and Vice-President Sally White. I am also indebted to the support from my department Chairperson, Dr. Kathleen Dougherty, and fellow philosopher Dr. Desiree Melton. Their support and friendships have greatly increased the quality of my life.

I also wish to thank several colleagues at the Saint Mary's Seminary and University, including the Rector, Father Thomas Hurst; the Dean of the Ecumenical Institute, Dr. Michael Gorman; Ms. Zenaida Bench; the Director of the Library at St. Mary's, Mr. Thomas Raszewski, and well as members of his staff, particularly Susi Ridenour, Anita Prein, and Patricia Brown.

Many colleagues and friends have discussed portions of this manuscript and/or made thoughtful suggestions about it. These include: Dr. Christopher Dreisbach; Dr. Margaret Steinhagen; Dr. Alison Dray-Novey; Dr. Rhetta Wiley; Professor Kingsley Price; Dr. John Lipsey; Dr. Thomas Benson; Catriona MacLeod; Dr. Bruce Burch; and Ms. Maria Wong. It goes without saying that any errors or mistakes in this book are entirely my own.

I'd also like to thank my students at the College of Notre Dame, Johns Hopkins University, St. Mary's Seminary, and the Maryland Institute of Art who continues to make this job of teaching a very great pleasure.

Gratitude goes to people at Wipf and Stock Publishers, including K. C. Hanson and Patrick Harrison whose support and guidance has been immense in this project. I also must recognize the deep support from Ms, Tryn Lashley, my editorial assistant who now has helped me complete work on five published books. Tryn's work has always been clear, concise, and thorough. She has been much help in this book, and for this I am deeply grateful.

Finally, to my two sons Reed and Jack, as well as my wife Sandra and my in-laws Tom and Mary Lee Parsons, I owe the greatest debt for continually making my life a satisfying and rewarding one.

Introduction

IN THIS INTRODUCTION WE have three main goals. First, to give a brief introduction to the religion of Islam and its sacred book, the Qur'an. Our second goal is to show that many European and American views on Islam are primarily misconceptions on the part of non-Moslems. Our third and final goal is to describe and discuss what materials the reader will find in the chapters that follow this introduction.

ISLAM AND THE QUR'AN

One evening in the year 610 CE, a forty-year-old Arab man was in a cave on Mount Hira, near the city of Mecca in the western part of the Arabian Peninsula. This man was holding a night vigil and thinking about his life, as well as the turbulent times in which he lived. The man said he heard a voice like it was a reverberating bell. The voice said, "Recite!" The man was startled. He stammered and said he did not know what to say. Again the voice commanded him to recite, and again the man, whose name was Muhammed ibn Abdullah, said he did not know what to say. Finally, the words came to him: "Recite in the name of the Lord who has created, created man out of a germ cell. Recite for your Lord is the Most Generous One Who has taught by the pen, taught humans what they did not know."

Muhammed, whose nickname was *Al-Amin* (the trusted one), did not know what to make of this experience. Where did the voice come from? Was it an evil spirit, a *djinn* speaking to him? Maybe he was going mad. Muhammed consulted with his wife, Khadija who assured him he was not going mad. She suggested they consult her cousin, a Christian man named Waraqa ibn Qusayy. She thought he might know about such things because Christianity has prophets. Waraqa told Muhammed that the voice had been sent down by Allah through an angel identified as Jibril (Gabriel). He also told him that Muhammed was to be a prophet to his people.

This night in Islam came to be known as "the Night of Power and Excellence." It was first in a series of visions that lasted from 610 to 632. These visions were later collected in a book appropriately called "The Recitation," or in Arabic, the *Qur'an*. Muhammed eventually was accepted as a prophet by his fellow Arabs. He became known as the *Rasul* (messenger), and his religion as *Islam*, related to the Arabic verb to submit.

Muhammed was born around 570 in the city of Mecca. He came from a tribe known as the Quraysh. Arabic religious practices at the time centered around a variety of gods and goddesses, as well as a group of spirits known as Djinn. Hubal was the god of the moon. He was the principal deity among the Meccans before the time of Muhammed. Hubal had three consorts, Al-Lat, Al-Manat, and Al-Uzza. A fourth god named Allah was responsible for creation.

In Mecca there was a shrine called the *Ka'ba*. It contained statues of various gods, as well as a sacred Black Stone, which, it was believed, was dropped from heaven. The Ka'ba had become a major pilgrimage site in Arabia. When Muhammed returned to Mecca from the cave, he began to convince others that "There is no god but Allah and Muhammed is his prophet."

In addition to these indigenous Arabic religions, there were also Christians and Jews living in Arabia in Muhammed's day. Indeed, it is clear that Muhammed knew many of the stories in both the Old and New Testaments, especially about Abraham, Moses and other prophets including tales about Jesus. Muhammed came to believe that he was the last in a series of Semitic prophets, extending back through Jesus, Abraham, and all the way to Adam, the first man.

Subsequent Islamic history can be divided into two parts around 1500. The year is often used as the dividing line between traditional Islam and modern Islam. In the late fifteenth and early sixteenth centuries, three Islamic empires arose, in Anatolia (Ottoman), Iran (Safavid), and the Indian subcontinent (Mughul). These empires lasted until the beginning of the modern era, until growing European interests and eventually colonialism, among other factors, hastened their collapse.

Other scholars suggest that the year 1300 should be the dividing line between classical and modern Islam. In the year 1258, the Mongols destroyed the imperial office of the Caliphate in Baghdad, thus bringing to an end the practical hope of a universal Sunni Islam under one Muslim ruler.

After Muhammed's death, there was some resentment and disagreement over the issue of succession. The two main competing groups came to be known as the Sunni and the Shi'ite, who now comprise about 80–85% of all Moslems. Sunni Moslems are those who follow an elected Caliph. They consider themselves traditionalists who emphasize the authority of the Qur'an, as well as that of the Hadith and the Sunnah, the sayings and practices of the prophet collected under the Sunni caliphs. The Sunnis believe that Muhammed died having not appointed a successor, and left the matter to the *Ummah*, the Moslem community.

Shiite Moslems are ardently devoted to the memory of Muhammed's close relatives: Ali, Fatima (Muhammed's daughter), and their sons Husayn and Hasan. Husayn was murdered in the city of Karbala, and the act is held by Shiites as a symbol against oppression. The martyrdom of Husayn is commemorated every year. Shiite Islam puts great emphasis on the touching tales of Ali and Husayn. Rather than recognizing the Sunni caliphs, Shiites pay their allegiance to a string of seven or twelve Imams (leaders or guiders). The first three were Ali, Hasan, and Hasayn.

Shiite Moslems believe that these twelve Imams were legitimate hereditary successors to Muhammed. The twelfth Imam, they believe, was commanded by Allah to go into hiding in 940. He is to continue to guide his people and he will return publicly on the Day of Resurrection and the coming of the Mahdi (Messiah). Another sect of Shiites, called the Ismailies or Seveners, recognize another man as the seventh and final Imam.

During the first two hundred years after Muhammed's death, collections of hadith began to appear on a variety of subjects. The number of *aHadith* (the plural) grew substantially, and systematically were organized in the ninth and tenth centuries. These collected ahadith filled 12 multivolume collections. The Sunnis came to recognize nine of these collections, but the two most authoritative are the two *Sahih* (authentic), Sahih Al-Bukhari and Sahih Muslim. The first was collected by a noted ninth century Islamic scholar Al-Bukhari. The second collection was compiled by a student of Bukhari named Muslim ibn al-Hajjaj who died in 875.

Among the Shiites there are three collections called *Akhbar*, rather than Hadith. According to tradition, they originated from Ali and the first Imams. These are the only authoritative traditions on the Qur'an in Shiite Islam.

Among Sunni Moslems believers adhere to what are called the "Five Pillars of Islam." These are five principal obligations of the Sunnis. The first pillar is called the *Shahadah*, which is a declaration of faith that there is no god but Allah, and that Muhammed is his prophet. The second pillar in Sunni belief is the *Salat*, which is an obligation to say daily prayers five different times a day. The third pillar is the *Zakat*, an obligation to pay alms to the poor. The *Sawm* is the fourth pillar of Sunni Islam. It is a requirement of fasting. Specifically, one must refrain from eating, drinking, and engaging in sexual intercourse from dawn to sunset during the month of Ramadan, which is the ninth month of the Islamic lunar calendar. The fifth pillar of Sunni Islam is the *Hajj*, a requirement to make a pilgrimage to the holy city of Mecca. This pilgrimage must be done during the month of *Zul Hijjah*, and it is compulsory. All devout Moslems must make the Hajj at least once in their lifetimes.

A few Moslems hold that there is a sixth pillar, the *Jihad*, which comes from the Arabic verb "to struggle." It refers to a moral obligation to struggle against one's conscience at the personal level, as well as struggling in the name of Allah against oppressors of the faith. Many westerners misunderstand the word *Jihad*, as we shall see in the section after next in this introduction.

THE NATURE OF THE QUR'AN

The Qur'an is roughly equal in length to the New Testament, and is divided into 6,000 sentences, 80,000 words and 114 *suras*, each is anywhere from a few lines to many pages in length.

The Qur'an is the foundation of Islam. It is universally believed by those of the Muslim faith that the Qur'an is the uncreated word of God, sent to humanity by the way of his servant, Mohammed, through the medium of the angel Gabriel. Most Moslems hold that the language of the Arabic Qur'an is unequaled anywhere in world literature.

The language of the Qur'an is quite beautiful. Muslims the world over love to recite it in low monotonous chants. Memorizing the Qur'an is still regarded as both praiseworthy and meritorious. Islamic tradition has it that Mohammed completed the Qur'an over a period of 23 years. It is said to have been written down on leaves, bones and parchment.

The Qur'an is thought of as the culmination and perfection of a series of messengers sent to guide humanity through a chain of prophets beginning with Adam, and ending with the last and final messenger of Allah, the prophet, Mohammed. It is universally believed that after the Qur'an, the "Final Testament," there will be no further revelation from Allah until the Judgment Day.

The Qur'an is written in an obscure dialect related to Syriac, Aramaic, Chaldean, and Himyerita. For our purposes it is quite like the dialect of Aramaic popular during the time of Jesus.

The derivation of the word *sura* is unclear, and it is misleading to think of a *sura* as a chapter in the Judeo-Christian Biblical sense. The suras tend to be associative, while the chapters of the New Testament are thematic, usually having a beginning, a middle and an end. Most of the longest suras are compilations of originally independent material, and thus there are many abrupt changes in person, verb tenses and subject matter. The Qur'an was not completed until after Mohammed's death in 632. It was constructed partly on the basis of extant notes, and partly drawing from oral tradition. Thus, it should not be thought of as the compilation of a single set of hands anymore than the making of the Torah was.

Only the shortest of the suras form tight literary units, and most of these come at the end of the work. For the most part, the suras are arranged by length, with the longest appearing first. The only exception is the opening sura, the *Fatihah*, which serves as a ritual prayer. The earlier *suras* are frequently taken up with events at Medina, with Mohammed's Meccan revelations, for the most part, coming at the end of the work. Like other Semitic religious texts, the original written Qur'an contained only consonants. The names of the suras, the numbering of the verses, and the vowels and diacritical marks were added long after the founder's death, during the Medina period. Thus, the Qur'an in places suffers from the same kind of confusion about vowels, and about where words and sentences begin and end, that sometimes lead to the kind of ambiguity and uncertainty of the Hebrew Bible.

The Qur'an is thought by many devout Moslems to be an exact replica of the Qur'an in heaven. In fact, it is believed by the most devout Moslems that the Qur'an is not supposed to be translated, for it would no longer be the direct word of Allah. Indeed, the speaker in the Qur'an is almost always God, who uses the royal "we," suggesting an intimate connection between the mind of God and the composition of the Qur'an. In the modern period, this stricture against the Qur'an appearing in other languages has been loosened somewhat with the movement of the Moslem religion into the Pacific Rim, into America, and deeper into Africa.

Allusions to biblical personages from both the Hebrew Bible and the New Testament are frequent in the Qur'an. They most often are given without introduction, as though the patriarchs and prophets of the Hebrew Bible, as well as Jesus, John the Baptist and other characters of the New Testament, were well enough known to first generation followers of Mohammed that no exposition was needed. From the Hebrew Bible Adam, Noah, Lot, Abraham, Isaac, Jacob, Ishmael, Moses, and Job, among others, make frequent appearances in the Qur'an.

Retributive justice was, from the beginning of Islam, the central explanation for suffering. On Judgment Day, as in Daniel 12:1–3, in the Islamic tradition the dead will be raised to be judged by God. The good will be rewarded in a heaven where:

> They shall recline on jeweled couches face to face, and there shall wait on them immortal youths with bowls and spoons and a cup of purest wine that will neither pain their heads nor take away their reason; with fruits of their own choice and flesh of fowl they relish. And there shall be dark-eyed houris, chaste as hidden pearls, a guardian for their deeds. There shall be no idle talk, no sinful speech, but only by greeting, "Peace, peace!"[1]

The wicked shall be dealt with harshly in a fiery hell: "they shall taste neither refreshment nor drink, save boiling water and decaying filth."[2] As in the noncanonical Jewish myth of the fallen angels, in the Qur'an,

---

1. Qur'an 3:25–26.

2. The edition of the Qur'an used in this chapter is *The Holy Qur'an: Text, Translation, and Commentary* edited and translated by Abdullah Yusuf Ali (Cambridge: Murray, 1947) I have also consulted the translation of J. M. Rodwell (London: Everyman's Library, M. Dent and Sons, 1909); commentaries on the Qur'an I have examined include: A.J Arberry, *The Koran Interpreted* (New York: MacMillan, 1976); M.M. Pickthall, *The Meaning of the Glorious Koran* (New York: New American Library, 1963); Khursshid Ahmad, *Islam: It's Meaning and Message* (Leicester: The Islamic Foundation. 1980); Mustanir Mir, *Coherence in the Qur'an* (Indianapolis: American Trust Publications, 1986); and Fazlur Rahman, *Major Themes in the Qur'an* (Minneapolis: Bibliotecha Islamica, 1989). I have also profited greatly from the work of John Wansbrough. In *his Quranic Studio* (Oxford: Oxford University Press, 1977) and *The Sectarian Mileaux* (Oxford: Oxford University Press, 1978), Wansbrough has applied some of the methods of modern biblical studies to the Qur'an. Another very useful reference tool for English-speaking reader of the Qur'an is Hanna Kassis' *A Concordance to the Quran* (Berkley: University of California Press, 1982), as well as *The Koran* translated by N. J Dawood (New York: Penguin, 1975).

Shaytan (Satan or *Iblis*) previously occupied a place in Allah's heavenly court. He fell from grace by an act of pride in refusing to honor Adam, the first man. Since then, the *Shaytan* has roamed the earth, leading vulnerable human beings into sin. But his activities will cease on Judgment Day, and he will be thrown down into the fiery pit, along with those who weakened under his temptations, to experience an eternity of suffering.[3]

Many of the Qur'an's suras explicitly or implicitly deal with the problem of innocent suffering. Sura 8, also called Al-Anfaal or, "the Spoils," for example, deals with why sometimes wicked people prosper. Sura 8 more specifically deals with the spoils of war and the theological ramifications of the practice. Through most of the history of Islam, the problem of reconciling the moral nature of the spoils of war is resolved by a Divine Plan theodicy, where all injustices are reconciled in the next life.

In effect, then, most suffering is explained in the Qur'an as retributive justice, punishment for sins committed. Any innocent suffering is attributed to the malevolent actions of the *Shaytan*. But early Islamic thinkers realized soon enough that this solution does not solve very well the mystery of innocent suffering. About that thorny question early Islam took a different tact. In short, the writers of the Qur'an conceived of innocent suffering as a kind of test of moral character, in much the same way the writers of the *Testament of Job* and the Epistle of James, and Clement's first letter construed the question. This point of view is nowhere more apparent than in Quranic and early Medieval Moslem commentaries on the man from Uz and his book.

ISLAM AND MODERN HISTORY

During the period of empires (the Ottoman in Turkey, the Safavid in Persia, and the Mogul dynasty in India) at least three major changes came to Islamic society. The first was the transformation of the Islamic Near East from a commercial economy based on money and bartering to a feudal economy based on subsistence farming.

The second big change in Islam during the period of the dynasties was the replacement of people in authority in Arabic speaking lands with Turk leaders. The Arab tribes held together in the desert regions; but in the cities and cultivated areas, like the plains in Iraq, Syria, and Egypt, the Arabs became completely subjugated. The Turks grew accustomed to

---

3. Qur'an 78:24–25.

taking the initiative and commanding, while the Arabs grew accustomed to passivity and subjection.

The third major change in Islamic culture was the transfer of the seat of Islam from Iraq to Egypt. Iraq was too remote from Turkey and the Mediterranean to be the base of the eastern wing of Islam, so Egypt—which was on the other principal trade route and which was the most unified area geographically—became the new center of the east.

As a result of these changes, Turkish and to a lesser degree Farsi became the languages of Islam. At first, many of the subjugated people welcomed the Ottoman takeover from the Mamluks as a return to political order; but by the eighteenth century, the Ottoman Empire was in decay. It had become corrupt, anarchic, and stagnant. The principal religious revolt during this period was Sufism. At first, the Sufis were mainly an escape from oppression, but with the organization of more brotherhoods, it became a social movement that was especially powerful among artisans. This period of stagnation came to an end with increase in contact with the West.

From the beginning of the sixteenth century, European expansion brought some of the new learning of the Renaissance and Reformation to the East. The French in particular had great influence in the Middle East. Napoleon's conquest of the Ottoman Mamluks at the close of the eighteenth century was the final blow.

Napoleon's conquest gave rise to a Moslem movement known as the Wahabis, whose founder was Muhammed ibn Abd al-Wahab. They called for a return to the doctrines and practices of earlier generations of the ancestors whom they venerated. In law, the Wahabis favored the rigorous interpretation of the Hanbalite School, and they shunned the veneration of saints which they considered superstitious.

The Wahabis were based in Arabia, where they waged a war with their dissenting neighbors. They went down to military defeat in the 1818 Turco-Egyptian War, but their puritanical reforms had much success in the rest of Islam. One immediate effect of the Wahabi Movement was a great hostility toward the Sufi Brotherhoods. Indeed, orthodox Moslems saw the Sufis as their great enemies.

One of the great leaders of the nineteenth-century reform in Islam was Jamal al-Din al-Afghani, who proposed the unification of all Islam through the Turkish caliphate. Afghani's movement came to be known as Pan-Islam or Pan-Arab Movement. This movement looked for a widespread response to western modernity. In India and Egypt conservative groups arose that gravitated to the Wahabi Movement. Many of the Sufi organizations lost their influence, and those that survived tended toward a return to traditional theology.

Even before this conservative threat came, the Sufis sponsored a number of missions in Africa, India, and Indonesia. Sometimes these conquests involved military ventures. Particularly, the Indian Wahabis and the Mahdists in the Sudan attempted to conquer by the sword. Organizations that have grown in the recent past like Al-Qaeda, the Moslem Brotherhood, and others seem in good measure to be an effort to fill the void created by the demise of earlier reform movements. The new movements operate in a pluralistic culture, while the Sufi orders drew on a homogeneous culture that was secure in its faith.

One major characteristic of Islam in the modern world is the invasion of Western ideas on the heels of Western takeovers in the Middle East, at first through the administrations of the Europeans who governed the newly acquired territory and then through the educational systems, which were westernized. This gave rise to a new professional class in places like Pakistan, where doctors, lawyers, journalists, and scholars frequently got their training abroad. One political effect of this training was to raise Muslim feelings of national identity and government.

The development of groups like Al-Qaeda has given rise to a number of misconceptions that Westerners have of Islam. In the next section of this introduction, we shall look carefully at these misconceptions.

MISCONCEPTIONS ABOUT ISLAM

Do not kill yourselves, for Allah is compassionate toward you. Whoever does so, in transgression and wrongfully, shall roast in a fire. (Qur'an 4:29–30)

For the past several years, I have been studying the Arabic language, as well as the history of Islam. I have gotten to the point where I now can do simple translations, and as I have increased my knowledge of the language, I increasingly have come to understand that people in the west have a number of misconceptions about Islam, the Qur'an, and the Arabic language. Among these chief misconceptions are three worthy of comment. They have to do with Holy War, virgins, and motivations.

The first of these misconceptions about Islam has to do with the word *Jihad*, which many news agencies over the last five years suggest should be translated as "Holy War." This is a grossly inaccurate understanding of the term. The word *Jihad* is the subject of 164 verses in the Qur'an. The word comes from the Arabic verb, *jahada*, which means "to struggle," or "to strive," resisting evil both individually and collectively. These two prongs of *Jihad* are sometimes called the Greater Struggle and the Lesser Struggle.

The Greater struggle is a striving against the self. It is the internal fight between right and wrong, error and truth, selfishness and selflessness, between hardness of heart and an all-embracing love. On the other hand, the Lesser Jihad involved the protecting the way of Allah against the forces of evil. This Jihad is the safe-guarding of one's life, faith, livelihood, honor, and integrity of the Muslim community. The Lesser Jihad makes possible the ability to fight back if attacked.

The Lesser Jihad is to be waged by *Muhadjadim*, fighters for the path of Allah. Support for the Lesser Jihad can be found in the Qur'an, where arguments for both pacifism and for active opposition to aggression both can be found. This defensive nature of Jihad is discussed at surah 22:39–40 of the text; the killing and treatment of non-combatants is talked about at 2:190-193; and the limits on killing in general is discussed at 4:29. The Qur'an makes it clear that suicide is forbidden (4:29), and it advocates kindness, even to non-Muslims at 60:8. The Qur'an does make a distinction between suicide victims and *Shahid* (martyrs) at 3:169–174 and 22:58, but nowhere in the Qur'an will one find the words, *al-harb muhadassa*, which would be one translation of the expression "Holy War."

The second misconception of Islamic ideas follows from the first. Among newspapers, television reports, and news accounts in the last few years have been the claim that the *Qur'an* guarantees the suicide bomber seventy-two virgins in *Jahanaam* (Paradise). There is among some contemporary Islamic scholars some debate about whether this is true. The closest the *Qur'an* comes to such a statement is 56:12–17, where Ahmad Ali's translation of the text tells us:

> In the gardens of tranquility, a number of earlier peoples
> And a few of later ages,
> On couches wrought of gold,
> Reclining face to face,

Youths of never-ending bloom
Will pass round to them.

The Arabic plural, *Abkarun* in the fifth line above is sometimes translated as "virgins," but surah 55:72–74 contains another Arabic word, *hur* that is also sometimes translated that way. Other scholars say both words should be translated as "angels," which may make more sense in arriving in Paradise. At any rate, there is nothing in the Qur'an that suggests the number of these "youths" is seventy-two. A later *hadith* (a recording of the sayings of Muhammed and his followers) does mention the number seventy-two. It comes in a collection of traditions by Al-Tirmidhi, a ninth-century Moslem scholar. The same number is quoted by Ibn Kathir, a fourteenth-century Islamic scholar, whose Qur'anic commentary on surah 55 quotes Muhammed as saying, "The smallest reward for the peoples of Paradise where there is an abode of 80,000 servants and seventy-two wives;" but the notion of seventy-two virgins does not appear in the Qur'an itself.

The final misconception of Islam is the one that has the most theological value. It is the belief that the motivation for suicide bombings in New York, Washington, in Israel, Iraq, and in Lebanon is religious. I say this is a misconception because of work done by Professor Robert Pape of the University of Chicago. In his book, *Dying to Win: The Strategic Logic of Suicide Terrorism*, Pape revealed his findings on an in depth study in which he explored the motivations of suicide bombers.

In a lecture delivered recently at the FBI Academy in Virginia, Pape revealed his findings regarding 462 suicide bombers across the globe. His main conclusion is that suicide bombings are less about religious fundamentalism than about social or political complaints. In an interview he gave ABC television, Pape said: "There's a faulty premise in the current strategy on the war on terrorism. That faulty premise is that suicide terrorism and Al-Qaeda suicide terrorism in particular is mainly driven by an evil ideology Islamic fundamentalism independent of other circumstances."

Professor Pape continued:

> The facts are that since 1980, suicide terrorist attacks from around the world over half of them have been secular in nature. What over 95% of suicide attacks around the world are about is not religion, but rather a specific strategic purpose—to compel modern democracies to withdraw military forces from the territory that the terrorists view as their homeland.

In the same lecture at the FBI Academy, as well as in a piece he did for the *New York Times*, Pape suggested that western democracies should withdraw their troops from Muslim lands, and instead support efforts of governments there to deal with the extremists. Pape points out that the presence of western troops in the region rarely occurred in the 1970s and 80s, and the activity of suicide bombers was also considerably less frequent than those of the present.

If Professor Pape's observations are correct, then the view that Moslem suicide bombers are motivated by religion is incorrect, and thus a misconception of Islam and some of its practitioners.

One final misconception that Westerners often have of Islam is the use of the Arabic word, *fatwa*. The word became current in the English-speaking world when on February 14, 1989, the Ayatollah Khomeini issued a *fatwa* on novelist Salman Rushdie because of Rushdie's novel, *The Satanic Verses*. In the *fatwa*, the Ayatollah told "all zealous Muslims of the world that the blood of the author of this book . . . which has been compiled, printed, and published in opposition to Islam, the Prophet, and the Qur'an, and also those involved in its publication who were aware of its content is hereby declared forfeit."

The *fatwa* continued: "I call on all zealous Muslims to dispatch them quickly wherever you may find them, so that no one will dare insult Islamic sanctities again. Anyone who is himself killed in this path will be deemed a martyr."[4]

From all this, many Westerners got the impression that the issuing of a *Fatwa* was the equivalent of "taking out a contract" on someone's life in the West. This is an absurd conclusion. The word *fatwa* is a technical term used in Islamic jurisprudence. It generally refers to a legal opinion or ruling on a point of law. A *fatwa* is only to be issued by a *mufti*, an Islamic scholar who interprets or expounds the *Sharia*, Islamic law.

4. Bernard Lewis, *The Crisis of Islam* (New York: Random House, 2002) 14.

In some theocratic societies like Iran and Saudi Arabia, and in some Islamic cultures where the government is based on *Sharia*, the Grand Mufti is often given the last say. The Ayatollah Khomeini was not the Grand mufti of Iran in 1989. Thus, the issuing of his *fatwa* against Salman Rushdie was outside the bounds of traditional Islamic law.

The opening chapter of this study is concerned with the existence and attributes of God in the Islamic faith. Like Judaism and Christianity, the Moslem faith assents to many of the traditional attributes of God in these earlier traditions, including Omnipotence, Omniscience, and Omnibenevolence; but, as we shall see, Islam also posits a number of other attributes of Allah that are not discussed in the Old and New Testaments.

In Islam, Allah is said to have 99 names. In a separate section of this chapter, we explore those names. There is also a tradition among Moslems that Allah has a 100th name—the most secret and most holy of Allah's names. In another section of this chapter we discuss this tradition of the 100th name of Allah.

The Qur'an, as well as later Islam, speaks of Allah in anthropomorphic ways, including Allah's face, His hands, His Throne, etc. In a third section of this chapter, we explore how Islam has dealt with these passages. In a final section of this first chapter, we make some general conclusions about the concept of Allah and His attributes.

In chapter 2 of this work, we explore the roles that Abraham, Isaac, and Ishmael play in the Islamic faith. As you will see, for the most part Islam saw Abraham as Christianity does, with one notable exception. In Islam, the son that Abraham nearly sacrificed in chapter 22 of Genesis is not Isaac. In Islam, it is Abraham's first born son, Ishmael.

The role of Moses in Islam is the topic for chapter three of this study. In Islam, as we shall see, great emphasis is placed on Moses' miraculous birth, as well as being saved by being put in a basket in the river. As a grown man, after being raised in the Pharaoh's family, Moses was given the ability to perform miracles. Among these miracles were the abilities to turn his staff to snakes, as well as making water flow from a rock. We have dealt, as well, with two later Islamic traditions about Moses. First, the nature of Moses' bodily disfigurement; and second, the claim that Moses had horns in Islam.

In chapter 4 of this study, we deal with a number of other Old Testament patriarchs and the role they play in Islam. Among these figures are Adam, Noah, Lot, Jacob, and Joseph. Again, for the most part, these figures play similar roles in Islam that they do in Judaism and Christianity; but there are also some differences. The figure of Joseph in Islam, for example, has a much loftier status in the Moslem faith than he does in Judaism and Christianity. In fact, Joseph has the longest continuous narrative in the Qur'an than any other biblical figure.

Chapter 5 of this work deals with one final Old Testament figure, Ayyub, the Arabic name for Job. Like Judaism and Christianity, in Islam Job is seen as a patient prophet, a man of profound moral virtue; but in Islam Job is often seen as the patron saint of skin diseases, as well as a man whose sickness was healed by the gushing of a stream that flowed from hitting the ground with his stick.

The remaining chapters of this study are concerned with the place of New Testament figures in Islam. In chapter five, Jesus is the center of the analysis. Isa (Jesus in Arabic) is among the greatest of Islamic prophets. He is known for his moral purity in Islam, but the Moslem faith does not see Jesus as the son of God. This is a curious fact when we consider that Islam does see Jesus as the Messiah. Islam believes that Jesus will return at the end of time, where he will participate in a great battle between the forces of good and evil.

The Islamic views of Mary, Joseph, and John the Baptist are the subject matter of chapter six of this study. Jesus' earthly father is not given a name in the Qur'an, but it does say he was a carpenter. The figure of Mary in Islam is more exalted than any other woman in the Islamic faith, but Moslems do not see Maryam (Mary in Arabic) as the mother of God. Yah Yah (John the Baptist in Arabic) is numbered among the greatest of Islamic prophets. He is noted for his faith, and he is seen as the cousin of Jesus in Islam, but most of what is said about him in the Moslem faith has to do, as we shall see, with his miraculous birth.

Chapter 7 of this study is devoted to an analysis of the figure of Iblis (the Devil in Arabic), as well as the role that Hell plays in Islam. As we shall see, there are many similarities to the role of Shaytan (another name for Iblis) and the Judeo-Christian perspectives on the demonic, but there are also some differences that are explored at length in chapter seven.

In chapter 8 of the work we explore and discuss the role of the *Djaal*, the Arabic word for the Anti-Christ. In Islam, the major discussions of the Anti-Christ come in connection with the end of the world. In Islam, as we shall see, both Jesus and the Anti-Christ have key roles to play in the End Times. In Islam, the *Djaal* is often associated with the people of Gog and

Magog in the Old Testament. There is also a tradition in Islam, which we explore in chapter eight, that the Anti-Christ has only one eye. Finally, in chapter nine we make some general conclusions we have garnered in chapters one through eight, as well as making some important comments on the nature of hermeneutics in the Islamic faith.

The Concept of God in Islam

God is only and Divinely like Himself.

—John Donne

It is from human reference that they derive their content. Only so are language and literature possible. Only so is it feasible to pray, to theologize, or to speak of God at all.

—Kenneth Cragg, *The House of Islam*

This indeed is the true story, and there is no God but Allah, and Allah is truly the All Mighty and the All Wise.

—Qur'an 3:62

INTRODUCTION

THE CONCEPT OF GOD in the Islamic faith is significantly like the concept of God in the Judeo-Christian tradition. Like the Old and New Testaments, the Qur'an tells us that Allah has many of the same attributes as are predicted of God in Judaism and Christianity. Chief among these are his omniscience (All Knowing), omnipotence (All Powerful), and omni-benevelence (All Good). Like God in Judaism and Christianity, Allah is unique; but, as we shall see in this chapter, there are a variety of other names for God in Islam. Indeed, Islamic tradition suggests that Allah has 99 names.

In this chapter, we take a close look at the names and attributes for God in the Islamic faith. In addition to the concept of Allah in the Qur'an, we also explore in this chapter, some views of God in subsequent Islam. As we shall see, the period of Islamic philosophy from the tenth to the fourteenth centuries was particularly fruitful in finding comments of Moslem thinkers on Allah and His attributes.

THE WORD *ALLAH* IN ARABIC

The word *Allah* is a compound word from the article *al* and the noun, *ilah*, God. The word *ilah* appears to have been the common word used when discussing divinities in the Pre-Islamic Arabia. Gradually, with the addition of the article, the word came to mean one of these divinities who has dominion over everything. The word *Allah*, then, came to be the name of the only God in Islam. The root of the word occurs in all Semitic languages as a designation of divinity.

The word Allah is not a proper name but a contraction of the word *al-ilah*, meaning simply "the god." Like his Greek counterpart, Zeus, Allah was originally an ancient rain/sky deity who had been elevated to a supreme status of the pre-Islamic Arabs. Though Allah was a powerful god to swear by, like most high gods in other cultures in the Middle East, He was beyond the supplications of ordinary people. Only in times of great peril would He be turned to. Otherwise, it was more expedient to turn to lesser, more accessible deities who acted as Allah's intercessors. These lesser deities were not only represented in the Ka'ba, they also had their own individual shrines throughout Arabia.

It was to these lesser deities that Arabs prayed when they needed rain, when their children were ill, or when they went into battle. It was also to these lesser deities that Arabs turns when they were to journey out into the desert, a treacherous place full of *Djinn*, those imperceptible beings made from smoke.

The word *Allah* in Arabic does not have a plural form, thus the name itself implies the unity of God in Islam. In Islam, the word *Allah* is always written with an *alif* to spell the long *a* sound. In vocalized Arabic, on the other hand, a small diacritical *alif* is added to the top of the *shadah* to indicate the pronunciation.

The one exception to these rules is a pre-Islamic inscription which ends with an ambiguous sign that may be an *h* sound, with a lengthened sound, or it may be a conjoined *l* and *h* sound. This text is the earliest known translation of the word *Allah* into another language. It is dated from the early seventh century, and is translated into Greek as *ho theos monos*, literally "the one God."[1]

The word Allah is the common word for God in all Arabic speakers, whatever their religious traditions, including Arabic Christians and Jews. A number of cognates of the word Allah appear in other Semitic languages, including the Hebrew El, Eloah, and Elohim. These words in turn probably derived from the Canaanite "El," and the Mesopotamian "Ilu."

The Hebrew words, *El* and *Eloah* are cognates of *Allah*, as are the Aramaic *Elaha* and the Syriac *Alaha*. When Jesus speaks on the cross in the Aramaic version of the New Testament, the Peshitta's Mark 15:34, he says, "Blessed are the pure in heart for they shall see *Alaha*."[2]

The word *Allah* is used in a number of principal sayings of the Islamic faith. Chief among these are: *La ilaha illallah*, "there is no God but Allah"; *Allahu Akbar* "God is great"; *Bimi-llah*, "in the name of Allah"; and *In sha Allah*, "If God is willing." The word *Allah* is never used as a proper name in Islam, it has no gender in Arabic, and it has a numeric value of 66 in Islamic mysticism or gematria.

CONCEPT OF GOD IN THE QUR'AN

The *Asma al-Husna*, the Excellent Names for God, are a significant part of Islamic doctrine and devotion. Many Moslem men and women, with a string of beads, run through his or her fingers the many names of Allah. Some seventy names for God appear in the Holy Book. Many of these are duplicates of each other. Some are active participles, and others are adjectives.

Like the Scholastic Period in Christianity, as well as the rabbis of the Talmud, the Qur'an speaks of Allah in anthropomorphic terms. It applies to expressions like "the Hand of Allah," or the "Face of Allah," as well as to adjectival name and attributes. There is no greater reluctance in any of the world's religious traditions to concede that the gulf between humans and Divine is one that cannot be fully described.

This does not mean that Allah is not involved with humans, but the true nature and attributes of Allah are well beyond human comprehension.

---

1. This inscription is described at length in Patricia Crone and Michael Cook, *Hagarism: The Making of the Islamic Word* (Cambridge: Cambridge University Press, 1977). The inscription is associated with the tomb of Abassa Bint Jurajj, an eighth-century grave.

2. RSV translation of Mark 15:34.

In the tenth and eleventh centuries, Moslem philosophers used the neat expressions, *bila kaif* ("without implying how") and *Bila tashbih* ("without representational intention") to speak of Allah and his predicates.

The two most notable names for God in the Qur'an are those that stand in the *Basmillah* or invocation that stand at the head of every surah of the Qur'an but the ninth, the expression, *Al Fahman al-Rahim*, the "Merciful Lord of Mercy." Others translate the phrase as "In the name of God, most Gracious and most Compassionate." The word *bismillah* is made up of three elements. The *bi* is a preposition. It means by, through, for, and by means of. The next part of the word is the root *ism*, which is the root for the words Islam and Moslem. The end of the word, the third part, is *Allah*, God in Arabic. Thus, the word means something like "By the means of the very essence of God." The implication is that whatever we do, each breath we take, every word we utter, is done because of and through the essence of the One.

The two terms, *rahman* and *rahim* are both from the Semitic root RHM. It is connected to the Arabic words for protection, tenderness, and compassion. The philosopher Ibn Qayyum, a fourteenth-century thinker, translates *rahman* as "Abounding Grace." The term, *rahim*, on the other hand, Ibn Qayyum suggests, is the effect of that grace on human beings.

Another dominant phrase often used in the Qur'an to describe Allah is *Rabb-al-Alamin*, usually translated as "Lord of the Worlds." The *rab* is connected to the word *abd*, the most frequent description of humans in the Qur'an. It is often translated as "Servant," as opposed to the Master, Allah. The word *rab* may also be connected to the Arabic words for "rule" and "nurture." The word *alamin* is connected to one of the verbs for "to know" in Arabic. The clear implication in this phrase is that Allah knows of the existence of and controls all that goes on in every world that is. This notion is summed up in the Qur'an's 3:83:

> Do they seek another way but Allah's? But whoever is in the heavens and on the earth is submissive to Allah and obedient to Him, by choice or constraint, and will be returned to Him.[3]

3. Unless otherwise stated, all the Arabic translations in this chapter are those of the author. I have also used the translations of the Qur'an by Ahmed Ali (Princeton University Press, 1993), and Majid Fakry's *An Interpretations of the Qur'an* (New York: New York University Press, 2000).

Divine Lordship over all worlds is sometimes interpreted to view all of nature, as well as humanity, in some sense to be Moslem. Kenneth Cragg speaks of this notion: "There is the concept of a natural cosmic Islam, in which stars and molecules, species and elements, plants and creatures, all worship by the conformity of the laws to their being."[4]

In Islam, that Allah is over humans and that humans are under Allah is a belief that rests as one of the foundations of the rest of the faith. In Islam, humans are invited to will their true being by heeding the Divine Will which conditions and describes it. The Divine Calling to humans also calls for the dethroning and the disowning of false gods. "There is no God but Allah." The Qur'an's 31:13 tells us, "To associate others with Allah is a grievous wrong."[5]

The most common word to refer to idolatry in the Qur'an is *Zulm*. The word means something that is intrinsically wrong. To associate something with Allah is *shirk*. C. T. R. Hewer describes *shirk* as "giving God partners."[6] Hewer continues: "God alone is worthy of worship, without any intermediary between the human being and God."[7]

Hewer also points out that Islam does not rule out the making or worshipping of idols, they simply cannot be worshipped the way that Allah is. Islam also seems to rule out the modern idols of power, wealth, prestige, high birth, racial superiority, nationalism, etc; but nothing can be allowed in Islam to distract from the love of Allah.

The Qur'an in several places speaks specifically about believing in other gods but Allah. Surah 37:95 speaks of the falsity of alleged gods, as does 13:16 and 21:22. The Qur'an also suggests that the doctrine of the Trinity in Islam is a claim that there are three gods. It also states quite explicitly at 23:91 that Allah does not have a son:

> Allah has not taken to Himself any son, nor is there any god with Him: for then each god would have taken of that which He created and some of them would have risen over the others.[8]

---

4. Kenneth Cragg, *The Religious Life of Man: The House of Islam* (Belmont, CA: Dickenson, 1969) 10.

5. *The Holy Qur'an*, 31:13 (author's translation).

6. C. T. R. Hewer, *Understanding Islam: An Introduction* (Minneapolis: Fortress, 2006) 91.

7. Ibid.

8. Qur'an 23:91 (author's translation).

Surah 21:22 speaks of the possibility of other gods:

> If there were in the heavens and the earth others gods beside Allah, there would have been a confusion in both. But glory to Allah, the Lord of the Throne High is He above what they attribute to Him.[9]

One of the most familiar themes having to do with the Lord of the Worlds has to do with time, and destiny in history. It is in the modern world a common assumption that members of the Islamic faith are fatalists. But many Western interpreters have misconstrued the matter. Again, as Kenneth Cragg suggests:

> The sense of God over all, omniscient, omni-competent, and omnipotent certainly dominates, even oppressively, in orthodox thinking and assumption. Some have readily identified history with God's will, in an arm grip of celestial necessity, inflexible and inescapable, to the point of denying natural and historical causation, any genuine place. All is seen without mediating causes as God's decree and God's deed. When puzzled about the moral accountability of men, if God is the sole author of all their deeds, the theologians found refuge in a verbal solution by saying that God willed the deed in the will of the doer.[10]

The Qur'an's 7:179 refers to the names of Allah as "good names." Some of the 99 names are gruesome like "Bringer of Death," "The Avenger," and "Dishonor." One of the names for God in the Qur'an, *Ad-Darr*, "The Distressor," is also used as a name for Shaytan.

The Qur'an at 7:180 and 59:22–24 speaks explicitly about the names for God. Surah 7:180–181 tells us:

> All the names of God are beautiful, so call him by them, and leave alone those who act profanely towards His names. They will be retributed for their deeds. Yet there are others among you who lead people to the truth and act justly in its light.[11]

---

9. Ibid, 21:22

10. Cragg, *The Religious Life of Man*, 10.

11. Qur'an 7:179 (author's translation).

The Qur'an's 59:24 also tells us that Allah's names are beautiful:

> He is the God, the Creator, the Maker, the Fashioner. His are the beautiful names. Whatever is in the heavens and the earth sings his praises. He is All-Mighty and All-Wise.[12]

References to Allah's names can also be seen in the Qur'an's 20:7-8, where His names are called both Beautiful and Excellent. Other references to Allah's "Beautiful Names" can be seen at 7:180 and 17:110 of the Qur'an. Moslems never cease to memorize Allah's Beautiful Names and to meditate on them. The list of names in Arabic is called *Al-Asma Al-Hunsa*. Several key surahs of the Qur'an sum up the Holy Book's view of Allah. Surah 112 is a good example:

> In the name of Allah, Most benevolent, ever-merciful.

> Say: "He is God
> The One, the most unique.
> God the eminently indispensable.
> He has begotten no one,
> And is begotten by none.
> There is no one comparable to Him.[13]

The word *Assamuad* is difficult to translate in Surah 112. It means something like "Absolute Existence," in the sense that all other existence is temporal and conditional. It also implies that Allah is not dependent on any thing, but all persons and things are dependent on Him. This notion of Allah being beyond anything human is reiterated in the Qur'an's 6:103: "No vision can grasp Him. But His grasp is over. All vision: He is above all comprehension, yet is acquainted with all things."[14]

In the Qur'an, Allah is unique, indispensable and uncreated. We get a similar view from Surah 64: "All that there is in the heavens and the earth sing the praises of Allah. His is sovereignty and His is praise, and He has power over everything."[15] Similar thoughts are expressed in Surah 61: "All that is in the heavens and the earth sing the praises of Allah. He is All mighty and All Wise."[16]

---

12. Ibid., 59:24.
13. Ibid., 112:1–4.
14. Ibid., 6:103.
15. Ibid., 64:1.
16. Ibid., 61:1.

Surah 59 begins the same way, as do surahs 1, 11, 39, 40, 42, 57, and 59. In short, the Qur'an sees Allah as One, Unique, All Knowing, All-Wise, All-Powerful, and the Creator of the Universe. He is called indispensable, uncreated, and Bestower of all that is Good.

Another significant difference between Islam and Christianity is that the latter often recognizes intermediaries that may stand in aid of Christians to communicate with the Divine. Sometimes Christians pray to Mary the mother of God or to other saints in their tradition. In the Moslem tradition there are no intermediaries between Allah and believers. Moslems pray directly to Allah, and seek guidance from Him alone. Humans need no intermediary, for, as Surah 5:7 tells us, "Allah knows well the secrets of your hearts."[17]

The Qur'an is very specific about how far Allah's attributes extend, particularly traditional Judeo-Christian attributes like Omnipotence, and Omniscience. The Qur'an tells us that Allah's knowledge extends to the smallest action of the smallest created thing. He knows there is no seed in the darkest parts of the earth, no green shoot or dry one that God does not know about (6:59) "No female conceives or brings forth life without the knowledge of Allah (35:11). The Qur'an tells us that Allah even knows every thought a man will have beforehand (1:16). He is closer to human beings than they are to themselves (34:50).

In the Qur'an Allah is Compassionate, Merciful, Loving, and Wise. He is the Creator, the Sustainer, the Healer. He is the One Who Guides, the One Who Protects, the One Who Forgives. In Muslim understanding, Allah is beyond our sight and understanding, yet at the same time, as the Qur'an's 50:16 tells us, "closer than our own jugular veins."[18]

THE CONCEPT OF GOD IN LATER ISLAM

The 99 names for God are discussed throughout Islam. Ibn Maja, ninth-century Persian thinker, says, "Oh Allah, I invoke you with all your beautiful names."[19] The Sahih Muslim, one of the six major collections of hadith,

---

17. Ibid., 5:7.

18. Ibid., 50:16.

19. Yahya ibn Sharaf al-Nawawi and Ibrahim Ezzeddin, *Forty Hadith* (London: Islamic Texts Society, 1997) 173.

tells us, "There are 99 names for Allah, one hundred minus one. He who explains them will get into Paradise."[20]

Abu Huraira, the late seventh-century Sunni narrator of hadith, also tells us, "There are 99 names of Allah, he who commits them to memory will go to Paradise."[21] Huraira continues: "Truly, Allah is Odd, He is One and He loves odd numbers."[22]

The most popular period of Islamic speculation about the nature and attributes of Allah was from the tenth to the twelfth centuries. In this period, most of the traditional questions in the philosophy of religion were dealt with by a number of thinkers. Al-Ashari, a tenth-century Moslem philosopher, responding to the problem of human free will and God's omniscience, puts the onus of responsibility on Allah when he writes, "It has no agent, who makes it as it really is, save God, and no one with powers over it so that it will be as it really is, in the sense that he creates it, save God."[23]

Ashari, one of the most famous writers of *Kalam* (scholastic theology), continues about God's attributes against those who claim Allah does not have free will, and those who say Allah can commit evil:

> The proof that God is free to do whatever He does is that He is the supreme Lord, subject to no one, with no superior over Him who can permit, command, forbid or perceive what He shall do and fix bounds for Him. This being so, nothing can be evil on the part of God. For a thing is evil on our part only because we transgress the limits and bounds set for us and do what we have no right to do. But since the Creator is subject to no one and bound by no command, nothing can be evil on His part.[24]

Al-Kindi, a ninth-century Moslem thinker, was among the first of the Islamic Aristotelians. He wrote works on geometry, astronomy, music, physics, medicine, and politics. He made a distinction, as Aristotle did, between the Active and Passive intellects. He also thought that discursive reasoning and demonstration are a third and fourth intellects.

---

20. *Sahih Muslim: English Translation* (Idara, India: Islamic Book Service, 2001) 1:98.

21. Nawawi, *Forty Hadith*, 134.

22. Ibid.

23. Ibid, 347.

24. Ibid.

The existence and attributes of Allah were taken up by a number of other Medieval Islamic philosophers. Al-Farabi, another tenth-century Moslem thinker, attempted to reconcile Platonic and Aristotelian ideas with the Qur'an. He made a distinction between theoretical philosophy and practical theology. Theoretical philosophy includes physics and metaphysics, while practical philosophy is about ethics.

Ibn Sina, known as Avicenna in the West, a tenth and eleventh-century philosopher and physician, wrote voluminously on various metaphysical ideas, many of them related to God. He too divides philosophy between theoretical and practical. His view of the soul is very much like that of Aristotle, and he thought that Allah's existence could be proven with the traditional Cosmological argument.

Al-Ghazali (1085–1111) an Iraqi philosopher criticized many of the arguments of Farabi and Ibn Sina. Chief among his criticisms was his argument against the eternality of the universe. Ghazali staunchly defended the view that the universe was created in time and out of nothing. Ghazali makes a distinction between revealed truths and natural truths, and he thought that mystical intuition is another way of apprehending truths about Allah and His nature.

Al-Nafasi, a twelfth-century Moslem thinker, also wrote voluminously about Allah and His attributes. In his *Aqa'id*, Nafasi tells us:

> God most High, the One, the Eternal, the Decreeing, the Knowing, the Seeing, the Hearing, the Willing: He is not an attribute, nor a Body, nor an essence, nor a thing formed, nor a thing bounded, nor a thing numbered, nor a thing divided, nor a thing compounded, nor a thing limited. He is not described by *mahiya* [whatness], nor by *kaifiyyah* [howness], and He does not exist in time or place. There is nothing that resembles Him ... He has qualities from all eternity existing in His essence. They are not He, nor are they any other but He ... His word is a quality from all eternity, not belonging to the genus of sound and letters, a quality that is incompatible with coming to silence.[25]

Ibn Rushad (1126–1198) was a Spanish philosopher from Cordoba. He is known in the West as Averroes. Like Avicenna, he was both philosopher and physician. Averroes, like Ashari and Al-Kindi, was famous for his commentaries on Aristotle. Thomas Aquinas read Averroes. Averroes

---

25. Majid Fakry, *A History of Islamic Philosophy* (New York: Columbia University Press, 2004) 149. Also see Cragg, *The Religious Life of Man*, 14.

had a Neo-Platonic theory of emanations. Averroes also gave substantial arguments for immortality of the soul, as well as resurrection of the body. Another Spanish Moslem philosopher from the same period was Solomon Ibn Gabriol Avicebron. Avicebron, who lived from 1020 to 1070, was Neo-Platonic in his orientation. His views were opposed by Thomas Aquinas but found favor with thirteenth-century Franciscans and Augustinians.

Averroes in his "The Decisive Treatise," writes a great deal about the concept of God. He calls Allah, "Blessed and Exalted, Who is the Maker, Giver of Being, and Sustainer of the universe. May He be praised and His power exalted."[26] Averroes points out that in addition to traditional attributes of God that are found in Judaism and Christianity, like omniscience and omnipotence, in Islam other attributes for God can be found that are not anything like the Judeo-Christian tradition.

Among these attributes and names are *Dhul Fazl al-Azim*, the Lord of Infinite Grace, which is mentioned at the Qur'an's 2:105; 3:74; 8:29; 57:21; and 62:4. The Lord of Infinite Grace is not generally included in the 99 names for God in Islam, but *Al-Qahhar*, "The Subduer, " *Al-Wahhab*, "The Bountiful Donor," and *Al-Fattah*, "The Opener, the Judge" generally are included.

Other names for God that one generally does not see in the Judeo-Christian tradition are *Al-Khafid*, "The Abaser or Humbler," *Al-Mudhill*, "The Humiliator or Degrader," and *Al-Hamid*, "The Praiseworthy."

THE 100TH NAME FOR GOD

Many Moslem traditions teach that in addition to the 99 names for Allah, there is also a 100th name that is hidden. Some say that this 100th name is the true name for God, unknown to human beings. Others say that the 100th name is *Allah*. The idea of the 100th name has great religious value among the Sufis. Some Sufis claim that through their rituals, they can reach an understanding of the 100th name. Full understanding of God, they argue, can only come with the knowledge of the 100th name.

Among some Shiite traditions is a belief that the 100th name will be revealed by the Mahdi, the Messiah, on the Day of Resurrection. The Bahai faith claims to be the fulfillment of the prophecy of the Mahdi,

26. Majid Fakry, *Averroes: His Life, Works, and Influence* (London: National Book Network, 2003). For this section of the chapter I have also consulted Oliver Leaman, *An Introduction to Classical Islamic Philosophy* (Cambridge: Cambridge University Press, 2001).

and that the 100th name was revealed as *Baha,* an Arabic name meaning "glory" or "splendor."

In Arabian folklore there are a number of stories about the 100th name for God. One tradition suggests the camel knows the 100th name but will not communicate it to other beings. This is why the camel moves with his head high defiantly across the desert, keeping the secret of the 100th name to himself. Others claim that the 99 names are actually adjectives of Allah, and do not tell us about the true identity. In this view, the 100th name is really the name for God.

Another Moslem tradition regarding the 99 names is that no Moslem is to be given any of the 99 names in the exact form they appear in the Qur'an and Hadith. The name *Al-Malik,* (The King) for example, may not be used as a first name, but just *Malik* (King) is often used in Islamic culture.

Another tradition suggests that the number "99" written in Arabic is imprinted on the palms of human's hands. These marks which look like this: A''A, are the Arabic numerals for 81 and 18, which together make 99. This claim, of course, has no Qur'anic basis, and most likely was another myth that developed early in Arabia.

Shulamith Levy Openheim's *The Hundredth Name,* published by Boyd's Mill in 1995, tells the tale of an Egyptologist walking past a sleeping camel on the edge of some fields. The man suggests the camel may be contemplating the 100th name for Allah. The *Kirkus Review,* in reviewing the book, tells us:[27]

> Salah worries at his beloved camel Qadiim's air of sadness until he thinks of a way to help; having heard it said that mankind knows only 99 of God's 100 names, Salah goes out into the night to pray that the last one be revealed—to Qadiim alone.[28]

The review continues: "The next morning, the camel's head is high, in its eyes is (Salah fancies) of wisdom."[29]

Presumably, the look of wisdom has come with the camel knowing the 100th name for Allah. *Publisher's Weekly* also provides a review of the Oppenheim book. It describes the plot:

---

27. Shulamith Levy Oppenheim, *The Hundredth Name* (London: Boyd's Mill, 1997).

28. Review of Oppenheim's *The Hundredth Name* in *Kirkus Review* (June, 1995) 7.

29. Ibid.

Salah is distressed because his camel, Quadiim, seems sad. His father tries to reassure him. "Here on earth we poor mortals must live and die knowing only 99 names for Allah, our god; in truth there are 100 names for God, and the last one of the most importance . . ." Salah prays fervently to let his camel know the 100th name. The following day, the camel stands proud and tall, "a look of infinite wisdom on his face."[30]

Both of these reviews of the Oppenheimer book, and the book itself, rely on this very old Egyptian tale that camels know the 100th name of Allah.

ALLAH AND ANTHROPOMORPHISMS

One group of verses of the Qur'an is called *mustashabah*. The word is often translated as "ambiguous." These ambiguous verses are distinct from those that are *Mukkam*, where the literal sense is quite clear. Thus, Allah is said to dwell on His throne (20:5 and 57:4). He "comes" or moves in places (89:22). The Qur'an speaks of the "hand of Allah," (48:10 and 51:7); it also speaks of Allah's "face," (55:27), His eyes (11:37, 52:48, and 54:14). These ambiguous verses were later the object of exegetical and theological controversy.

Since the beginning of Islam, many anthropomorphisms have been used to discuss Allah. The Qur'an's 48:10 speaks of the "hands of Allah." Other verses in the Qur'an suggest that Allah sits on a throne, has a face, and other anthropomorphic characteristics. Surah 2:115, for example, tells us: "Wherever you turn, the face of Allah is there."[31]

The Qur'an's 38:75 refers to "the hands of Allah." 39:67 tells us that on the day of the resurrection, the whole earth will be in the fistful of Allah. 2:255 of the Qur'an tells us that "Allah sits on his throne over all on heaven and earth." 25:59, 32:4, 40:15, and 69:17 all refer to Allah's throne. The Qur'an's 40:15 tells us that Allah's throne is "high above all ranks." 25:59 informs us that what was created in the heavens and the earth is firmly established on Allah's throne. The same language is used at 57:4. Surah 69:17 speaks of eight angels bearing the throne of Allah.

These anthropomorphisms, and many like them, can be found in the Qur'an. This raises an important question about how to interpret these

---

30. Review of Oppenheim's book in *Publisher's Weekly* (June, 1995) 11.

31. Qur'an 2:115 (author's translation).

anthropomorphisms. Indeed, one theme that turns through the history of Islamic understandings of Allah is how to deal with these anthropomorphisms. Islamic speculations about these anthropomorphisms were particularly popular in the Medieval period.

Later in the eighth to eleventh centuries these ambiguous verses were a subject of debate between the Mutazalite School and the Asharite School of Islamic philosophy. The former wished to reconcile these verses of the Qur'an with the God of reason, particularly the God of Greek philosophy. The Asharites reacted to this view. For them, the anthropomorphic verses are beyond human understanding.

In still later Islamic philosophy, the Asharites began to suggest that the anthropomorphic passages were metaphors. The "hand of Allah" was interpreted to mean the "protection that extends over human beings." His eyes denote "the intensity of His Providence."[32]

Al-Ghazali, twelfth-century Aristotelian philosopher, writes of the problem of the "Throne of Allah." Ghazali tells us:

> He is seated firmly on His throne after the manner which He has said and in the sense in which He willed a being seated firmly, which is far removed from contact and fixity of location and being established and being enveloped and being removed. The throne does not carry Him, but the throne and those that carry it are carried by the grace of His power and mastered by His grasp. He is above the throne, and the heavens and the earth and above everything unto the limits of the stars.[33]

A number of hadith deal with some of these anthropomorphisms. One tradition that discusses the Throne of Allah suggests that the highest part of Paradise is the Throne of Beneficence. Indeed, from the Throne, the rivers of Paradise flow. Sahil Bukhari suggests that "Allah's throne has legs and sides. Moses will be holding one of the legs of Allah's throne. You don't believe it? You'll see for yourself."[34]

Abu Huraira tells us that "Allah's Throne has tight security. He can see everything from it. He is firmly established on it." Huraira and Bukhari make similar comments about the "hands of Allah," and "the face of Allah." A number of other hadith speak of the "shin of Allah." Abu Sa'id

---

32. "Allah," in *Encyclopedia of Islam* (Leiden: Brill, 1979) 1:412.

33. Quoted in Cragg, *The Religious Life of Man*, 14.

34. Nawawi, *Forty Hadith*, 93.

Al-Khudri, another medieval Sunni commentator, for example, tells us this about the shin of Allah:

> Then the Almighty will come to them in a shape other than the one which they saw the first time, and He will say to them, "I am your Lord." And none will speak to Him but the prophets, and then they will say to Him, "Do you know any sign by which you can recognize Him?" They will say, "The shin!" And Allah will uncover his shin whereupon every believer will prostrate before Him, for showing off and gaining a good reputation. These people will try to prostrate but their backs will be rigid like a piece of wood, and they won't be able to prostrate. Then the bridge will be laid across Hell.[35]

This comment by Al-Khudri may be related to a line from the Qur'an, which tells us, "On the day that the great calamity falls and they are called to bow in homage, they will not be able to do so." Several other hadith make it clear that on the day of the resurrection, there will be no problem in seeing Allah in His physical form. He will be recognized by his shin.

ALLAH'S BODY

Directly connected to these comments on anthropomorphisms is a question that we find throughout Moslem philosophy, "Does Allah have a body?" Some hadith point to the claim that faithful Moslems will "see" Allah on the Day of Resurrection. Abu Huraira, for example, responds to this question of "seeing Allah," by asking: "Do you have any difficulty in seeing the moon on a full moon night? Do you have trouble seeing the sun when there are no clouds? So will you see Him like that."[36]

This same tradition is repeated in this hadith narrated by Abu Sa'id al-Kudri: responding to the question about seeing Allah on the Day of Resurrection, Khudri asks: "Do you have any difficulty in seeing the sun and the moon in a clear sky? So you will have no difficulty in seeing your Lord on that day."[37]

Another hadith of Bukhari narrated by Jarir tells a similar story: "We were sitting with the Prophet and he looked at the moon on the night of

35. Ibid., 181.
36. Ibid., 182.
37. Ibid., 183.

a full moon and said, 'You people will see your Lord as you see this full moon, and you will have no trouble in seeing Him.'"[38]

All of these comments made above come from Sunni commentators. They apparently hold the view that in the afterlife human beings will be capable of a "sight" that they do not possess on earth. These comments are in direct opposition to perspectives from Shiite Moslems. The traditional Shiite point of view is that Allah does not have a body.

The Twelver Shiites believe that Allah has no shape, no physical hand, no physical leg, no physical body, no physical face. They believe God has no visible appearance. Allah does not change in time, nor does he occupy a physical place. Under no circumstances, the Shiite argues, does Allah change. There is also no time frame regarding Allah.

As support for their view, Shiite scholars often point to Surah 6:103 of the Qur'an: "No eyes can penetrate Him, but He penetrates all eyes. And He knows all the mysteries for He is All-Knowing."[39]

Thus one fundamental difference between Sunnis and Shiites is that the former believes that followers will "see" their Lord on the Day of Resurrection, while the latter holds that Allah cannot be seen because He is beyond space and time.

THE VOICE OF ALLAH

The Voice of Allah is a recurrent theme in the Qur'an. Allah speaks directly to a number of His prophets through a small voice. This voice acts as a kind of conscience, as well as a continual remembrance that Allah is to be found in the hearts of all true believers.

In a number of passages in the Qur'an, Allah is said to speak to human beings. 42:51, for example, tells us: "He is not given to man that Allah should speak to him except by suggestion, or indirectly, or send a messenger to convey by His command, what ever He pleases."[40]

The Qur'an 4:164 speaks of Allah speaking directly to Musa (Moses). At 2:253, the Qur'an speaks of *Rasulin* (apostles) to whom Allah spoke. At 38:82, the Holy Book tells us that "when Allah wills a thing, He has only to say, 'Be!' And it is."[41] In several passages, Allah is talked about as a voice in

38. Ibid.

39. Qur'an 6:103 (author's translation).

40. Qur'an 42:51 (author's translation).

41. Ibid., 2:253.

the heads of various of his followers. The Qur'an's 41:43–44 suggests that "Nothing is said to you which has not been said to other apostles before you."[42]

Many of the explanations of these passages often point to the difference between literal and metaphorical language about Allah. Imam Ali, for example, speaks of sura 38 and says:

> When Allah wishes to bring something into being, He says, "Be!" But He does not do it with a voice, nor with a voice that has sound, nor with a call that could be heard by humans. For the speech of Allah is one of His actions whereby a thing is endowed with its existence.[43]

This same understanding is seen throughout hadith and Islamic philosophy. Indeed, one of the major preoccupations of Moslem philosophers in the Medieval period was an attempt of harmonizing the literal truths of philosophy with the metaphorical truths of the Qur'an. Often these philosophers responded by suggesting a Two Truths Theory that look similar to Thomas Aquinas' distinction between Natural Truths and Revealed Truths.

Some Islamic scholars have raised the question that is Allah is said to have speech, does that limit Him in any way? These scholars always respond by pointing out a distinction in the Judeo-Christian scholarship that suggests that God's existence and His essence are not distinct, but rather are one and the same. This, coupled with claims about Allah's perfections like omniscience, omnipotence, and eternality, lead these Moslem philosophers to conclude that Allah is not limited simply by saying He has speech.

THE UNITY OF GOD IN ISLAM

In several places the Qur'an talks about the Unity of Allah. Sura 112:1–4 is a representative example:

> Say He is Allah, and One and Only.
> Allah, the Eternal, Absolute.
> He does not begot, nor is He begotten.
> And there is none like unto Him.[44]

42. Ibid., 41:43–44.
43. Imam Ali, "Peak of Eloquence," sermon 184.
44. Qur'an 112:1–4 (author's translation).

The Qur'an speaks repeatedly about there being only one God. It also regularly argues against the concept of the Trinity, as well as the belief that Jesus (Isa) is God. It also tells us in several places that Mary (Maryam) was simply a human being, and not the mother of God. When the Qur'an speaks of the Unity of Allah, it frequently uses the Arabic word, *tawheed*.

The Arabic work, *tawheed* means belief in one God, but it also means much more than that. The word comes from the Arabic root, for "to unite" or "to consolidate." The term *tawheed* is used in three different ways in relation to Allah. The first sense in which the word is used is in the Arabic expression, *Tawheed ar-Ruboobeeyah*. It means something like "the unity of Lordship"—that Allah alone is the sole Creator, Cherisher, and Sustainer.

The second sense in which the word *tawheed* is employed in relation to Allah is related to the Arabic expression, *Tawheed al-Asmaa was-Sifaat*. This refers to the unity of Allah's attributes. This expression is often associated with the Qur'an's 42:11: "There is nothing whatever like Him, and He is the One that hears and sees all things."[45]

The third and final use of the word *tawheed* comes in relation to the expression, *Tawheed al-Ibaadah*. The expression means something like "the unity of worship." The Arabic root of the word, *Ibaadah* is *Abd*, "slave" or "servant," the most common Arabic term for talking about a Moslem believer.

All three categories of *Tawheed* are used in the Qur'an. The first can be seen in 10:31 of the Holy Book: "Say, 'Who is it that Sustains you in life from the sky and from the earth?'"[46] It can also be seen at 43:87: "If you ask them, 'Who created you?' They will certainly say, 'Allah.' How then are they unified with the Truth?"[47]

The Qur'an at 3:64 speaks of the unity of worship: "Oh People of the Book. Come to common terms as between us and you that we worship none but Allah."[48]

This third sense of unity, the unity of worship suggests that Allah alone deserves worship. He alone can destroy worship, and He alone can bring worship into being.

45. Ibid, 42:11.
46. Ibid, 10:31.
47. Ibid, 43:87.
48. Ibid, 3:64.

TWO-TRUTH THEORY IN ISLAM

One way that medieval Islam got around using these anthropomorphisms is to make a distinction between literal and mystical levels of interpretation much like can be seen in the Alexandrian Jews who wrote the Septuagint and Christian figures like Gregory the Great. Averroes, for example, made a distinction between the literal interpretation of the Qur'an, which was proper for the common person, and the allegorical interpretation, which is the proper interpretation for scholars. The latter interpretation, Averroes believed, gives one an access to higher truths in Islam. It may not be in harmony with the literal interpretation which is powerless to access these higher truths.

This notion of Averroes came to be known as the "Double Truth Theory," or the "Two Truth Theory." It claims that what is true in religion may not be true in philosophy, and vice versa. Similarly, what is true at the literal level of interpreting the Qur'an may not be true at the allegorical level.

This distinction between a literal and an allegorical interpretation of the Qur'an is employed by Averroes, specifically on dealing with Ghazali's teachings on the temporal origins of the universe with Aristotle's teaching of the eternality of the universe. In a recent article by Ebrahim Moosa on allegory in Islam Moosa also suggests that Al-Ghazali makes a distinction between what Moosa calls the "imaginary or symbolic" interpretation, and the literal view of the Qur'an.

Al-Ghazali in the eleventh century represented a critical backlash against the Aristotle orientation of Avicenna. In his work, *The Incoherence of the Philosophers,* Al-Ghazali attacks what he saw as inconsistent with many truths in the Qur'an. In Al-Ghazali's view, the truths of the Qur'an supercede those of the philosophers. One of the repercussions of Al-Ghazali's views and his followers was that philosophy in the Islamic East came to an end, although it would soon have a revival in the Islamic West in the work of Averroes.

Averroes in his *The Incoherence of the Incoherence* (a direct response to Al-Ghazali), seeks to defend a coherent Aristotelian view with the Qur'an. He begins by defining philosophy as "The investigation of existing entities insofar as the point to the Maker."[49] Averroes goes on to quote two passages from the Qur'an, 59:2 and 7:184. The first urges "believers to

---

49. Fikry, *History*, 117.

reflect." The second passage asks, "Have they not considered the kingdom of the heavens and the earth and all the things Allah has created?"[50]

Averroes goes on to discuss two different kinds of passages in the Qur'an, those which the Qur'an refers to as "unambiguous," which may be interpreted literally, and those which are "ambiguous," which may be reflected upon and interpreted. The net upshot of Averroes' view is that the truths of philosophy do not contradict the truths of philosophy.

CONCLUSIONS

In this chapter we have explored the concept of God in the Islamic traditions. We began the chapter by looking carefully at the etymology of the word *Allah*. We saw in this section that the word is a cognate of other names for God in Hebrew, Aramaic, and in classical Syriac.

We continued this first chapter by examining the concept of God in the Qur'an. Much of the concept of God and His attributes in the Qur'an are like comments about the existence and attributes of God in Judaism and Christianity. Like in the Old Testament, in the Qur'an Allah is called All-Good, All-Knowing, and All-Powerful; but the Qur'an, as we have seen, also contains names and attributes for God that do not appear in the Old and New Testaments. Some of these names are Bringer of Death, The Avenger, and The Dishonerer.

In the third section of this chapter, we explored a number of comments made in post-Qur'anic Islam about the nature and attributes of Allah. In this section we also introduced the Islamic notion that Allah has 99 names. We have shown there are a number of them in the Qur'an with regards to Allah, and we have also explored how some later hadith have responded to these verses.

Connected to the subject matter of the fourth section of this chapter, we have explored the question of whether Allah has a body. The Sunni tradition seems to think that He does, and that they will see Him at the Resurrection of the Dead. The Shiites, on the other hand, do not believe they will see Allah's body at the end of time, for they do not hold that Allah has a body. Indeed, in the Shiite tradition, Allah is beyond space and time. In the fifth section of this chapter, we have discussed the uses of the Arabic term, *Tawheed* and its use in Islam in relation to God. As we

50. Ibid.

have seen, this Arabic term is used to discuss the "Unity of Allah" in three distinct and separate ways.

In the sixth and final section of this initial chapter, we have explored what is sometimes called the "Two Truth Theory" or the "Double Truth Theory." As we have shown, this theory was a belief among many Scholastic philosophers in the medieval period. The belief was developed as a response to the question of whether the truths of the Qur'an were contradictory to claims in the philosophy of Aristotle.

Chief among the participants in this debate were Al-Ghazali and Averroes. The former believed that the truths of philosophy were superceded by the truths of the Qur'an, while the latter thought Aristotle and the Qur'an were compatible. Other Medieval Moslem participants in this debate were Al-Farabi and Avicenna. Both of these philosophers held a view closer to that of Averroes. They did not believe that the truths of the Qur'an were contradicted by the truths of Aristotle. This led Avicenna and Farabi to what came to be called the Two Truth Theory, which later was adopted by Averroes.

In the second chapter of this work, we take a close look at Islamic views of two Old Testament patriarchs, Ibrahim and Isaq (Abraham and Isaac). As we shall see, one of the fundamental differences between the Judeo-Christian traditions and Islam is that the Jews and Christians believe that Abraham nearly sacrificed his son, Isaac, while the Moslem tradition suggests the sacrificial son was Ismail (Ishmael). We shall also discuss in the next chapter the traditional roles played by Abraham and Ishmael in the Islamic tradition.

2

Abraham, Isaac, and Islam

We are the remnants of prophecy. And that was the prayer of Ibrahim regarding us.

—Muhammed al-Baqir

Allah, the exalted, has given Ibrahim the glad tidings, and he has bestowed a favour and multiplied it and placed in his progeny twelve mighty personalities.

—Ibn Kathir

Remember when his Lord tried Ibrahim, by a number of commands which he fulfilled. Allah said, "I will make you a leader among men."

—The Qur'an

INTRODUCTION

IN THIS CHAPTER, WE take a close look at the figures of Abraham and Isaac in the Islamic tradition. We begin the chapter with a description of the treatment of Abraham in the early Qur'an. We continue the chapter by looking more specifically at what Islam has to say about the story in Genesis 22, the binding and sacrificing of Isaac. In a third section of this chapter, we explore the other Qur'anic traditions about Abraham, as well as the place of Abraham in later Islam. We conclude this chapter with a number of conclusions on the place of the prophet Abraham in Moslem history.

IBRAHIM IN THE EARLY QUR'AN

Ibrahim is the Arabic name for Abraham, one of the earliest patriarchs in the Hebrew Bible. He is considered one of the first and greatest of Moslem prophets. He is mentioned in greater or lesser details in twenty-five principal suras of the Qur'an. Moses is the only prophet of Islam mentioned more often than Ibrahim. This is not to say, however, that Abraham is inferior to Moses. Indeed, Ibrahim is called *Khalil Ullah* in Arabic, "friend of Allah."[1]

In two suras, which are dated from the Meccan period, there are references to the *suhuf* (leave scrolls) of Abraham and Moses.[2] In the latter of these two passages, Ibrahim is called a man who "has paid his debt in full,"[3] presumably a reference to Ibrahim holding steadfast in faith in light of Allah's command to kill Isaac. In another passage, Ibrahim is referred to as one who "speaks the truth" (*siddik*).[4]

In a whole series of suras from the second and third Meccan periods, the Qur'an tells of how Ibrahim attacked the idol worship of his father, named Azar in 6:74. In this tradition, there is a belief that Azar was a maker of idols, and Ibrahim advocated instead belief in one God. These beliefs are discussed at length in 37:83–98; 26:69–89; 19:41–50; 43:26–28; 21:51–73; 29:16–27; and 6:74–84.

Sura 37 speaks of Ibrahim asking why his father/uncle worship idols, as do suras 19, 21, 26, and 43. Sura six discusses Allah's ability to control the movements of the moon and the sun. 29:16–27 also speaks of the worshipping of idols, and it also provides a number of admonishments

1. The edition of the Qur'an I have used in this chapter is Ahmed Ali, *Al-Qur'an* (Princeton: Princeton University Press, 1993). I have also consulted the following translations: Sayed Razwy and Abdullah Yusufali, *The Qur'an Translation* (London: Asir Media, 2002); A. J. Arberry, (editor) *The Koran Interpreted* (New York: Touchstone, 1996); and N. J. Dawood, *The Koran: With Parallel Arabic Text* (New York: Penguin Classics, 2000). I have also consulted the following secondary sources: Ibn Warraq, *The Origins of the Koran* (New York: Prometheus, 1998); Mateen Elass, *Understanding the Koran* (London: Zondervan, 2004); Thomas Cleary, *The Essential Koran* (San Francisco: Harper Collins, 1994); Arthur N. Wollaston, *The Religion of the Koran* (London: Kessinger, 2004); and Henry Bayman, *The Secret of Islam* (New York: North Atlantic Books, 2003).

2. Qur'an 87; 18f. and 53:36f.

3. "Ibrahim," in *The Encyclopedia of Islam* (Leiden: Brill, 1979) 3:980.

4. Qur'an 37:112. The principal hadith I have used in this chapter are Bukhari, *Anbiya*, 8–11; Muslim, *Fada'il*, 150-154; Tabari, *Annales*, I; 252–319; Ibn al-Athir, *Chronicon*, edited by Tornberg (1867).

to believers. Among these are not to ask about the nature of how Allah created, nor ask whom or why he punishes.

In the Median period of the development of the Qur'an, Ibrahim becomes a more prominent figure in Islam. Indeed, Ibrahim and his son, Ishmael no longer lead a shadowy and isolated existence. Instead, they become responsible for building the Ka'ba in Mecca as a symbol of pilgrimage. Indeed, Ibrahim and Ishmael are given credit in Islam for making the Ka'ba, a monotheistic place of worship.

There is also a tradition in Islam that Ibrahim is buried in Hebron. This is most likely connected to the fact that Ibrahim's wife, Sarah, died in Hebron, and thus he wished to be close to his wife. In the Masjid al Haram in Mecca there is an area known as *Maqam Ibrahim* ("the stations of Abraham,") where the impressions of the prophet's footsteps can be seen. Ibrahim also plays an important role in one of the Pillars of Islam, the Hajj, which is the requirement to travel to the Holy Mosque. One of the most important aspects of the Hajj is remembering Ibrahim's faith and willingness to sacrifice his son.

About Abraham's death the rabbinic tradition suggest, and Islam adopts, that the Angel of Death had no power over him. One account suggests that when God wished to take Ibrahim's soul, Allah sent an angel in the form of a decrepit old man. Ibrahim was at table with some guests, when he saw an old man walking in the heat of the sun. He sent an ass to carry the man to his tent. But the old man did not have the strength to put the food to his mouth, and even then he had the greatest difficulty in swallowing it.

This tradition continues:

> Now a long time before this, Ibrahim had asked Allah not to take his soul until he (Ibrahim) should make the request. When he saw the actions of this old man he asked him what ailed him. "It is the result of old age, Oh Ibrahim!" he answered. "How old are you then?" asked Ibrahim. The old man gave his age as two years older than Ibrahim, upon which the prophet exclaimed, "In two years time, I shall be like him. Oh Allah, take me to Thyself." The old man was none other than the Angel of Death, and he took away Ibrahim's soul.

One tradition has it that on the way to the altar of the Holy Mosque, Iblis, the Evil One, attempted three times to dissuade Ibrahim from sacrificing his son. These places where Iblis appeared are marked by three symbolic stones, where traditional Moslems throw stones to ward off the enemy.

The *ramy al-jamarat*, or the "Stoning of the Devil," is part of the Islamic Hajj. Pilgrims throw stone at three walls called *jamarat*. Traditionally, the three *jamarat* (singular, *jamarah*) were three tall pillars, which have been replaced in the 2004 Hajj with three 85 foot walls. On the tenth day of Dhu al-Hijjah (Eid ul-Adha), pilgrims throw seven pebbles at the largest of the *jaramat*. On both of the following two days, they throw seven pebbles at each of the three walls. The purpose of this ritual is to ward off the Devil.

Another aspect of the Hajj is the commemoration of the sacrifice and faith of Ibrahim's wife, Hajre (Hagar), who attempted to find water for her son Ishmael, when he was near death from thirst. The tale has it that Hajre ran between the two hills, Safar and Marwa, seven times. In lieu of this incident, *saaee* (effort or struggle) is mandatory for all pilgrims traveling to Mecca. The story has it that in this quest for water, Hajre saw a spring of fresh water that erupted where her son had fallen. This spring became the basis of the founding of the city of Mecca, since fresh water is scarce in that part of the world. This spring has been running for thousands of years. Ibrahim settled his wife and family there, and eventually, the prophet Mohammed was born there.

In some Moslem traditions, a specific *dua* (prayer) is recited daily to honor Ibrahim. The traditional *Salaat*, that occurs five times a day, also has a number of references to Ibrahim, the father of all believers. He is mentioned as an upright man, who is nether Christian nor polytheist, nor Jew. As the Qur'an tells us:

> O those who believe. Bow down and prostrate yourselves, and worship your Lord, and do good, that happily you many prosper. And strive for Allah with the effort which is his right. He has chosen you, and He has not laid down any religious requirements; the faith of your father Ibrahim is yours. He has named you Moslems in the old days, and in his Scripture, that the messenger may be a witness against you, and that you be a witness against mankind. So establish worship, pay the poor their due, and hold fast to Allah. He is your protecting Friend, a blessed Patron, and a blessed Helper.[5]

In the Islamic tradition, the faith of Ibrahim frequently is called *Millat-e-Ibrahim*, "the religion of Ibrahim," because of the Moslem belief

---

5. *Encyclopedia of Islam*, 3:981.

that Ibrahim was the first believer in Allah and Islam, as well as the view that Islam's history traces back to Ibrahim through his son Ishmael, not Isaac, as in Judaism and Christianity.

A final Moslem tradition, mentioned above, is the role that Ibrahim played in establishing monotheism in Islam. The Qur'an 6:76–83 tells us that anything subject to disappearance is not worthy of worship. Azar's idols were subject to disappearance, so Ibrahim was a monotheist. Although some Moslems believe that Azar was Ibrahim's father, the majority of Islamic adherents believe that Tarakh was Ibrahim's father, and Azar was his uncle. These Moslems suggest that Ibrahim destroyed his uncle's idols, not those of his father. This tradition further holds that Ibrahim was thrown into a fire, which miraculously failed to burn the prophet.[6] This scene of Ibrahim surviving in a raging fire is one of the most common themes depicted in the Islamic iconography of Abraham. Another important scene depicted in Islamic art is Abraham's sacrifice of Isaac, which we explore in the next section of this chapter.

IBRAHIM AS A MODEL OF FAITH

More than any figure in Islam, with the exception of Muhammed himself, the figure of Ibrahim is seen as a model for Islamic faith. This becomes clear in a number of passages in the Qur'an. The Qur'an's 16:120–123 is a good example:

> Ibrahim was certainly a model of faith, obedient to God and upright, and not one of the idolaters. Grateful to Him for his favors; so He chose him and guided him to the path that is straight, and gave him what is good in the world, and in the Hereafter. He will be among the righteous and the good. So We commanded you to follow the way of Ibrahim, the upright who was not of idolaters.[7]

This general conclusion about the moral character of Abraham in the Islamic faith is held throughout the Qur'an, as well as the major ahadith (the plural of hadith) on the prophet. Consider this passage from the Qur'an's sura 60:

> You have an excellent model in Ibrahim and those who were with him, when he said to his people, "We are through with you and

---

6. Qur'an 18:50.

7. The Holy Qur'an 16:120–123 (author's translation).

those who you worship other than Allah. We reject you. Enmity and hate have come between you and us forever."[8]

The figure Ibrahim is not only seen as the founder of the Religions of the Book, he is also at times displayed as having the same status as Moses (Musa), particularly with respect to the bringing of scripture to Islam. Consider these verses from sura 87 of the Qur'an:

> Surely he will succeed who grows in goodness. And recites the names of his Lord and serves with devotion. But no, you prefer the life of the world, though the life to come is better and abiding. This is surely in the earlier Books. The Books of Abraham and Moses.[9]

There is no indication elsewhere in the Qur'an or in ahadith what the "books of Abraham" might be. Nor is there any indication in the Hebrew Scriptures that he was responsible for sacred texts. What is clear about Abraham is that in Islam he is considered to be one of the greatest of the prophets, a man most often referred to as "The friend of the Merciful."

ISLAM AND THE SACRIFICE OF IBRAHIM'S SON

The Islamic tradition, by and large, believes that it was Ishmael rather than Ishaq (Isaac) whom Allah told Ibrahim to sacrifice. Islamic scholars point out that despite specifying Ishaq as the sacrifice, Ibrahim is told to "Take your son, your only son, whom you love." Since Ishaq was Ibrahim's second son, there was never a time when he would have been his father's "only son." Thus, some scholars contend there must have been an earlier tradition of Genesis, where Ishmael was the intended sacrifice. The Qur'an itself does not specify by name which son was the object of sacrifice. It simply says it was Ibrahim's "only son." The Qur'an puts the matter this way:

> And he said, "I am going away to my Lord who will show me the way."
> And he prayed: "Oh Lord, grant me a righteous son."
> So we gave him the good news of a son. When he was old enough to go about with him, he said, "O my son, I had a dream that I was sacrificing you. What do you think of that?"
> "Father," he said, "do as you are commanded. If God pleases, you will find me steadfast."

8. Ibid., 60:4.
9. Ibid., 87:14–19.

When they submitted to the will of God, and Ibrahim laid his son down prostrate on his temple, we called out: "Oh Ibrahim, you have fulfilled your dream." Thus do we reward the good.

This was indeed a trying test, so we ransomed him for a great sacrifice. And we left this holy memory for posterity. Peace be on Ibrahim. That is how we reward the good. He is truly among our most faithful creatures.[10]

In Islam, Ibrahim's dream is seen as a test from Allah. When Ibrahim told the dream to Ishmael, it was his first son that convinced his father to fulfill God's command. In this sense, it is a test for Ibrahim, whom had longed for a son, as well as Ishmael. When the Devil tempted them before the sacrifice, some Moslems argue, Ibrahim and Ishmael threw stones at Iblis, thus the origins of throwing stones at the Devil in Islam.

This sacrifice of Ishmael is celebrated in Islam at the feast of Eid ul-Adha. This feast occurs on the tenth day of Dhul Hijja, a month in the Moslem calendar. The chief purpose of Eid ul-Adha is to celebrate Ibrahim's willingness to sacrifice his son. Some Moslems also celebrate Eid ul-Adha as a mark for the end of the Hajj, for the millions of Moslems who make the pilgrimage to Mecca each year.

Many Moslems believe that Allah revealed in a dream to Ibrahim that he should sacrifice his son, Ishmael. Thus, Ibrahim and Ishmael set off for Mina, the Arabic name for Mount Moriah. As they went, Iblis attempted to dissuade them from the sacrifice; but Ibrahim stayed true to Allah, and the Holy One gave him a sheep to sacrifice in his son's stead.

The celebration of Eid ul-Adha is one of two major festivals in Islam. The other is called Eid ul-Fitr, which celebrates the end of Ramadan—the month of fasting. It is a joyous occasion, a happy celebration that one could survive a month long fast. Moslems dress is festive attire. A common greeting on this celebration is *"Eid mubarak,"* which is roughly translated as Happy Ending.

Eid ul-Fitr is generally considered to be a three day festival, while Eid ul-Adha is supposed to last a day longer. On the first day, people dress in their finest clothing and perform prayers together in a large gathering. Moslems who can afford to do so, sacrifice animals, usually sheep, as a symbol of Ibrahim's sacrifice of his son. In Arabic, this sacrifice is called *Qurba*, the Arabic word for both martyr and sacrifice. The meat from the *Qurban* is distributed among neighbors, relatives, and the poor.

10. Ibid. 6:76–83.

The feast of Eid ul-Adha comes immediately after the Day of Arafat, when Mohammed pronounced the final seal on the religion of Islam. On this day, Moslems stay in the city of Arafat until sunset. They say ritual prayers and spend the remainder of the day glorifying Allah and asking for forgiveness.

Eid ul-Adha also has a number of other names in Islam. In West Africa, it is known as *Tobaski*; in Bangladesh, as *Qurbani Eid*; in Turkey, Eid ul-Adha is called *Kurban Byrami,* or "sacrificial feast" in Turkish; Moslems in Bosnia call Eid ul-Ahda *Kurban*, the Bosnian word for "sacrifice." What all these names have in common is they all celebrate the faithful willingness of Ibrahim to sacrifice his son Ishmael.

In more modern Islamic scholarship, several scholars have contributed to the understanding of Ibrahim's sacrifice of his son. Hamid al-Din Farahi, an Indian Moslem scholar born in 1863 and died in 1930, in his Arabic work, *Al-Ray al-Sihih fi man huwa al-dhabih*, revived the Isaac or Ishmael question, coming down decidedly on the side of Ishmael. Abdus Sattar Ghawri, a contemporary Moslem scholar, has affirmed Farahi's work in his "The Only Son Offered for Sacrifice: Isaac or Ishmael." Ghawri uses a passage from Deuteronomy 21:15–17 as a proof text for the Ishmael view.[11]

The Hebrew of Deuteronomy 21:15–17 goes like this:

> If a man has two wives, one of them loved and the other disliked, and if both the loved and the disliked have borne him sons, and the first born is the son of the one disliked, then o the day that the man wills his possessions, he is not to treat the son of the loved wife as his preference to the son of the disliked, who is the first born. He must acknowledge as his first born the son who is the one that is disliked, giving him a double portion of all that he has; since he is the first issue of his virility, the right of the first-born is his.[12]

Clearly early Islam found this Hebrew Bible text attractive for it outlines the relative importance of Ibrahim's two sons, Ismail, the first born, and Isaq. From its inception, Islam exalted the life of Ishmael, the progenitor of Islam, while leaving the figure of Isaq in the shadows.

Most Islamic sources speak of Ibrahm leaving his family after he lost hope that he could convert his father and their people. Ibrahim then

11. Ibid. 11:71.
12. Deuteronomy 21:15–17 (author's translation).

devises a plot to destroy the idols. One source suggests that Ibrahim knew that a big celebration was coming, where everyone would leave town for a big feast on the riverbank. After making sure that nobody was left in town, Ibrahim went to the temple armed with an axe. Statues of all shapes and sizes were in the temple. Plates of food were being offered to them, but the food untouched. "Why don't you eat," says Ibrahim, "It is getting cold?" Then with the axe he destroyed all the idols except one, the biggest of them. He hung the axe around its neck and left.

In other Islamic versions of the sacrifice of Ibrahim's son, the prophet has the same dream of sacrificing his son on three consecutive nights, or that it was seven nights in a row. In every account, Ibrahim asks Ishmael what it means, and the son tells his father to do whatever Allah commanded.

OTHER ISLAMIC TRADITIONS ON IBRAHIM

In addition to the material mentioned above, there are also a number of Moslem traditions that often attempt to fill in some of the details of these traditions. Among the topics of these traditions are the rescue of Ibrahim from the fire; Ibrahim's intercession on the part of his pagan father; Ibrahim's quarrel with the autocratic Nimrod; and the killing of four birds depicted in Genesis 15:9ff. Many of these scenes are also popular in Moslem iconography about Ibrahim.

Two representative images in Moslem iconography are a modern Islamic folk drawing of the sacrifice of Ishmael. The surrounding text comes from the Qur'an 37:104: "And when he reached the age to work with him, he said, 'Oh my boy, I have seen a dream that I should sacrifice you, what do you think of that?' The boy said, 'Oh sir, do what you have been bidden. I hope to please Allah and be one of the patient.'"[13]

The other representative image of modern Islamic iconography is a sixteenth-century miniature from *Zubdat al-Tawarikh* by Luqman-i-Ashuri. The lower register shows Ibrahim about to sacrifice Ishmael. Beneath the image is a genealogy of Ishmael, the beginning of Islam. In the upper register, Ibrahim emerges from Nimrod's fiery furnace. The first

---

13. Abdus Sattar Ghawri, "The Only Son Offered For Sacrifice: Isaac or Ishmael," (Lahore: al Mawrad Institute, 2004).

of these images is owned by the Oxford University Library; the other is owned by the Chester Beatty Library in Dublin.[14]

Mentions of Nimrod in the Hebrew Bible are rather limited. He is called the first to become "a mighty one on the earth," and "a mighty hunter before the Lord." He is also said to be the founder and king of the first empire after the flood, and that his empire is connected with the Mesopotamian towns of Babel, Uruk, Akkad, Calneh, Nivevah, Resen, Rehoboth-Ir, and Calah. Nimrod's kingdom is sometimes called the "land of Shinar," as well as the "land of Nimrod," but nowhere in the Biblical materials is there any indication that Nimrod had a relationship with Abraham/Ibrahim. In fact, there is a gap of seven generations between Abraham and Nimrod. Nimrod was Noah's grandson, while Abraham was 10 generations removed from Noah (Genesis 10:11). Nevertheless, later Jewish and Islamic traditions bring the two of them together in a cosmic battle between good and evil, and polytheism and monotheism.

Beginning the confrontation between Nimrod and Ibrahim, in one Moslem tradition, Nimrod is portrayed as an enemy to monotheism. A dream and gazing of the stars tells Nimrod of the impending birth of Ibrahim. Nimrod, therefore, orders the killing of all newborns in his kingdom. Ibrahim's mother escapes into the fields and secretly gives birth.

In this account, Ibrahim grows up and begins the worshipping of Allah, the only God. He confronts Nimrod and tells him to his face to cease idolatry, whereupon Nimrod orders him burned at the stake. In some Islamic versions of the tale, Nimrod has his people gather wood for four years before the fire for Ibrahim. After the lighting of the fire, Ibrahim walks out unscathed, and then declares war on Nimrod.

When Nimrod appears as the head of a great army, Ibrahim produces an army of gnats, which destroy Nimrod's forces. Some Islamic accounts have a gnat enter the ear of Nimrod and drive him out of his mind. In other Moslem accounts of the two figures, Nimrod repents and accepts Allah. Other accounts explain Ibrahim's leaving Mesopotamia as an escape from Nimrod.

Whether or not Nimrod repented, Nimrod remained in Islamic tradition a symbol of evil and an archetype of idolatry. Indeed, in the Talmud, Nimrod is referred to as "Nimrod the Evil," and in Islam as *Nimrod Al-Jabbar*, Nimrod the Tyrant.

14. "The Sacrifice of Ishmael," Oxford University Library.

Nimrod is referred to in the Qur'an at sura 21:68–69, where Nimrod says of Ibrahim: "Burn him and save your gods, if you are men of action." But Allah responds to Ibrahim being placed in the fire by Nimrod's followers: "'Turn cold, oh fire,' we said, and gave safety to Ibrahim. They wished to entrap him, but We made them greater losses."[15]

Other Moslem accounts have it that when Ibrahim emerges from the fire, Nimrod exclaims, "You have a powerful God. I wish to offer him hospitality," but Ibrahim tells Nimrod that his god needs no hospitality from anyone.

Another version of Ibrahim, Nimrod, and the fire suggests the following:

> A huge pit was dug up and a large quantity of wood was piled up. Then the biggest fire people have ever seen was lit. The fire flames were so high up in the sky that the birds could not fly over it for fear of being burned. Ibrahim's hands and feet were chained, and he was put in a catapult to throw him into the fire. At that time, Angel Jibril came to him and said, "Oh Ibrahim, is there anything you wish for?" Ibrahim could have asked to be saved from the fire, to be taken away, but no, he said, "I only wish that Allah be pleased with me." The catapult was released, and Ibrahim was thrown into the heart of the fire. But Allah would not allow his prophet to be killed. He ordered the fire, "O fire! Be cool and safety for Ibrahim!" And the miracle happened. The fire obeyed and burned only the chains. Ibrahim came out of it as if he were coming out of a garden, peaceful, his face illuminated, and not a trace of smoke on his clothes. People watched in shock and said, "Amazing! Ibrahim's god has saved him from the fire."[16]

Another version of the Ibrahim and Nimrod (or Namrod, or Namrud) has it that Nimrod asks Ibrahim to explain to Nimrod's people who his god is. Ibrahim says that his God is the one that gives life, and who takes it away. The King responds by saying he does that every day. Ibrahim says that his God brings the sun from the east. He asked the King that if he has the power have his god make the sun rise in the west. Clearly, Nimrod was unable to carry out this task.

Ibrahim's intercession on the part of his pagan father is also a popular tale in Islam. In some Moslem accounts, the name of Ibrahim's father is

15. "The Sacrifice of Ishmael," from *Majma al-Tawrikh* by Hafiz-Ii (Persia, 1425) Cheester Beatty Library, Dublin.

16. Qur'an 21:68–69.

Azar. Others give the father's name as Terah. Still others say Azar was his name, and Terah his surname. What all accounts of Ibrahim's father have in common is that Azar was a great worshipper of idols, and devotee of astronomy. Ibrahim had to work hard in dissuading his father from these practices. In sura 21:53, we get a description of Ibrahim's attempts to reconcile his father with the worship of Allah, and this scene is commented on in later Islamic history.

The Qur'an tells us:

> We had earlier given Ibrahim true direction, for We knew him well when he said to his father and his people, "What are these idols to which you cling so passionately?" They replied, "We found our fathers worshipping them." He said, "You and your fathers were in clear error."[17]

Various accounts of Ibrahim have the prophet destroying the idols of his father with an axe. The following day, Ibrahim's people saw what he had done and were angry with him. When the leader of his village asked Ibrahim why he had done it, the prophet asked why the idol gods have not saved themselves from ruin. In this account, Ibrahim is then sentenced to be burned alive.

The angel Jibril (Gabriel), the account has it, came to Ibrahim and asks if there is anything that Ibrahim desires. Ibrahim says no, and then Allah brings the cool breeze to save Ibrahim from the fire. This cool breeze makes Ibrahim feel as though he was in a cool garden, and he walks unharmed from the fire.

In still another Moslem account, Ibrahim and his wife Sarah visited Egypt calling the people there to Allah. During the visit, the Pharaoh of Egypt gives Ibrahim a slave woman name Hajirah. Ibrahim took the woman as his second wife. Hajirah becomes pregnant and gives birth to Ibrahim's son, Ishmael. In this account, Allah instructs Ibrahim to take Hajirah and Ishmael to Hejaz, a desolate place in the desert. Ibrahim placed a bag full of dates and a skin of water on the ground next to his son. Ibrahim started to walk away, when Hajirah begged her husband not to leave them in the desert. She asks if Allah had commanded that they be left there alone. Ibrahim says He has, and he leaves them in the desert with a sorrowful heart, placing their lives in the hands of Allah.

---

17. The Holy Qur'an 21:51–54 (author's translation).

Hejirah and Ishmael quickly runs out of supplies, and she begins running between two hills, in search of water or help. Seven times she runs from the hills of Safa to Marwah in the search for water. Ishmael became so thirsty that he began crying, kicking the ground with his heels. A great stream rushed from where Ishmael's heels had struck the ground, and a great stream rushes forward. This stream is still running today, according to Moslem legend, and it is called the Zam Zam.

The Well of Zam Zam (or the Zam Zam Well), or simply Zam Zam is a well located within the Masjid al Haram in the city of Mecca. It is near the Ka'ba, the holiest of places in Islam. The Zam Zam is 30 meters deep. There are a number of springs contributing to the well. Many Moslems believe that the waters of the Zam Zam are sacred. Thus, they make every effort to drink from the well during the pilgrimage.

Some Moslems believe the waters of the Zam Zam not only satisfy hunger and thirst, but also is said to heal sickness and disease. The water from the well is served in coolers stationed throughout the Masjid al Haram. Pilgrims often fill canisters with the water from spigots provided by the Saudi government. Some even dip their clothing in the Zam Zam water and then preserve the garment for use as a burial shroud.

As the Islamic population has increased throughout the world, increasing demands for the water has made it difficult to supply all that is demanded. In many cities throughout the world there is a trade for Zam Zam water. The trade for fake Zam Zam water is said to be ever increasing.

In another account of the origin of the Zam Zam, Allah sends forth the Angel Jibril who scrapes the ground, causing the stream to appear. In this account Hagar confines the pool of water with sand and stones.

The grandfather of Muhammed, a man named Abdul Muttalib, is said to have rediscovered the well after it had been neglected and filled with sand. Muttalib became the guardian of the Zam Zam. He is said to have maintained the well for many years, giving its water to those who make a pilgrimage to Mecca.

A tribe that had been searching the desert for food and water known as the Banu Jaham, came upon Hejirah. They were sitting by the stream in awe. The Jaham sat down with them and decides to set up a temporary camp that later becomes the city of Mecca. Numerous stories have arisen about the appearance of the Zam Zam. One account suggests that some Arabs traveling through Makkah saw birds flying around al-Marwa.

"They must be flying around water," they said. Eventually, these Arabs also brought their families and friends to the spot.

Ibrahim continues to call people to the worship of Allah, but until then, no place of worship had been built for them. When Ibrahim prays for a place of worship, Allah commands Ibrahim and Ishmael to build the Ka'ba, a Sacred House of worship. The Qur'an 2:125–127 gives a full account of these events. It reads:

> Remember, we made the House (of Ka'ba) a place of congregation and safe retreat, and said, "Make the spot where Ibrahim stood the place of worship;" and enjoined upon Ibrahim and Ishmael to keep our house immaculate for those who shall walk around it and stay in it for contemplation and prayer, and for bowing in adoration.[18]

Later Moslem tradition says that the Ka'ba is an exact replica of the Ka'ba in Heaven, thus Ibrahim and Ishmael were not working from scratch when they built the Ka'ba. Other versions of the construction of the Ka'ba suggest that Ibrahim and Ishmael inserted a Black Stone in one of the corners of the building in accordance with the will of Allah. Thus, the ritual of the Hajj was initiated that day, and continues to this day.

In Islamic accounts, Ibrahim is often called the "father of hospitality." Long accounts are given of Ibrahim's visits by angels, particularly Jibril (Gabriel). Ibrahim is also said in Islam to be the first whose hair grew white. In Moslem tradition, Arabs trace their ancestry back to Ibrahim through Ishmael. Because Ishmael was circumcised (Genesis 17:25), so are all Moslems. An analogous to Paul's reversal of the figures of Isaac and Ishmael (Galatians 4.24–26), the Islamic tradition makes Ishmael rather than Isaac the son that Ibrahim was commanded to sacrifice. Both sons appear at Ibrahim's funeral (Genesis 15:9), suggesting in Islam that both sons have a lofty place in the history of Judaism.

In Qur'an 3:60, we are told that "Ibrahim was not a Jew, nor yet a Christian, but he was a *hanif*, but he was not an idolater." Those who are most worthy of him, the Qur'an tells us, "are those that follow him and his prophets, and those who believe." Indeed, in several places Mohammed

---

18. Clearly, 73. For more on the relationship between Abraham and King Nimrod in Islam, see D. Sidersky, *Les Origenes des legends musulmanes dans les Coran* (Paris, 1933) 31–54; H. Schutzinger, *Ursprung und Entwichlung der arabischen Abraham-Nimrod legende* (Bonn, 1961); and M. Hayek, *Le mysterie D'Ishmael* (Paris, 1964). Other early sources are A. Geiger, *Judiasm and Islam* (Madras, 1898); A. Sprenger, *The Life and Learning of Mohammed* (Berlin, 1862), particularly 276–85.

says in the Qur'an that the *Millat Ibrahim* (religion of Abraham) is the one that he desires his people to follow. Mohammed makes this observation at Qur'an 16; 124; 2:124; and 12:77.

One final Islamic tradition on Ibrahim is the view that the prophet died in Palestine and was buried in a cave called Al-Mikfela, near Hebron. This view can be seen early on in Islam, continued during the Middle Ages, and exists in the Modern Period. Genesis 23 gives an account of the death of Sarah. 23:3 tells us that Sarah died at Kiriatharba (that is, Hebron). Thus, in Islam Ibrahim desires to be buried near his first wife, Sarah.

DISAGREEMENTS OVER THE SON FOR SACRIFICE

The Qur'an 37:99–110, the main narrative on the sacrifice of Ibrahim's son, does not identify the name of the son. Thus, at times in Islam, there has been some disagreement in Islam over the identity of that son. Muhammed himself declared the intended one to be Isaac. This is also the point of view of his colleague, Omar ibn al-Kattab, and of Ali ibn Ali Talib, a member of the second generation of Moslem scholars.

Over and against this view is the Persian scholar, Al-Tabari (838–923). Tabari quotes all the hadith of the Arab Masoretes and exegetes, who were divided over whether the son was Isaac or Ishmael. Umayya ibn Bi al-Salt, another contemporary of Muhammed, gives a lengthy description of the binding (29:9–21), as it is told in the Bible and midrashim. Tabari discusses the sacrifice in both his *Tarikh* (history) and his *Tafsir* (commentary), but he points out in both that there is some confusion about the identity of the son for sacrifice.

In a fragment of the genizah at al-Samaw'al al'-Kurazi there is a mention of the *Dhabih* ("the bound one"), as Isaac, and sometimes Ishmael, is referred to in the Moslem tradition. In some Islamic accounts, the son, whether Isaac or Ishmael, is redeemed for a lamb, while in others it is for a ram.

Like in Biblical accounts of Abraham, in the Quranic discussions of Ibrahim the prophet is put to the ultimate test to see if he would submit absolutely to the Divine will of Allah. He was asked to sacrifice his son. Hewer comments on the differences between the two:

> In the Bible, it is Isaac who was to be sacrificed, but in the Islamic tradition it was Ishmail. The Qur'an is not explicit that the son to

be sacrificed was Ishmail, but the overwhelming Muslim tradition interprets it that way . . . Here lies an important difference between Jewish and Islamic traditions.[19]

What all Islamic accounts share is that just before Ibrahim is to come down with the knife an angel appears and tells him to stop, and that an animal is provided in the son's stead for the sacrifice. In some Islamic accounts the angel is identified as Jibril (Gabriel), while in others the angel is not identified.

Generally speaking, the angel is identified in Islamic traditions as Jibril, the Angel Gabriel, who is also said to have struck the ground to find the Zam Zam, as well as, as we shall see in a later chapter, commanded Ayyub (Job) to strike the ground, whereupon a stream appears at Job's feet.

ISLAMIC MIDRAHS ON IBRAHIM

The stories told of Ibrahim in the Qur'an naturally became the basis for further midrashic expansion among Moslems. The likeness of the history of Ibrahim to certain features in the accounts of the life of Mohammed made Ibrahim a favorite among Islamic commentators and historians. Islamic writers had two major sources from which they drew their knowledge of Ibrahim. The Hebrew Bible and the *akhbar*, the rabbis from earlier commentaries.

Like the rabbis of the Talmud, most discussions of later Islamic commentaries on Ibrahim are about the sacrifice of Ishmael. Among the earliest commentaries on the Ibrahim and Ishmael story was Abd al-Rahman ibn Sakhir, also called Abu Haraira. Haraira lived in the seventh century and died around 678. He was among the first writers of ahadith, and among the first commentaries to suggest that Ibrahim wished to sacrifice Ishmael, not Isaac.

Muhammed al-Bukhari (810–870) was born in the city of Bukhara, in what today is Uzbekistan. Bukhari was among the most important of early Sunni writers of ahadith. Bukhari is important for our purposes because of a hadith that says that Ibrahim lied on three occasions. Bukhari then enumerates the three lies. In one, Ibrahim tells Sarah to tell anyone who asked her about him was to say "He is my brother."[20]

---

19. C. T. R. Hewer, *Understanding Islam: An Introduction* (Minneapolis: Fortress, 2006) 20.

20. Qur'an 2:125–127.

Islamic commentaries are full of discussions of whether Ibrahim did or did not lie. Some say he did lie, others that he did not; a third camp has it that Ibrahim had the proper intentions, but the listener did not properly understand those intentions. Some commentators say that Ibrahim lied because of certain consequences that would follow if he did not. Ahadith are full of this kind of philosophical discussions of the life of Ibrahim. A third Islamic commentator on Islamic views of Ibrahim and Ishmael is Abu Jafar Muhammed ibn Jarir ibn Yazid ibn Kathir al-Tabari. Al-Tabari (838–923) wrote a major commentary on the Qur'an and compiled an exhaustive history of Islam to his time. In his commentary on the Qur'an, Tabari points out that the Qur'an does not explicitly say which of Ibrahim's sons was to be prepared for the sacrifice. He also points out that Hagar, Ishmael's mother, is not mentioned in the Qur'an.

Abu Hurairah, a Yemenite Moslem scholar who lived in the seventh century, has an extensive discussion of whether Ibrahim lied. His conclusion is that "Ibrahim did not lie, except on three occasions. One was for the sake of Allah when Ibrahim said "I was sick," in Qur'an 37:89:

> When he said to his father and his people, "What is this you worship?" Why do you solicit false gods instead of Allah? What do you imagine the Lord of the worlds to be?" Then he looked up to the stars that they worshipped, and said, "I am sick of what you worship." But they turned their backs on him and went away. (Qur'an 37:86–90)

The second lie came, Hairara says, when his people came to Ibrahim and asked who destroyed the idols, Ibrahim responded, "The biggest idol did it," when in fact it was Ibrahim. The third lie occurred with Ibrahim tells Sarah that when she is asked who Ibrahim is, she should say, "He is my brother."

Tabari repeats the story that Ibrahim has a dream to kill his son, but Tabari suggests it was Ishmael to be sacrificed. Tabari also maintains that the prophet Mohammed was one of the descendents of Ishmael. The oldest extant commentary on the life of Mohammed, that of Mohammed ibn Ishak, also makes the same claim.

Ibn Kathir, an Islamic scholar born in Busra, Syria in 1301, also wrote a lengthy commentary on the Qur'an, including a number of observations about Ibrahim and Ishmael. The principal works of Kathir, who died in 1373, include: *Signs Before the Day of Judgment, The Birthday of the Prophet,* and *Sins and Their Punishments.*

Kathir rehearses the account of Ibrahim's father being a maker of idols, and that the boy very early on adopts monotheism and the worship of Allah. Kathir suggests that Ibrahim smashed the idols of his father in the temple, and was punished by being thrown into a fire. Kathir also reports the story of the angel Gabriel coming to Ibrahim, asking if there is anything the prophet desires. When Ibrahim says no, Allah brings a cool breeze to save Ibrahim from the fire.

Kathir also repeats the story of the battle with "Namrud," as he calls him, and he also tells the story of the migration into Egypt, Hagar and Ishmael, and the forming of the Zam Zam. Kathir also tells the tale of Ibrahim asking Allah to reveal how the Almighty brings people back from the dead. Allah commands Ibrahim to take four birds, cut them up, mingle their body parts, divide them into four portions, and then place them on the tops of four different hills. Then Allah told Ibrahim to call the birds back in the name of Allah; and immediately, the birds flew back to Ibrahim.

Other traditional Islamic commentators who have made comments on the figure of Ibrahim are Abdullah ibn Abbas, a cousin of the prophet Mohammed; Musnad Ahmad ibn Hanbal, an eighth-century collector of Sunni hadith; Sunan Abu Dawud, a ninth-century collector of Sunni hadith; Jami al-Tirmidhi, another collector of hadith; Kanz al-Ummal, the author of an eight volume set of hadith; and Ali ibn Abd-al-Malik al-Hindi, the late sixteenth-century editor of the hadith of Kanz al-Ummal.

For the most part, these later Moslem commentators do little more than repeat the stories about Ibrahim from earlier traditions, particularly those related to the miracle of Nimrod's furnace, the building of the Ka'ba, the finding of Zam Zam, and, of course, the sacrificing of Ishmael Hanbal, Dawud, and Ummal give particularly good accounts of the sacrificing of Ibrahim's son. Tirmidhi and Al-Hindi gives excellent accounts of Ibrahim's faith in emerging from Nimrod's furnace. All of the above, suggest that Ishmael and Ibrahim could not have built the Ka'ba alone. They each suggest that the two must have had some angelic help with the construction.[21]

---

21. For more on the building of the Ka'ba by Ibrahim and Ishmael, see F. E. Peters, *The Hajj: Muslim Pilgrimage to Mecca and the Holy Places* (Princeton: Princeton University Press, 1994); and Reuven Firestone, *Journeys in the Holy Lands: Abraham-Ishmael Legends* (New York: State University of New York Press, 1990).

IBRAHIM AND THE ANGELS

Various tales about Ibrahim in Islam have spurred a belief in a series of visions where it is thought an angel appears to Ibrahim. In addition to being saved from Nimrod's furnace by an angelic miracle, other stories in Islam often associate Ibrahim with angelic apparitions. Among these traditions are the founding of Zam Zam by Ishmael and his mother, and the building of the Ka'ba by Ibrahim and Ishmael. About the latter, many Moslem thinkers point out the difficulty two men alone would have in the building of the Holy Shrine. Thus, some Islamic accounts suggest that the prophet and his son had divine or angelic assistance in building the shrine.

Similarly, in the conceptions of both Ishmael and Isaac in the Islamic tradition are often accomplished through the help of supernatural powers, as well as in the fact that Ibrahim was willing to go through with the sacrifice of his son. Some Islamic commentators suggest that Ibrahim could not have gone through with the sacrifice unless he was provided with angelic help. In this regard, the providing of a ram for sacrifice in the place of Ibrahim's son is also seen in Islam as a miracle.

In Islam, Ibrahim is seen as a prophet, a founder of Islam, and as a man who frequently was aided by divine or angelic assistance. This can be seen in no better place than the various miracles associated with Ibrahim.

IBRAHIM AND DEATH AND RESURRECTION

There are also a number of accounts in Islamic commentaries that one day Ibrahim asks Allah for the secret of bringing people back from the dead. In some accounts, Allah asks Ibrahim if he has doubts about the issue. Ibrahim usually responds by saying he has no doubts about the absolute power of his God, but he wanted to satisfy his curiosity over the mechanisms of resurrection. In most hadith, it is at this point that Allah tells Ibrahim to gather the four birds, kill them, mix their body parts, and then scatter the parts on the top of four different hills. Allah commands that Ibrahim should call the birds by name, and the four birds will come to the prophet.

Most Moslem commentators suggest that thus Allah showed Ibrahim the keys to resurrection that will come on Judgment Day. Allah will call to his creation as He wills, and Moslems will rise from the grave. There are a number of different accounts of this tale. Sometimes they vary on the number of birds and hills; sometimes they differ over the kind of birds, or the story is told using a different kind of animal; but what they all share is that Allah knows the secret of bringing back the dead.

The best account of this story in the Qur'an is seen at 2:260. There the text tells us:

> Remember when Abraham said, "Oh Lord, show me how you raised the dead." He said, "What, do you not believe?" "I do," answered Abraham. "I only ask for my heart's assurance." The Lord said, "Trap four birds and tame them, then put each of them on a separate hill, and call them, and they will come flying to you. Know that Allah is All-Powerful and Wise."[22]

The origins of this tale are most likely a story in Genesis 15:7–11, where Abraham is commanded to cut several animals in half, including birds. There is a similar mention of birds in the Qur'an at 2:260. Most of the mention of the tale of the four birds in Moslem commentary comes in connection with Qur'an 2:260.

Among Medieval hadith, the tale of Ibrahim and the four birds is told by Abu Haraira, Kathir al-Tabari, Ibn Kathir, and in the work of Ahmad ibn Hanbal. In Hairara and Tabari, there are four birds, while in Hanbal and Kathir there are three. In all four accounts the birds in question are crows or black birds. Tabari suggests Ibrahim may have had doubts about the resurrection, but the other three commentators do not.

CONCLUSIONS

In this chapter, we explored two major issues. First, how is the figure of Abraham (Ibrahim) portrayed in the Qur'an? The other major question is "How is Ibrahim portrayed in later Islam?" There are many conclusions to be made about the first question. Ibrahim is seen as the founder of Islam through his son Ishmael. He is also seen as one of the greatest of Moslem prophets.

The other question for this chapter, ideas about Ibrahim in later Islam, can be answered in a number of ways. First, Ibrahim was commanded to sacrifice Ishmael, not Isaac. Second, Ibrahim miraculously escaped from a fire after his confrontation with Nimrod. Third, Ibrahim attempted to

---

22. The Holy Qur'an 2:260–261 (author's translation).

intercede for his pagan father. And fourth, Ibrahim was visited by a series of angelic beings, and chief among them was Jibril (Gabriel).

Other beliefs about Ibrahim in later Islam include: the notion that Ibrahim and Ishmael built the Ka'ba; that Hijirah and Ishmael founded the Zam Zam; that Ibrahim had a dream that he would sacrifice his son, and he saw it as a message from Allah; that Ibrahim learned from Allah the method for bringing people back from the dead; that the Angel of Death had no control over Ibrahim's soul; that Iblis (the Evil One) three times attempted to dissuade Ibrahim from sacrificing his son; that Ibrahim's sacrifice is celebrated at the feast of Eid ul-Adha; and that Ibrahim and Ishmael built the first house of worship in Islam.

All of these traditions mentioned above can be seen in early commentators on the Qur'an like Bukhari, Abu Hairara, and Tabari, as we see as well in later ahadith among scholars in the modern period. As we have seen, in modern Moslem scholarship, and in Islamic iconography as well, the two principal themes about Ibrahim to be discussed are the battle with Nimrod and escaping from the fire, and the sacrificing of Ishmael.

These two themes predominate discussions of Ibrahim in modern Islam. A third theme that was popular in Islamic scholarship on the figure of Ibrahim is when in the prophet's life did he begin to have these major beliefs? Late nineteenth-century scholar, Snouck Hurgronje, maintained that all of Mohammed's pronouncements about Ibrahim came after the hidjra. It was only at this juncture that Ibrahim became the forerunner of Islam.

This thesis of Snouch-Hugronie became more widely known through a supplement which A. J. Wensinck added to the article on Ibrahim for the *Encyclopedia of Islam*. Its publication brought bitter responses, mostly from Moslems. Edmund Beck, in an article for *Le Museo*, revived the Snouck-Hugronie thesis in 1952. A few years later, French scholar, Youakim Moubarac, a pupil of Louis Massignon, attempted to act as a mediator between French Arabs and the followers of Snouck-Hugronie.

In general, Abraham is revered in the Islamic faith more than all but a few of its prophets. He is revered for his faith, his establishment of the Zam Zam and the building of the Ka'ba. In the following chapter, we explore the Moslem views of perhaps, next to Muhammed himself, the most revered of Islam's prophets, the figure of Musa (Moses).

3

The Prophet Musa (Moses) in Islam

Muslims do believe in the Prophet Moses in as much as they believe in all the other Prophets and Messengers without discrimination.

—Ahmad H. Sakr, *Prostration Sujud*

Commemorate Moses in the Book. He was a chosen one, both an apostle and a prophet.

—Qur'an 19:51

The prophet Musa was a shy man and used to cover his body completely because of his extensive shyness.

—Mohammed al-Bukhari

INTRODUCTION

IN THIS CHAPTER, WE take a close look at the figure of Moses (Musa, in Arabic) in the Islamic tradition. We open the chapter, with an account of the figure of Musa in the Qur'an, a man mentioned more often in the Islamic sacred text than any other figure. We continue the chapter by looking at what could only be called a Moslem biography of the prophet. In section three of this chapter, we take a close look at what subsequent collectors of hadith have had to say about the prophet Musa; and we bring the chapter to a close with some general conclusions about what Islam has to say about Moses, as well as the place of Musa in Islamic history.

C. T. R. Hewer describes the relationship of Islamic prophets to the Judeo-Christian tradition:

> For Jews and Christians especially, this has a profound message. Of the twenty-five prophets named in the Qur'an, twenty-one are

Biblical figures. A Muslim is required to believe that Abraham, Moses, and Jesus, among others, were prophets sent by God to teach essentially the same message as Muhammed and the Qur'an. Islam never sees itself as a new religion . . . Islam is part of that revelation from God that goes right back to Adam and Eve and encompasses every human being who has ever lived. The Qur'an is a restatement of the essentially identical revelation, which is there to reinforce and clarify earlier revelations.[1]

In addition to this relationship between the Bible and the Qur'an, Hewer also points out that these earlier revelations, from the Old and New Testaments, may be contradicted by the revelation to Muhammed. Hewer continues: "To the extent that earlier revelations have been lost or misunderstood, the Qur'an comes to correct those errors and to restate the revelation of Islam."[2]

These comments by Hewer may aid us in more fully understanding Islamic views of Biblical characters. We already have seen in the second chapter that the son to be sacrificed by Abraham in chapter 22 of Genesis is not Isaac in Islam. In the Muslim faith, the son to be sacrificed was Ishmael. Thus, the revelation to Muhammed supersedes the one in the Old Testament. Similar comments about Moses are made in Islam that supersede earlier revelations found in the Old Testament.

MUSA IN THE QUR'AN

Musa (Moses) is the most frequently mentioned prophet in the Qur'an. He is mentioned in 34 different suras. We can find extensive information about Musa's life in three of the largest suras: al-Araf, Ta Ha, and Al-Qasas. All three offer detailed accounts of Musa's difficulties with the Pharaoh of Egypt, beginning in his childhood, and moving on to the evil conduct of his people, and his struggling of communicating Allah's message to them. The overarching Islamic view of Musa is that through his unyielding courage, and under the most stringent circumstances, Musa is presented as one of the great prophets of Islam, and as an example to his people.

Sura 20, called *Ta Ha*, includes an account of how Musa was chosen (20:9–36), as well as an account of the birth of Musa (20:37–76). The story

1. C. T. R. Hewer, *Understanding Islam: An Introduction* (Minneapolis: Fortress, 2006) 9.
2. Ibid.

of how Musa was chosen and told of his mission is a highly mystical account. Musa was true to his family and solicitous for their welfare. While they were encamped in the desert, he saw a fire off in the distance. When he approached the fire, he saw that it was holy ground and he removed his shoes. Musa saw life in things without it, and a great light in his hand. Armed with these signs, Musa is told to go forth, whereupon he sees a burning bush.

Sura *Ta Ha* also gives an account of how Musa's mother was directed to place her new born son in a basket and into the river, to be brought up in Pharaoh's house under the supervision of Allah. Eventually Musa is to preach to Pharaoh and declare the glory of Allah.

In Islam, Musa was prepared for his mission from the start. His mother received guidance so that Allah's purpose could be fulfilled. Musa was brought up in Pharaoh's palace and trained in all the learning of Egypt. After a stay with the Midianites, Musa was called to his double mission: to preach to Pharaoh and his people, and to free the Hebrew people. Musa and his brother Harum (Aaron) went to Pharaoh, who rejected Allah and his signs, but appointed a trial between Musa and Pharaoh's magicians. Musa wins the contest, converting some of the Egyptians, but not Pharaoh.

In 20:77–104, the Hebrew people are rescued from Egyptian bondage and led on the way to the Promised Land. Allah's grace gives Musa, Harun, and the Hebrew people light and guidance; but the people rebelled under the leadership of Samiri, who melted the gold of the peoples' jewelry, and made a golden calf as an idol of their worship. Musa destroys the calf, and cursed the man who led the people astray.

Sura 28, *Al-Qasas* also gives an account of Musa's mother:

> And We inspired the mother of Musa, saying, "Suckle him, Musa,
> But when you fear for him, cast him into the river, and fear not, nor
> should you grieve. Awe shall bring him back to you, and We shall
> make him one of Our messengers.[3]

Al-Qasas also contains an account of giving Musa the Ten Commandments:

---

3. Most of the Arabic translations in this chapter are those of the author. Unless otherwise stated, I generally have used the translation of the Qur'an by Ahmed Ali, published by Princeton University Press, 1993.

And indeed We gave Musa, after we had destroyed the generations of old, the Scripture, the *Taurat* (the Torah), as an enlighten-
ment for mankind, and a guidance, and a mercy, that they might
remember.[4]

Sura 28 (verses 15–16) also describes Musa murdering an Egyptian
man. The Qur'an describes the event this way:

And Musa struck the man with a single blow and finished him off.
"This is of Satan's doing," he said. "He is an enemy and a corruptor."
"Oh Lord," he prayed, "I have done wrong, forgive me." And Allah
forgave him.[5]

Sura 7, *Al-Araf,* supplies an account of Musa going to Pharaoh, as
well:

Then after them, We send Musa with signs to Fir'aun (Pharaoh)
and his chieftains, but they rejected the signs. So see how was the
end of the *Mufsidun* (mischief-makers).[6]

Al-Araf also gives an account of Allah bringing the plagues to Egypt:
"So We send on them the flood, the locusts, the lice, the frogs, and the
blood, as a series of signs. Yet they remained arrogant, and they continued
to be *Mujirimun* (criminals)."[7]

Al-Araf also has an account of the parting of the Red Sea. "And we
brought the children of Israel across the sea."[8] The narration continues:

And they came upon a people devoted to idol worship. They said
to Musa, "Make for an *Ilahan* (a god), for they have *Alitha* (gods)."
Then Musa said, "You are a people who do not know the majesty
and greatness of Allah, and what is required of you, to worship
only Allah alone: the one and only God that exists.[9]

Sura 7 also has an account of Musa being given the Ten Commandments:

And We wrote for him on the tablets the lessons to be drawn from
all these things and their explanations. And We said, "Hold on to

4. Ali translation, sura 28.
5. Qur'an 28:15–16 (author's translation).
6. Ibid, sura 7.
7. Ibid.
8. Ibid.
9. Ibid.

these things firmly, and enjoy your people if they follow these things.
I shall show you the house of *Al-Fasiqun* (the disobedient).[10]

Al-Araf also tells the tale of the golden calf (148–150), dividing the Hebrew people into twelve tribes (160), the contest with Pharaoh's magicians (106–109), and the leading of the people into the Promised Land (138).

In addition to references to Musa in these major suras of the Qur'an, there are also a number of other mentions of the prophet in the Holy Book. Sura 19:51–53 gives a narrative of bringing Haran to Musa. The Qur'an also contains two other accounts of the parting of the Red Sea (20: 77 and 26:63), as well as two accounts of the forty nights Musa spent on Mount Sinai (2:51 and 7:42).

Other mentions of Musa in the Qur'an can be found at 2:51–61; 3:84; 4:153; 5:20–25; 6:84; 6:154; 11:96–99 and 110–111; 14:5–8; 17:2, and 101–103; 18:60–82; 19:51–53; 20:9–98; 22:44; 23:45–49; 25:35–36; 26: 10–67; 27:7–10; 28:3–43; 48:76; 29:39; 32:23; 33:7; 33:69; 37:114–120; 40:23–27, 37, and 53; 41:45; 42:13; 43:46; 46:12 and 30; 51:38; 53:36; 61:5; 79:15; and 87:19.

Some of these refer to Musa and other prophets receiving their revelation (3:84; 4:153; 6:84; 6:154; 17:2); some of these passages recall Musa's battle with Pharaoh (29:39); some refer to Allah giving Moses the Book (33:23); and one passage mentions the maligning of Musa (33:69), which we shall discuss at length later in this chapter.

The Qur'an also speaks at length about the behavior of the Jews when Moses was on Mount Sinai getting the Ten Commandments. The Qur'an's 4:153 to 155 tells us:

> The people of the book demanded of you to bring them a book from heaven, but of Moses they had asked a bigger thing, and demanded, "Show us God face to face." Then they were struck by lightning as punishment for their wickedness. Even then they made a golden calf, when clear signs had reached them. Still We forgave them, and We gave Moses full authority.[11]

In several other passages in the Qur'an, the status of Moses is elevated, while the behavior of the Jews is condemned. The Qur'an's 2:60, for

---

10. The translation of Sahih Bukhari I have used in this chapter is that of M. Muhsin Khan, *The Noble Quran* (London: Dar-us-Salam Publications, 1999).

11. The Holy Qur'an 4: 153–54 (author's translation).

example, gives this account of Moses striking the rock: "And remember when Moses asked for water for his people. We told him to strike the rock with his staff, and behold, twelve springs of gushing water came forth, so that each tribe has a separate place of drinking."[12]

This Islamic view that Moses striking the rock yields twelve different streams is quite different than the account given in Numbers 20, where Moses is instructed by God to talk to the rock, so that it yields its water. Instead of doing that, Moses strikes the rock twice, water gushes forth, and, for his disobedience, Moses is barred from entering the Promised Land. In the Qur'an's 7:160 we get another account of the coming forth of the twelve streams. In this account, Allah tells Moses that if he strikes the rock twelve springs of water will gush forth. Of course, there is nothing comparable to this tale in the Hebrew Bible.

In countless other passages in which Moses appears in the Qur'an, he is described as having a lofty status, and as possessing powers that go beyond other prophets or ordinary human beings. Indeed, because of these powers, Moses' stature seems considerably more elevated in Islam than he does in the Hebrew Scriptures.

The same relative importance of Moses and his people can also be seen in the Qur'an's 7:137 that tells us:

> We then made the people who were weak and oppressed owners of the land East and West which We had blessed. Thus the fair promise of your Lord to the children of Israel was fulfilled, for they were patient with adversity, and whatever Pharaoh and his people erected, the structures were destroyed.[13]

In the beginning of this narrative, the Israelites are called "weak," and a few verses later, Moses is praised for leading them across the Red Sea. About Moses, the text says: "Remember the day when he saved you from the people of Pharaoh who oppressed and afflicted you, and killed your sons and spared your women. In this was a great trial from your Lord."[14]

Throughout the Qur'an, the people of Israel are denigrated, while the figure of Moses is exalted. He is praised for his role at the Red Sea, for his bringing water to the people of Israel, and for bringing scripture

---

12. Ibid., 2:60.

13. The Holy Qur'an 7:137–38 (author's translation).

14. Ibid., 7:141.

to his people. At the same time, Moses is said to have faults, like doubting Yahweh about talking to the rock to get water.

The Qur'an talks in several places about Musa being given Scripture. One exemplary passage is from sura 4: "The people of the Book demanded of you to bring to them a book from heaven. But of Moses they had asked a bigger thing and demanded, "Show us God face to face." They were struck by lightning then as punishment for their wickedness."[15] This passage talks about Musa being given the Torah, the people asking to see God face to face, and then people being struck down by lightning. It is followed by one of several accounts in the Qur'an that tells of the making of the golden calf. In all of the references to the golden calf in the Qur'an, they emphasize the disbelief of the people of Israel, while at the same time, emphasize the faith of Musa.

ISLAM'S BIOGRAPHY OF MUSA

To add details to the account of Musa we already have given, Musa is said in Islam to have been born into the House of Imran, in the clan of Lavi, one of the twelve clans of Banu Israil. Some accounts have Musa's mother fearful of the destiny of her child. They also suggest that Musa's basket was found by the Queen of Egypt's maids, whom brought the baby to the palace. The hungry baby needed to be fed, some Moslem accounts have it, but the baby did not accept any of the foster mothers brought in.

Some accounts suggest that Musa's sister followed the baby into the palace, and offered to the Queen to bring a proper mother for the baby. When she returned, she had Musa's mother with her, and the baby responded immediately to her nursing. After several years, some accounts have it, Musa began to show extraordinary intelligence, and the young Musa was recognized by the Pharaoh. Eventually, the young boy is appointed as one of the King's top astrologers.

Later, Islamic commentators suggest, Musa was naturally inclined to help his people. One day, while trying to free an Israelite in a scuffle with an Egyptian, Musa is said to have killed the Egyptian with one blow. This gave Musa a reputation among the Egyptians. The Egyptian officials plan to try Musa for murder and then execute him; but a noble person in the clan of the Pharaoh (called *Momine Ale-Fir'on*), informed Musa of the plot, and helped the prophet escape into the desert.

15. The Holy Qur'an 4:153 (author's translation).

Islam gives very arduous accounts of Musa in the desert. When he reached the land of Midyan (the Midianites), he stopped to rest at a well, where shepherds were busy watering their herds. Musa saw that there were two young beautiful women waiting for their place at the well. Musa offers to pull the rope for these women whose father was too sick and weak to pull the rope. After helping the women feed their animals, Musa returned with the women to their home. When their father asks why the daughters are home so quickly, the daughters tell the story at the well. The father, whose name is Sho'ayb (Jethro in the Old Testament), recognized the deed as one only done by a man of Allah. He sent one of his daughters to bring Musa to him.

Musa marries one of Sho'ayb's daughters, Safoorah (Zipporah in the Old Testament), and the prophet stays with the Midianites for ten years, living a simple life in contrast to his life in the Egyptian Palace. After several conversations with his father-in-law, Musa decides he is going to free the Israelites, so he leaves for Egypt with his family in tow.

Most Moslem accounts have it that on the way to Egypt, they stopped one night and pitched their tents near Mount Sinai. It was cold and they needed fire for warmth. Musa sees what looks like a fire higher in the mountains. Musa tells his family to remain in the tent, while he goes to explore the fire.

Most Islamic commentators say that when Musa went to explore the fire, he finds a burning bush instead. It was on Mount Sinai, that Musa was given his Divine command. Indeed, Allah bestowed on Musa the gift of miracles to be performed before the Pharaoh and his people. Allah also instructed Musa to return to Egypt. Musa was afraid of being arrested for murder if he returned to Egypt, and he also begins to stutter. Musa prays to Allah that he be granted fluent speech. He also asks that his brother Harun be designated as his deputy in the travails ahead.

Allah granted Musa's requests, and told him he could take his brother along. He also told Musa to be gentle and patient with his language and he would be fine. Musa was overwhelmed by the experience of the burning bush, and the brilliant light emanating from the bush disappears. Musa came down from the mountain, told his wife the story, and she acknowledged that her husband is a prophet of Allah.

They make their way to Egypt and to the house of Imran, her father. He took his brother aside and told him of his appointment as a prophet.

Harun was pleased and assures his brother that he will help in the tasks ahead.

When Musa and Harun arrive at the Egyptian court, they tell the Pharaoh that he worships false gods, and that there are no gods but Allah. After Musa showed the Pharaoh his miracles, and wins the contest with the magicians, the prophet is granted permission for the Israelites to leave Egypt.

Musa issues a specific order for his people to collect all their belongings and leave their homes before sunrise. The remains of Yusaf (Joseph) already had been collected in a box. Musa led his people out of Egypt, and right to the shores of the Red Sea. When the day dawned, the report of Musa's departure reached the Pharaoh. He mounted his fastest chariot and led his forces after the Israelites. The Egyptians catch up to the Israelites at the Red Sea. Musa's people were caught between the Egyptians and the Sea. The Pharaoh laughed, and asked, "Where is Musa's god now?" At that point, Allah created a path for the Israelites, but when the Egyptians follow, they are drowned by the Sea.

Musa leads his people through the hot desert and arrives at the foot of Mount Sinai, the place where earlier Musa had seen the burning bush. The Israelites were short of water, and they begin to complain to Musa. The prophet hit a nearby rock with his staff, and twelve springs of water begins to flow from the rock. Musa tells the people he is going up on the mountain for a few days, and that Harun was in charge in his absence.

Musa returns to the spot where he was given his miracles, and was given the Ten Commandments, and the rest of the Torah. When Musa returned to the camp, he was infuriated that his people had built the golden idol, which he promptly destroys. When the people insist on a meeting with Allah, Musa took a selected seventy elders up to Mount Sinai. On the way up the mountain, they are nearly struck with lightning. The entire group fell to their knees and began to worship Allah.

Meanwhile, the Israelites had exhausted their food supply, and again they begin to grumble. Again, they blame Musa for their troubles. Musa begged Allah for relief, and Allah sends the gift of *Mann-O-Salwa* (heavenly meals). They were happy for a while, but then the people begin to complain about the monotonous diet. They ask for their traditional diet, garnished with garlic.

Eventually, the Israelites erected their tents in the desert, outside the land of *Kin'an* (Canaan). They could see the land from their high perches in the desert. Musa sent *Yusha bin Nun* (Joshua) to gather information. In the meantime, *Maryam*, Musa's sister, passed away. Yusha returns telling Musa that the land is fertile with fruit trees and vineyards; but the people, the *Banu Israil*, refused to enter the land.

At their refusal, Musa prayed for Allah's help. Allah tells Musa to lead the people back to the desert, where they would roam in wretchedness for another forty years. Musa continued in the desert for forty years as ordained by Allah. During this time, many of the old folks who had originally come out of Egypt had died. The new generation of *Banu Israil* was raised to believe in Allah, and to follow the instructions of the Torah. Musa took the people back to the land which their fathers had rejected forty years ago. The prophet told the people he would not be accompanying them into the Promised Land. Musa leaves the people in the care of his brother, Harun, and went up into the hills to pray. He went up to the mountains, but he never came back for Musa died there, and nobody knows the location of his grave.

There are no verses in the *Qur'an* that say that Musa went to the mountain and did not return. Although the Qur'an does not mention his death, many ahadith refer to it. In most of these, Musa is confronted by the Angel of Death who came to take peoples' souls. Being strong, Musa overcame the Angel of Death, and the angel returned without the prophet's soul. Later, in these traditions of hadith, Allah tells Musa to put his hand on a goat. The number of hairs on the goat Musa's hand covered would be the number of years Musa lived.

Another Islamic tradition involving Musa says that when Muhammed was on his Night Journey, the *Miraj,* the prophet was taken from Makka (Mecca) to Jerusalem. From there it is said that Muhammed was taken up into Heaven, where he had an audience with Allah. On the way to Jerusalem, it is said, Muhammed passed the grave of Musa, and he saw Moses there in prayer. Later on, when the prophet was ascended into Heaven, Musa was again one of the first to greet him.

MUSA'S MIRACLES

In several places in the Qur'an it is recorded that the prophet Musa performed a number of miracles. Among these are turning his staff to snakes, the parting of the Red Sea, the bringing of water from a rock. Other episodes in the life of Musa are also seen in Islam as miraculous events, like the phenomenon of the burning bush.

The parting of the Red Sea is described in detail in the Qur'an's 26:60–66, where the text tells us:

> But they pursued them at sunrise. When the two forces drew within sight of each other, the people said to Musa, "We shall certainly be overtaken." But Musa replied, "By no means, Allah is with me. He will show me the way." So We commanded Musa "Smite the sea with your staff." And it parted, and every parting was like a lofty mountain. Then We brought the others to that place. We delivered Musa and everyone with him. And We drowned the others.[16]

The drowning of the Egyptians is also told at 17:102–103, where the text tells us:

> Then he sought to turn them out of the land, but We drowned them and all their followers. After this, We told the children of Israel, "Dwell in the land. When the promise of reckoning comes, We shall bring you together from a motley crowd."[17]

Bringing water from the rock is described at 2:60 and 7:160. In both of these accounts, the Qur'an has Allah telling Musa to strike a rock with his staff, as in the Hebrew Bible; but the Islamic accounts of the story, twelve streams gush forth and not single stream, as in the Hebrew Bible: "When his people asked for water, We said to Musa, 'Strike the rock with your staff,' and behold twelve streams gushed forth, so that each of the tribes had place of its own to drink."[18]

The Qur'an also gives explicit accounts of Musa turning his staff to a snake, and the failure of the burning bush to be consumed. In both of these instances in the Qur'an the emphasis in the miracle is placed on the actions brought by Allah. Indeed, in both instances, Musa points out that it is the power of Allah that brought about the wonders.

MUSA AND INTERPRETATION

In Arabic the word *Sharia* means a road or a highway, a well worn path that leads to a particular place. In technical religion terms, *Sharia* is the

---

16. The Holy Qur'an 26:60–66 (author's translation).

17. Ibid., 17:102–3.

18. Ibid., 7:160.

way of finding the guidance of Allah that was left as a pattern for living a faithful Islamic life. In the case of Musa, Allah gave him the *Taurat* (the Torah). Subsequent references to the *Shari'a* are given to other prophets as well. To Muhammed, for example, Allah revealed the Qur'an, another indication of the way, the *Shari'a*.

Although the Islamic tradition recognizes that God revealed the *Taurat* (Torah) to Musa on Mount Sinai, the Qur'an, nevertheless, has some discrepancies when compared to the Torah. C. T. R. Hewer comments on these discrepancies and Islam's view in interpretation:

> This must mean that, while the Torah as it is currently preserved in the Hebrew Bible might contain some, perhaps much, that was originally given to Moses in the *Taurat*, it is incomplete and contains some errors. The presence of some errors means that it is unreliable as a complete guide to human living. How do we know how many other errors there might be, once we admit there are some?[19]

Much more will be said about Islamic hermeneutics in the final chapter of this study; but it is enough to say now that Moslem exegetes, both ancient and modern, see the *Taurat* as a flawed communication of Allah's revelation. Indeed, the Qur'an tells us that the ancient Jews were careless with the text of the *Taurat* that was given to Moses. The Qur'an's 2:75–79 informs us, "How do you expect them to put their faith in you, when you know that some among them heard the word of Allah and, having understood, perverted it knowingly?"[20]

These errors must have resulted from carelessness in copying the text or in preserving early manuscripts some Moslem scholars suggest. Or perhaps there have been deliberate changes written into the text of the *Taurat (Torah)*, such as the substitution of Isaac for the first-born Ishmael. At any rate, it is often alleged that ancient Judaism was careless in the way the Biblical text was passed down.

As we shall see later in this study, there are also a number of discrepancies between the way that Islam sees Jesus and approaches taken in traditional Christianity. It is enough now to point out that Islam does not see Jesus as the son of God; nor does Islam see Mary as the mother of God. Thus, Islamic scholars believe that like early Judaism, early Christianity

---

19. Hewer, *Understanding Islam*, 48.

20. *The Qur'an* 2:75 (author's translation).

also transmitted faulty information about the identities of Jesus and his earthly mother. Again, we will talk at more length about this Islamic view of hermeneutics in the final chapter of this study.

MUSA IN LATER ISLAM

In addition to the traditions we have seen in the first two sections of this chapter, a number of other aḥidith about the figure of Musa can be found throughout Islamic commentaries. Muhammed ibn Ismail al-Bukhari (810–870), for example, made a number of observations about the prophet Musa. Bukhari points out that Musa was a shy man. He tells us:

> The prophet Musa was a shy man and used to cover his body completely because of his extensive shyness. One of the children of Israel hurt him by saying, "he covers his body in this way because in some defect in his skin, either leprosy or a scrotal hernia, or he may have some other defect." Allah wished to clear Musa of what they said about him, so one day, while Musa was in seclusion, he took off his clothing and put them on a stone and started to take a bath. When he finished the bath, he moved toward his clothes, but the stone took his clothes and ran away. Musa picked up a stick and ran after the stone, saying, "Oh stone, give me back my clothes." Then he saw a bunch of people of Israel who saw him naked. Allah cleared Musa of what he had been accused. The stone stopped there, and Musa put his clothes back on, and started hitting the stone with the stick. The stone still had some traces of the hitting, three, four, or five marks. This is what Allah refers to when he says "Oh you who believe. Don't be like those who annoyed Musa." Allah proved Musa's innocence of that which was alleged, and he was honorable in Allah's eyes.[21]

This reference to Musa's nakedness was most likely borrowed from an earlier commentary by Abu Huraira, a seventh-century Sunni collector of hadith. Huraira tells the story this way:

> The people of Israel used to take their baths naked, altogether, looking at each other. The prophet Musa used to take his bath alone. The people said, "By Allah, nothing prevents Musa from taking a bath with us, except he has a scrotal hernia." So once Musa

---

21. Yahyaibn Sharaf al-Nawawi, *Forty Hadith* (London: Islamic Text Society, 1997) 138. I have also consulted Sahih Al-Muslim's eight-volume hadith, published by Adam Publishers and Distributors in London, edited by Abdul Hamid Siddiqi and published in 1991.

went out to take a bath, and put his clothes over a stone, and that stone ran away with his clothes. Musa followed the stone, saying, "My clothes, oh stone! My clothes, oh stone!" Until the people of Israel saw him and said, "By Allah, Musa has no defect in his body." Musa took his clothes and began to beat the stone. But by Allah, there are still six or seven marks present on the stone from that excessive beating.[22]

Needless to say, Huraira's account of Musa's nudity differs significantly from that of Bukhari. Bukhari says "four, five, or six" marks remain on the stone, while Huraira says it is "six or seven marks." In Huraira's account, there is a mention of all the people of Israel taking nude baths together, while Bukhari does not mention them. Both accounts mention a scrotal hernia, but Bukhari suggests Musa might have been shy due to the prophet having leprosy.

Whatever to make of these differences is not clear, but by the time we get to the work of Sahih Al-Muslim, ninth-century Persian interpreter from the Qushayr tribe and the second most famous hadith among Sunni Moslems, he adds some important elements to the tale:

> Musa was a modest person. He was never seen naked by the people of Israel who said he was afraid of exposing his private parts, because he had been suffering with a scrotal hernia. One day he took a bath and placed his garments on a stone. The stone began to run away with the clothes. Musa followed and said, "O stone, my garment! O stone, my garment! O stone!" until it stopped near a big gathering of people of Israel. And this verse was revealed pertaining to the incident. "Oh you who believe, don't be like those who malign Musa, but Allah cleared him of what they said, and he was worthy of regard by Allah."[23]

Most of the details are similar to the other accounts, but the quotation at the end of Muslim's account looks very much like a line from the Qur'an: "O yea who believe, do not be like those who malign Musa, while Allah cleared him of what they alleged; and he was held in high esteem by Allah."[24]

Thus, it is clear that the origins of hadith commentators on Musa and nakedness is a line in the Qur'an, but just where Mohammed got

22. Ibid, 139.
23. Ibid.
24. Deuteronomy 18:18 (author's translation).

this tale remains a mystery. Certainly, it was not from the Hebrew Bible. Nowhere does the Old Testament tell such a tale. There are a number of prohibitions in Leviticus 18:6–19 related to nudity. Exodus 20:26 and 28:42 both prohibit nakedness within the context of Yahweh's cult, and priests are commanded to wear linen pants "from the loins to the thigh" but nowhere do the Hebrew scriptures discuss Moses' shyness in relationship to nudity and a bodily defect.

In several places of the Babylonian Talmud there are discussions of *orioth* (nudity). Tractate Hagigah Mishnah Ain Dorshin suggests the subject of nudity may not be discussed among three or more people; but nowhere in the Talmud is there a discussion of Moses' nakedness and shyness. Thus, it remains a mystery where Mohammed and early Islam got the kernel for this tale. Whatever the source, this story has been told and retold among many generations of collectors of hadith. The tale appears in Tafsir al-Jalalayn, Tafsir Ibn Abbas, and in Tafsir ibn Kathir.

It is likely that the tale originated in certain interpretations of Exodus 34:29–35, where Moses is depicted as being disfigured due to a direct encounter with God. Various traditions arose about the identity of the disfigurement, including the Islamic views that Musa suffered from leprosy or a hernia. In either case, Musa would not want other Moslems to see him nude, due to the disfigurement.

Another issue regarding Musa in Islam relates to a certain interpretation of Deuteronomy 18:15–19. Specifically, verse 18 has God say "I will raise up for them a prophet like you from among their brethren; and I will put my words in his mouth."[25] Many discussions among Moslem commentators have identified this prophet as being Mohammed. Others suggest that Isa (Jesus) is the prophet being referred to in Deuteronomy 18:18. In modern Islam, after the sixteenth century, nearly all commentators suggest that the prophet in question is Mohammed. Other contemporary Moslem exegetes of the Hebrew Bible take another route to explain the passage in Deuteronomy. Alhaj A. D. Ajijola, for example, tells us:

> The first five books of the Old Testament do not constitute the original Torah, but parts of the Torah have been mingled up with narratives written by human beings, and the original guidance of the Lord has been lost in the quagmire.[26]

25. Alhaj A. D. Ajijola, quoted in Norman Geisler and Abdul Saleeb, *Answering Islam* (Grand Rapids: Baker, 1993) 148.

26. Mohammed Ali, *A Manual of Hadith*, 2nd ed. (London: Ahmadiyya Anjuman Ishaat, 1990).

Other modern scholars suggest that if one is to identify the prophet of Deuteronomy 18:18 as Mohammed, then this contradicts the Qur'an 29:27, where "prophethood and revelation" are to come through the progeny of Isaac and Jacob, and not Ishmael. When Abdullah Yusuf Ali, a Moslem translator who died in England in 1952, translated sura 29:27, he added the word "Abraham" in parentheses, so as to include Ishmael in the origins of the prophets. But the word "Ibrahim" does not appear in the original Arabic text from which Ali worked.[27]

Other Moslem scholars, through a sometimes circuitous route, identify the prophet of Deuteronomy 18:18 with Mohammed. They often do this by using Deuteronomy 34:10 as a proof text that the prophet in Deuteronomy 18:18 could not have been Jesus. The argument goes something like this. Deuteronomy 34:10 tells us: "And there has not arisen a prophet since in Israel like Moses, whom the Lord knew face to face."[28]

In the next step in the argument, Moslem commentators identify the prophet of Deuteronomy 18:18, with the comment in Deuteronomy 34:10. The conclusion they draw from this is that the prophet to come in the future mentioned in Deuteronomy 18:18 could not be a Jew.

In the third step of this argument, Moslem commentators use several passages of the New Testament to establish that Jesus of Nazareth was a Jew. From all of this, it follows that Jesus could not have been the prophet in Deuteronomy 18:18. The final step in the argument should be clear: if the prophet mentioned in Deuteronomy 18:18 is not Jesus, it certainly could be Mohammed.

This argument is sometimes bolstered by modern Islamic exegetes by comparing Moses to both Jesus and Mohammed, to show which prophet is more "unto Moses." And from this comparison, many modern Islamic scholars believe that Mohammed is far more like Moses than Jesus. This argument is used for a number of reasons in contemporary

---

27. Deuteronomy 34:10 (author's translation).

28. The Hebrew word for *Qaran* means both "horn" and "a ray of light." Hence the confusion regarding Moses' horns. In Psalm 69:31, *Qaran* is used to describe a young bull or ox. There "horn" seems appropriate; but in Exodus 34:29, *Qaran* is employed in conjuction with the phrase "skin of his face." Thus, the translation of "horns" seems inappropriate there. Saint Paul understood *Qaran* as "shone," and not as "grow horns," as evidenced by his remark in 2 Corinthians 3:7–13. For more on Moses' horns, see Ruth Mellinkoff, *The Horned Moses in Medieval Art and Thought* (Eugene, OR: Wipf & Stock, 1997); also see Margit Süring's thesis published as *The Horn-Motif: In the Hebrew Bible and Related Ancient Near Eastern Literature* (Berrien Springs, MI: Andrews University Press, 1980).

scholarship. Among those reasons is the desire to establish, among many modern Islamic scholars, that Islam is an older faith than Christianity, that Mohammed has a more exalted status than Jesus in the eyes of Allah, and that Abraham and Moses were prophets of Allah and not Jews.

MOSES AND HORNS

Another Islamic interpretation of Moses suggests that the prophet grew horns. This suggestion derives from a mistranslation of the Hebrew expression, *qaran panav*. The root may be read as "horns" or as "rays of light." *Panuv* means "his face." Thus, some Moslem interpreters suggest that Musa's face was "enlightened," while others argue that "Musa had horns around his face."[29] The Hebrew term *qaran* is also used at Exodus 35:30 and 35. In Psalm 69:31, the word *qaran* is used to describe an ox or a young bull. The translation of "horn" is probably appropriate in that context.

The Septuagint suggests that Moses "was glorified," and Saint Jerome translates the expression in question as *cornuta* ("horned" or "horns"). This tradition of the "horned Moses" also exists in the Christian tradition, beginning with the Old Latin text, continuing through the Vulgate, and culminating in Michelangelo's famous sculpture, depicting Moses with horns.[30]

There are images of Moses with horns in the glass of French Cathedrals, particularly Chartes, Paris, and Bourges. The Chartes window shows a horned and haloed Moses with a brazen serpent. Illustrations of Aelfric of Eynsham's *Paraphrase* in the eleventh century also show Moses wearing a hat with horns pointing out of it.[31]

---

29. The edition of the Septuagint I have used in this chapter is that of L. C. L. Brenton, *The Septuagint With Apocrypha: Greek and English* (Montville, NJ: Hendrickson, 1986). The edition of the Vulgate is that of R. Weber, *Biblia Sacra Vulgata* (New York: American Bible Society, 1990).

30. Various editions of Aelfric's *Homilies and Paraphrases* were illustrated in the High Middle Ages. Aug Naegle produced a German version of Aelfric in Vienna in 1903. More recently, Oxford University Press produced a version of Aelfric's homilies in modern English in a 1997 edition. Sir Thomas Browne (1605–1682) was one of the great English minds of the seventeenth century. He is best known for his *Religio Medici* ("The Religion of the Physician") which was published in 1642. Browne also wrote *Vulgar Errors*, from which his account of Moses' horns comes.

31. Thomas Browne, *Vulgate Errors* (London, 1646) chapter 9, p. 3.

Among some Christian thinkers, both Medieval and Modern, the horns of Moses are also identified with the horns of Satan. The mention of Moses in the window at the Chartes Cathedral above may well be related to that association. Indeed, in a number of Christian and Moslem images of Moses/Musa in the High Middle Ages, the patriarch is shown with horns and accompanied by a serpent. They may say more about the widespread Anti-Semitism in both traditions in the period more than anything else.

It was very widespread in the Medieval period and the early Renaissance to depict Moses with horns. These horns, in both Christian and Islamic art, made it as easy to identify Moses as it was to identify Saint Lawrence with his gridiron or Saint Catherine and her wheel.

In more modern times, Sir Thomas Browne (1605–1682), English polymath and scholar, wrote an essay entitled, "Of the Pictures of Moses with Horns." Browne, who was competent in both Greek and Latin, prefers the translation from Tremellius Scrofa, a second-century BC Roman Jew. Browne gives this for Tremellius' view: *Quod splendida facta esset cutis facei ejus.*[32] Browne provides his English translation of Tremellius: "His face was radiant, and disperses beams of light."[33]

In both Christian and Islamic art, Moses/Musa was depicted with horns, particularly in the period from the tenth to the fourteenth century. It is likely that the Islamic images borrowed them from the earlier Christian depictions that stretch back to the Dark Ages. By the seventeenth century, the tradition had halted in both Christianity and Islam.

In contemporary discourse, the issue of Moses and his horns can be seen in the work of Gerald A. Honigman, a Florida based educator who specializes on the Middle East. Mr. Honigman associates Moses' horns with those of the Devil.[34] But it is more likely that the association in the Michelangelo piece is part of a long tradition in both Christianity and Islam of the Devil-Jew that go all the way back to the Gospel of John. In fact, the earliest known picture of a Jew in England is called "Aaron, Son of the Devil."

32. Ibid.

33. Gerald A. Honigman, "Moses' Horns . . . Again," on Paleo Judaica.com, February 21, 2004.

34. Ahamd H. Sakr, *Understanding Islam and Muslims* (London: Foundation for Islamic Knowledge, 1990) 79.

OTHER MODERN VIEWS OF MUSA IN ISLAM

Another Moslem discussion of Musa is whether the prophet was a Jew or a member of the Islamic faith. Many modern scholars in Islam suggest that Musa was not a Jew. Contemporary scholar Ahmad H. Sakr, for example, tells us:

> Moses was not a prophet of the Jews. He was a prophet of Allah to the children of Israel. He was sent to save them from the persecution of Pharaoh of Egypt. However, Moses was a Muslim. He preached the message of Allah. He taught them to believe in Allah the Creator of the Universe. He instructed them to pray, fast, and pray Zakat as well.[35]

The Arabic word *Zakat* is the third of the Five Pillars of Islam. It refers to paying a fixed portion of one's earnings to the poor and needy. *Zakat* is prescribed in the Qur'an at 9:103: "Of their goods take zakat, so that you might purify and sanctify them; and pray on their behalf, verily your prayers are a source of security for them."[36]

Not all modern Moslem scholars agree that Musa was not a Jew; but many carry on the Islamic tradition that both Abraham and Moses (or Ibrahim and Musa) are to be seen as Moslems far more importantly than as Jews.

One final tradition of Islamic discussions about Musa involves a Moslem tradition known as the *Miraj*. It refers to an experience of Mohammed's that is recorded in Sura 17:92–95. One English translation of these lines goes something like this:

> Let pieces of the sky fall on us as You assert Your will, or bring Allah and the angels as a sure sign. Or you come to possess a house of gold, or ascend to the skies, though we shall not believe that you have ascended until you bring down a book for us that we could read.[37]

There is lots of disagreement among modern scholars about the meaning of the *Miraj*.[38] One interpretation goes like this: Mohammed went on a mysterious night journey into Heaven. While traveling in the

35. Author's translation.

36. Qur'an 17:92–95 (author's translation).

37. For more on the *Miraj*, see the hadith of Anas ibn Malik, who gives a lengthy discussion of the religious experience in question.

38. Ibid.

various levels of Heaven, Mohammed meets a number of the Hebrew prophets. In the sixth level, Mohammed meets Moses, and in the seventh heaven, the prophet meets Abraham. While in the sixth heaven, Musa tells Mohammed to go to the seventh heaven and inquire why daily prayers should be said there ten times. So the number of daily prayers was reduced to five in number in Islam, through the courtesy of the prophet Musa.

Some Moslem accounts of the *Miraj* suggest that the journey begins when the angel Jibril (Gabriel) or Mika'il (Michael) entered the house of Muhammed by breaking through the roof. Some accounts say that Muhammed made the journey on an animal called *Burraq*, who did not allow Muhammed to ride him until after he was scolded by the angel.

There are also some discrepancies in the Moslem tradition about whether the other prophets appeared to Muhammed in physical form, or as spirits. Another question is whether Muhammed himself was seen by the others as a physical being or as a spirit apparition. Others suggest that the entire vision came in a dream.

Various versions of the *Miraj* are told in modern Islam. Some of them to prove the capacity of the soul to survive death, others to explain why five time daily prayer is required by all devout Muslims. Whatever the reason for the telling of the *Miraj*, it is frequently used in modern Islam for various theological purposes, many of them related to survival after death.

Some modern Moslem thinkers point out the similarity of this tale to the eighth-century Sufi movement, where various mystical experiences are described, some while in the body and some while not. Other writers point out the similarity to modern day near-death experiences, and argue that Mohammed may have had one. Whatever interpretation we give to the *Miraj*, modern Islamic scholars frequently use it for theological purposes.

DIFFERENCES FROM THE BIBLE'S VIEW OF MOSES

Some details of Islam's view of Musa differ from the Biblical view. In Islam, it is the Pharaoh's wife that finds the infant Musa, not his daughter. Instead of assisting seven shepherdesses as the Bible has it, in Islam it is only two. The Qur'an speaks of bringing nine miracles, rather than ten plagues, as the Torah has it. In Genesis, Moses only strikes the rock a single time with his staff, while in Islam it is twelve strikes and twelve streams that come forth, one for each tribe. The account of the streams in Islam (Qur'an 2:57) is a memory of the twelve springs of Elim. Exodus 15:27 tells us: "Then there came to Elim, where there were twelve springs of water and seventy palm trees; and they made a camp there by the water."[39]

Another difference between the Qur'an and the Bible on the story of Moses/Musa is that Haman is made a minister to Pharaoh in the Qur'an, something not found in the Bible, where Haman is introduced in the Book of Esther as a great enemy of Aaron and Gideon and the Jews (see 12:6 and 16:10–17).

In Islam, Musa repents of having slain an Egyptian, something not found in the Genesis narrative. In Islam, Musa sees the burning bush at night, and wished to take a brand from the fire to his home (Qur'an 20:10 and 28:29), again, two elements not found in the Biblical account. In Islam's account of Musa, Pharaoh's magicians lose their lives in the encounter with Musa and Yahweh, while in the Bible they do not.

Another significant difference of the Qur'an and the Hebrew Bible's views of Moses involves the episode of the golden calf, which is discussed at the Qur'an's 7:152 and 20:85–98. In Islam, the calf is assembled through the leadership of one "Al-Samiri," the Arabic word for Samaritan— something not indicated in the Hebrew text.

Finally, in Islam, there is an account of Musa accompanying a wise man on a journey at 18:59–81. In verses 66–69, Musa asks the wise man a question:

> Moses said to him, "May I attend upon you that you may instruct me in the knowledge you have been taught in the right way?"
>
> The man said, "You will not be able to bear it. How can you understand that which is beyond your comprehension?"
>
> "You will find me patient if Allah wishes it," said Musa. "And I will not disobey you in any way."[40]

There is no Biblical parallel to this passage, nor is there any haggadic account that seems to be related to it.

CONCLUSION

In this chapter, we have attempted to describe and discuss the figure of the prophet Musa (Moses) in the Qur'an and later Islam. In the Qur'an,

39. Exodus 15:27 (author's translation).
40. Qur'an 18:66–69 (author's translation).

Musa is mentioned more often than any other Moslem prophet. In all, he appears in 34 different suras. In most of the major sections of the Qur'an where Musa is mentioned, it is primarily in the context of his confrontation with the Pharaoh of Egypt, and his contest with the Pharaoh's magicians. In many other sections of the Qur'an where Musa is mentioned, various other events in the prophet's life are recorded, including the giving of the Ten Commandments, the destruction of the golden calf, the receiving of manna in the desert, the episode of the burning bush, and the striking of the rock in the desert to receive water.

In the Qur'an, Musa is seen as one of the greatest of the prophets of Allah. He is the man who brought scripture to Islam, who led the Hebrew people out of Egypt, and who brought those people to the Promised Land.

In this chapter, we have also explored a number of traditions about Musa provided by Medieval Moslem commentators. Among these tales are stories about why Musa was shy, about whether he had a bodily disfigurement of some kind, how to interpret various events in and around Mount Sinai.

In this chapter, we have also described and discussed various perspectives from modern Islamic scholars on the figure of Musa. As we have shown, many of those discussions centered on the identity of the prophet mentioned in Deuteronomy 34:10, whether Musa did or did not possess horns, and what the proper meaning is of the *Miraj*, a kind of mystical experience Mohammed describes in sura 17 of the Qur'an.

In the close of this chapter, we explored a number of differences between the account of Moses in the Genesis narratives, and the view of Musa in Islam. Among those differences were the number of female shepherds Musa helps, Musa repenting for killing an Egyptian, and a conversation Musa has with a wise man—a conversation that does not appear in the Biblical materials.

In general, Islam's view of Moses is an exalted one. He is numbered among the greatest of Allah's Messengers. He was a holy and trustworthy leader, and a good role model for later generations of Islam. Unlike Moslem discussions of the ethics of Ibrahim that sometimes concentrate on whether he did nor did not lie, no moral misgivings are ever uttered about Musa in the Islamic tradition. In the history of Islam, Musa is numbered among the greatest men who ever lived. He is remembered in Islam for his great leadership, his ability to perform miracles, and for bringing scripture to the Peoples of the Book.

In the next chapter, we shall explore the roles played by a number of other prophets in the Islamic tradition. Many of these prophets are also patriarchs of the Old Testament. In the following chapter, we shall describe and discuss the roles of figures like Adam, Noah, Lot, Joseph, Samuel, and many others, play in the religion of Islam. As we shall see, sometimes those roles deviate considerably from those in Judaism and Christianity.

4

The Role of the Prophet Yunus (Jonah)
in the Islamic Faith

How he was stuck there, was reformed,
forgiven also—
and belched back as a word to grace us all.

—Hart Crane
"After Jonah"

So also was Yunus among those sent (by Us).

—The Qur'an 37:139

The modern Jonah
goes down like a stone
if he comes across a whale
he hasn't even time to gasp.

—Yvonne Sherwood
A Biblical Text and its Afterlives

INTRODUCTION

Another of the most important prophets in the Islamic faith is the figure of Yunus, the Arabic word for Jonah. The prophet swallowed by a great fish is mentioned in about a dozen places in the Qur'an. This chapter begins by exploring what the Holy Book has to say about Yunus and his ministering to the city of Nineveh. In the second section of this chapter, we discuss in some detail the role that Jonah has played in ahadith on the figure.

In a third section of this chapter, we explore the figure of the prophet Yunus in Moslem iconography. As we shall see, Islamic artists have frequently depicted the figure of Jonah, particularly in traditional painting.

In a final section of this chapter, we make some general conclusions about the importance of the figure of Yunus in Moslem life, particularly his role as a moral exemplar in the tradition. We also explore in the final section of the chapter the major differences between Jonah in the Judeo-Christian tradition and Yunus in Islam.

THE ROLE OF YUNUS IN THE QUR'AN

The figure of Yunus is mentioned four times in the Qur'an without any references to his father; once as *Dhu-i-Nun* (21:87); once as *sahib al-hut*, "He of the fish" (68:48); and twice as "An apostle of Allah," (4:163 and 6:86). The principal place the story of Yunus is told is Surah 37:139–148. Abdullah Yusuf Ali gives this English translation of this passage:

139. So also was Yunus among those sent (by Us).
140. When he ran away (like a slave from captivity) to the ship (fully) laden,
141. He agreed to cast lots, and he was condemned.
142. Then a big fish did swallow him and he had done acts worthy of blame.
143. Had it not been that he repented and glorified Allah,
144. He certainly would have remained inside the fish till the Day of the Resurrection.
145. But We cast him forth on the naked shore in a state of sickness,
146. And We caused to grow, over him, a spreading plant of the gourd kind.
147. And We sent him on a mission to a hundred thousand men or more.
148. And they believed; so We permitted them to enjoy their life for a while.[1]

This basic account in the Qur'an has a number of similarities, as well as some important differences to the account of Jonah in the Hebrew Bible. Like the Hebrew account, Yunus has the status of a prophet. The two traditions also agree on the notion that Jonah tried to escape on a ship; that the inhabitants of the ship drew lots; that the prophet was thrown into the sea; that he was swallowed by a great fish; that God caused a gourd to give Jonah shade from the sun; that he was sent by God to minister to

---

1. Abdullah Yusuf Ali, *The Qur'an: Text, Translation, and Commentary.* (London: Tahrike Tarsile Qut'an, 1987.) p. 143.

foreigners; and finally, that both Jonah and those to whom he ministers ultimately repent and are glorified.[2]

The differences in the accounts of the Hebrew Bible and the Qur'an on a figure of Jonah are also of some significance. First 37:142 tells us that Jonah "had done acts worthy of blame," a judgment not found in the Hebrew text. Secondly, the Arabic text suggests that if he had not been spewed up, Yunus "certainly would have remained inside the fish till the Day of Resurrection."[3] In a third major difference between the Hebrew and Arabic accounts, the latter argues that the prophet ministers to "a hundred thousand men or more,"[4] while the Hebrew text says:

> And I should not be concerned about Nineveh, that great city, in which there are more than a hundred and twenty thousand persons who do not know their right hand from their left, and also many animals. (4:11)[5]

In addition to these mentions of Jonah in Surah 37, there are a dozen or so other references to the prophet in the Qur'an. Some of these speak specifically of Yunus and the big fish. Among these are 21:87 and 68:48–49. The first of these gives a synonym for the name Yunus. The text tells us:

> And remember Dhu 'n-noon (Jonah of the fish) when he went away in anger and imagined We will not test him with distress.[6]

The account in Surah 68 says:

> Do not be like Jonah of the fish who called to his Lord when he was choked with anger. Had it not been from a favor from us he would not have been cast blame-worthy on a barren plain.[7]

Most of the other mentions of the prophet Yunus in the Qur'an speak of his great status as a prophet. Appraisals for the man, and for his teachings, can be found at 4:163; 6:86; 10:98; and 21:88. In the first of these passages, Yunus is mentioned along with a number of other prophets in the Islamic tradition. The text reads:

2. Ibid.

3. Ibid, 37:142.

4. Ibid, 37:147.

5. The Book of Jonah, (4:11) (author's translation).

6. *The Qur'an* 21:87 (author's translation).

7. *The Qur'an* 68:48–49 (author's translation).

We gave guidance to Ishmael, Elisha, Jonah, and Lot;
And we favored them over the other people of the world.[8]

At Surah 10:98, the Qur'an asks a question, "Why has there been no habitation that believed and profited by their faith, except the people of Jonah?" Presumably the text refers to the Ninevites to whom Jonah has ministered. Surah 21:87–88 is mentioned above. It again mentions Jonah in relationship to a group of prophets "who are delivered by their belief."[9]

Altogether the Qur'an mentions the names of 26 separate prophets. Four different Moslem prophets have a Sura of the Qur'an named after them (Hud, Ibrahim, Muhammad and Yunus). There are said to be more than 125,000 prophets in all in the Islamic tradition. Whenever a prophet dies, another is said to take his place. The Qur'an explicitly tells us this about the role of the prophets:

> These were the Prophets who received Allah's guidance. Follow the guidance that they received. (6:90)

In addition to the passages mentioned above, an entire Sura, Sura 10 is named after Yunus. It takes its name from the 98th ayat, which reads:

> Why has there been no habitation that believed and profited by their faith, except the people of Yunus.[10]

Tradition has it that Sura 10 was revealed at Makkah (Mecca). Some contemporary scholars think some of the verses of Sura 10 were revealed at Madinah (Medina). This is, however, a superficial view. The continuity of the theme suggests that the entire Sura is of a single piece.

There are a number of major themes in this Sura. Among these are the following: The Providence of Allah; the doctrine of the afterlife; and the admonishment and warnings of non-believers. A number of the prophets are also mentioned in Sura 10. In addition to Yunus, the Prophet Musa (Moses) is discussed in the Sura. At the end of Sura 10, Muhammad commands all believers to make a declaration to this effect: "This is the Creed and this is the rule of conduct that has been prescribed for me by Allah." Muhammad adds, "No change can be made at all in this. Whoever

---

8. *The Qur'an* 4:163 (author's translation).
9. *The Qur'an* 21:87–88 (author's translation).
10. 10:98 (author's translation).

accepts this will do so for his own good, and those who reject it, do it at their own peril."

One version of the mention of Yunus at 10:98 translates the ayat this way:

> And why, there was not a town which believed and its faith profited by it, except the people of Yunus. When they believed, We removed from them the torment of ignominy in the life of this world and provided them with comfort to enjoy it for a fixed while.[11]

The translation of Muhammad Asad renders the line this way:

> For alas, there has never yet been any community that attained to faith [in its entirety], and thereby benefited by its faith, except the people of Yunus. When they came to believe, We removed from them the suffering of disgrace [which otherwise would have befallen even them] in the life of this world, and allowed them to enjoy their life during the time allotted to them.[12]

Both versions suggest that no race of people have ever entirely turned to Allah; and both accounts mention the people of Yunus being blessed by Allah "for a fixed time." But the first account talks about Yunus having only two followers, while the other does not. The origins of this belief are not clear, but it is repeated in a number of ahadith.

THE FIGURE OF YUNUS IN HADITH

Among traditional hadith, there are very few comments on the prophet Yunus. One of the principal accounts on the prophet comes from Hafez ibn Kathir, and his book, *The Stories of the Prophets*.[13] Kathir was an 8th century scholar who was born in the city of Basra. He studied law and is considered one of the foremost authorities on *Fiqh*, Islamic jurisprudence.

In his account of the prophet Yunus, Kathir tells us that "Once Yunus admits that there is no God but Allah, and that Allah alone can save him, something wonderful happens." Kathir suggests that the wonderful thing is that the large fish, or whale in the Islamic tradition, begins to sing the

11. *The Holy Qur'an with English Translation and Commentary* Edited by Maulana Muhammad Ali. (London: Ahmadiyya Anjuman Ishaat, 1991) p. 242.

12. *The Message of the Qur'an*. Edited by Muhammad Asad. (London: The Book Foundation, Bilingual Editions, 2003) p. 99.

13. Hafez ibn Kathir, *The Stories of the Prophets*. (Islamabad: Dar-us-Salem Publications, 2003.) p. 107.

praises of Allah. Then a short time later, Kathir tells us, all the other fish began to sing the praises of Allah. Indeed, all the creatures of the sea, "each in its own way," sang Allah's praises until "there was a great chorus of praise."[14] It is at this point, Kathir suggests, that the whale swims to the surface and ejects Yunus onto the shore. Kathir concludes his analysis:

> Just as Allah had used the whale to save Yunus from the storm and from drowning in the sea, so He also uses it to bring Yunus safely to the shore again.[15]

But in Kathir's view the story does not end there. He says that Yunus is feeling sick and sore as he lies on the sand in the scorching heat, still not knowing what will become of him. Allah takes even more care of him and causes a plant to grow up over him, so that Yunus is covered with shade. Once he has recovered from his ordeal and his skin has ceased to hurt from the irritations caused by the acids in the fish's belly, Allah again tells Yunus to return to Nineveh, to see what has become of the city. When he arrives, to his great surprise Kathir informs us, the city and its people have not been destroyed. Rather, they have all turned to Allah; His message had finally gotten through to them.

Kathir says that when the inhabitants of the city saw a dark cloud and terrible storm hovering over the city, they saw in it an indication of what was to come for them and they did not repent. Kathir asks, "Who knows why they turned back to Allah, but they did. And Yunus, after all his adventures, is finally content with his mission to minister to the people of Nineveh."[16]

A number of other Moslem scholars mention the prophet Yunus in their ahadith. Abd Allah ibn Abbas, a cousin of Muhammad and revered for his knowledge of Islam, was a seventh century companion to the prophet. Abbas quotes the prophet as saying, "One should not say that I am better than Yunus bin Matta."[17] In another hadith, Abbas again describes Muhammad as saying, "No slave of Allah shall say that I am better than Yunus bin Matta."[18] Abbas adds, "So the prophet mentioned

14. Ibid, p. 108.

15. Ibid, p. 109.

16. Ibid.

17. Abdullah ibn Abbas, *Tafsir ibn Abbas: Great Commentaries on the Holy Qur'an* (London: Fons Vitae, 2008.) p. 99.

18. Ibid.

his father's name with his name."[19] Abbas makes the same claim in a third hadith. He says, "The Prophet said that his Lord said, 'It does not befit a slave that he should say that he is better than Yunus bin Matta.'"[20] This same observation is repeated by Imam Nawai, another seventh century, Syrian follower of Muhammad.

At the heart of all ahadith on Yunus is the notion of his moral character, and the judgment that no one is of a better moral character than the prophet Yunus. Sometimes this judgment compares Yunus to Muhammad, and sometimes to other followers of Allah; but the conclusion is always the same: no Moslem follower in more morally perfect than Yunus.

A fourth major hadith on the prophet Yunus can be found in the work of Abu Huraira, another seventh century companion of Muhammad, as well as the most often quoted author in Sunni Islam. Abu Haraira tells this tale of the Prophet Yunus:

> Once while a Jew was selling something, he was offered a price that he was not pleased with. So he said, "No, by He who gave Moses superiority over all human beings." Now hearing him, an Ansari man got up and slapped the Jew on the face, saying, "You say, 'By Him Who gave Moses superiority over all human beings, although the Prophet Muhammad is among us!'"
>
> The Jew went to the Prophet and said, "Oh Abu-I-Qasim! I am under the assurance and contract of security, so what right does so and so have to slap me? The prophet turned to the man and asked, "Why did you slap him?" And the man told him his version of the story. The prophet became angry until anger appeared on his face. Finally, he said, "Don't give superiority to any prophet among Allah's prophets, for when the trumpet will be blown the first time, everyone on the earth and in the heavens will become unconscious except those whom Allah will exempt.
>
> The trumpet will be blown a second time and I will be the first to be resurrected to see Moses holding Allah's Throne. I will not know whether the unconsciousness which Moses received on the Day of Tur has been sufficient for him, or has he got up before me. And I don't say that there is anybody better than Yunus bin Matta.[21]

19. Ibid.

20. Ibid, p. 100.

21. Theodor Noldeke, *Geschichte des Qorans* (Berlin: Adamant Media Corporation, 2004.) p. 168.

The "Day of Tur" refers to the place in the Sinai Peninsula where Musa (Moses) left to go to Mount Sinai to receive the ten command-ments. The place lies on the coast of the Gulf of Suez in southwestern Egypt. The same emphasis on the moral character of the prophet Yunus can be seen in a whole collection of similar hadith. Hurairah makes the same judgment in another hadith on Yunus when he writes, "The Prophet said, 'None should say that I am better than Yunus bin Matta.'"[22] Similar judgment have been made in ahadith by Yunus bin Yazid, another seventh century Moslem scholar and second Caliph of the Umayyad Dynasty.[23]

Umayya ibn Abi al-Salt, an older seventh century contemporary of Muhammad, gives accounts of a number of biblical characters, includ-ing Nuh (Noah) and Yunus (Jonah). Umayya describes Nuh's ship in the midst of a raging storm, not all that different from the account of Noah in the Hebrew Bible. Umayya writes:

> (It rose) upon the surface of the iridescent waters which until now
> no mariner thought navigable. And the ship sailed in it uninter-
> ruptedly for seven days and six nights.[24]

About Yunus, Umayya suggests that had the prophet not prayed in the belly of the great fish to Allah, he would have remained there until the resurrection of the dead agreeing with the Qur'an's judgment of 37:144. Umayya also says that Jonah "stayed only a few days in the belly of the fish, which may or may not be a contradiction of the account of Jonah in the Hebrew Bible."

Other ahadith on the prophet Yunus can be seen in the work of the ninth century Persian historian, Tabari; the 10th century thinker, Kisai Marvasi; in the 11th century, *al-Thalabi* by Ahmad ibn Muhannad; in Ali ibn al-Athir's 12th and the 13th century historical writings.

Tabari suggests that "none of Yunus' bones or members were injured" in his time in the fish. Al-Kisai informs us that Yunus was born when his father was 70 years old. His mother, Kisai says, became a widow soon after Yunus' birth, and she had nothing left but a wooden spoon, which proves to be a cornucopia. Al-Kisai also suggests that Yunus was conceived on the Day of Ashura, a traditional day of fasting among Shiite Moslems. Ibn

22. Ibid.

23. Ram Swarup, *Understanding the Hadith.* (New York: Prometheus Books, 2002.) p. 363.

24. Ibid, p. 364.

Al-Athir threw himself into "the jaws of the whale which had come from India."

Several ahadith record conversations between Allah and the whale. Al-Kisai says that "Allah commanded the whale saying, 'Oh whale, oh whale, We shall not make Yunus into your sustenance. Instead We make you a retreat for him, a sanctuary.'" Tabari gives a commentary on the three-fold darkness of the Qur'an's 21:87 as "the inside of the fish, the depths of the sea, and the darkness of the night" that envelope Yunus. Tabari also explains the three-fold darkness as referring to the fish being swallowed by a second fish which, in turn, was swallowed by a third fish. Tabari also says that Allah made the whale transparent, so that Yunus could see the wonders of the deep. In fact, Tabari thinks that Yunus heard the sounds of the whale, and of other fish, sing the praises of Allah in the bottom of the sea, in the same way that the angel Gabriel heard Yunus' prayer from the belly of the great fish.

There is some dispute in the Islamic tradition about how long Yunus remained in the belly of the fish. Some say three, seven, twenty, or even forty days. The *Thalabi* says Yunus was hurled to the shore "like an antelope." Kisai says "like a gazelle." Athir says "like a plucked chicken."

There is also some confusion in the Moslem tradition about the casting of lots and the number of times it takes place in regard to Yunus. In some accounts, the Captain of the ship flips a coin to determine who is responsible for the storm. In other accounts, it is the casting of lots. In some versions in Islam the casting of lots occurs once, while in others it happens three times.

Some accounts of Yunus in Islam suggest that the sailors of the ship knew Yunus to be among the most honorable men on the ship, so they are surprised of the result of the casting of the lots. They did not wish to throw him overboard because of his piety. This is the reason, usually given in the Islamic tradition for the casting of lots a second and third time.

There is also some disagreement among the writers of major ahadith about the identity of the shore to which the great fish spewed out the prophet. Some say it is on the shores of the Euphrates, near the ancient city of Nineveh, while others contend that the Prophet was deposited onto a remote island.

In a number of ahadith on the Prophet Yunus, remarks are made that Allah, because of His wisdom and mercy, withheld from the prophet knowledge of how the story was to end. Yunus came to know the whole plan after that plan was carried out and put into effect. Some point to the story of Ibrahim and his command to sacrifice his son, as a parallel example of the prophet not knowing how a story of a prophet eventually will turn out for the good. When writers of hadith make this claim, it is usually in reference to the Islamic version of the Providence of God, and Allah having knowledge of all things, past, present, and future.

Another legend on Yunus comes from al-Yafi'I 's *Rawd al-rayahin* which tells us that Yunus asks the angel Gabriel to show him the most pious of mankind. The angel shows him the man who loses in succession his feet, his hands, and his eyes, but still puts his confidence in Allah.

An article in the *Jewish Encyclopedia* sums up these Islamic references to the prophet Yunus:

> The story of Jonah was a favorite subject in Islamic legend; several motifs worthy of adaptation are found in it: the repentance of the inhabitants of Nineveh on the day of *'ashura*; the sojourn of Jonah in the belly of the fish; his prayers, etc.[25]

The Feast of Ashura in Shiite Islam celebrates a day of mourning for Husayn ibn Ali who was murdered in 680 at the Battle of Karbala. Sunni Islam believes that Musa (Moses) fasted on this day to express gratitude to Allah for leading the Israelites out of Egypt. Thus it has become a day of fasting for all Sunni Moslems. This tradition was most likely borrowed from the Hebrew tradition that the Book of Jonah is read on the Day of Atonement.

A final hadith on the prophet Yunus tells a tale about the Prophet Muhammad traveling to the city of Ta'if to see if its leaders would allow the Prophet to preach his message from there rather than from Makkah. What followed is Muhammad was cast from the city by urchins and children, and he sought refuge in the Garden of Utbah and Shaybah, two members of the Quraysh tribe. The two men sent their servant, a man named Addas, to feed Muhammad and his companions grapes.

Muhammad asks Addas where he was from, and he told him from Niniwah (Nineveh). "The town of Yunus, son of Matta," the Prophet replied. Addas was surprised that Muhammad knew who Yunus was, so he asks the prophet, "How do you know about Yunus?" Muhammad responded by saying, "We are brothers," said Muhammad. "Yunus was a

25. Article on the Prophet Yunus, *The Jewish Encyclopedia* (New York: Funk and Wagnalls, 1901.) pp. 225–27.

prophet of Allah and so am I." Addas immediately accepted Islam and kissed the hands and feet of the Prophet.

This hadith is told in a number of contexts in Islam, including the account of Umm-i-hani Abu Hasan, a 17th century Persion writer of hadith. In one version of this story, Addas responds, "The owner of this beautiful face and these sweet words cannot be a liar, so I now believe that you are Allah's messenger." So Addas became a Moslem on the spot, adding "I have been serving these cruel people for many years. They have been depriving people of their rights, They have been cheating others, they have no goodness in them. They will commit any baseness to get what they want." Then Addas concludes:

> I want to go with you, get honored with your service, to be the target of the irreverence which the ignorant and the idiots will commit against you, and to sacrifice myself to protect your blessed body.[26]

There is also some confusion in the Moslem tradition about why Yunus became angry when he was told to go minister to the people of Nineveh. Some scholars say that the destruction of Nineveh was so urgent that Yunus was not given time by the angel Gabriel to mount a steed or put his shoe on before leaving. Others say that Yunus was angry because his prediction of the fall of Nineveh was delayed, so he appears to have been a liar.

A commemoration of the repentance of the inhabitants of Ninive is on the 28th of February in the Eastern Orthodox Churches. A fasting occurs on the Monday, Tuesday, and Wednesday after the Sunday of the Pharisee and the Publican, in the third week before the beginning of the Fast of Lent. In an appendix to the Palestinian-Gregorian Calendar there is the mention of another three day fast associated with Jonah on July 13, 14, and 15.[27]

In several places Bukhari mentions a fast performed by the Quraysh tribe that was associated with Ashura and the 10th of Myharram. Muhammad ordered the same fast, but it appears to have become option-

---

26. Tahar Ben Jelloun, *The Sacred Nights* (Baltimore: Johns Hopkins University Press, 2000.) pp. 167–68.

27. Sidney J. Griffith, *The Church in the Shadow of the Mosque.* (Princeton: Princeton University Press, 2007.) p. 205.

al later on. Bukhari makes this point in at least three different ahadith.[28] There are also at least four other places where Bukhari talks specifically about the prophet Yunus. In two of these, he is related to fasting, in the other two he is not.[29]

THE FIGURE OF YUNUS IN ISLAMIC ART

Na'ama Brosh and Rachel Milstein, writing in their *Biblical Stories in Islamic Painting*, describe the figure of Jonah in Islamic art and architecture:

> Jonah is one of the five prophets who offered praise to God in the midst of a difficult ordeal and in the end was granted God's favor. The common feature of the ordeals was that they all took place in a confined, threatening space, and that, following the experience, the prophet emerged stronger and more reassured than ever before. According to Jami, Jonah belonged to the group of Sufis whom God retrieved from the belly of the fish of "destruction" (*fana'*) and placed besides the waters of "separation" (separation from God, meaning everyday existence), so that they could bring humanity toward salvation.[30]

Brosh and Milstein continue their analysis:

> Jonah and the fish, as symbols of salvation, are rooted in Pre-Islamic religious traditions, particularly Christianity and the Gnostic religions. Details and interpretations of the story reached Islam from these and Jewish sources. In Islamic sources, Jonah is called Dhu al-Nun, meaning owner of the fish (the *nun* in Semitic languages and in Sanskrit means either fish or boat, and its shape in Arabic script—a dot within a half-circle—may symbolize either one sailing in the hull of a boat or a child in the womb.[31]

Brosh and Milstein continue by giving a summary of the composite story of Yunus:

> The composite story describes Jonah as a man who led his home city or abandoned his people without God's permission, and, be-

---

28. Bukhari, *Hadith* Vol. V., Book 58, no. 169; vol. III. Book 39, no. 117; vol. III, Book 31, no. 66.

29. Ibid. Vol. IV, Book 55, no. 605; vol. 6, Book 60, nos. 77, 155; and vol. I, Book 1, no. 107.

30. Na'a,a Borsh and Rachel Milstein, *Biblical Stories in Islamic Painting* (Jerusalem: The Israel Museum, 1991.) p. 39.

31. Ibid.

cause of this, was destined for punishment in some state of hell (or purgatory, according to Christianity.)[32]

Brosh and Milstein go on to contrast the Quranic account of Yunus with that of Tabari:

> In contrast, Tabari emphasizes the story's theme of salvation, describing the belly of the fish as a mosque—large enough for Jonah to stand in and pray. Most of the historiographers agreed that Jonah remained in the belly of the fish for a period of forty days. This is identical to the length of time Adam is said to have spent in seclusion following his birth and exile from Paradise, and it corresponds to the number of days the Sufi customarily spends apart from society as part of his mystical experience.[33]

Brosh and Milstein continue their analysis:

> After Jonah prayed and fasted for a period of forty days, won God's forgiveness, and was purified, he emerged from the belly of the fish as a child comes out of the womb. According to Tabari, the prophet was indeed like a child—weak and thin—until a goat appeared at the site where he came ashore and nurtured him for forty days and nights.[34]

The tradition on Yunus being succored by a sheep or a lamb is also used by 15th century Persian chronicler Mirkhwand (1433–1498). Mirkhwand takes the image of Jonah as a child emerging from the womb a bit farther, suggesting that Yunus emerged from the belly of the fish clad in diapers.[35]

There is also another tradition on Yunus, beginning in the 15th century iconography, is the image of a nude Yunus appearing with an angel who presents the prophet with clothes. In these illustrations, Jonah appears partially or completely naked, or dressed in a white shirt similar to those worn by the prophet Yusef (Joseph) when he is in the pit.[36] Brosh and Milstein describe these images:

---

32. Ibid.

33. Ibid.

34. Ibid.

35. Na'ama Brosh and Rachel Milstein, *Biblical Stories in Islamic Painting* (Jerusalem: The Israel Museum, 1991.) pp. 39–40.

36. Ibid., p. 40.

> The motif of an angel presenting a righteous individual with a garment recalls illustrations of other prophets: Abraham in the fire; Joseph in the pit; Job after his ordeal of suffering; and even Jesus after his baptism.[37]

These elements above are precisely those most commonly featured on the prophet Yunus in Islamic art. In an illustration from a 14th–15th century Persian manuscript, *Jami at-Tawarikh*, completed by Rashid ad-Din, Yunus is shown being cast upon the shore by the great fish. The naked prophet remains with his legs still in the fish, while an angel hovers above the scene. Rays of bright sunlight emanate from the angel's right hand. In his left hand the angel offers Yunus some clothing. This manuscript is owned by the Metropolitan Museum of Art in New York City.[38]

There are a number of copies of Rashid al-Din's *Jami al-Tanarikh* "The Universal History." One is owned by the Royal Asiatic Society in London; another copy is owned by the Edinburgh University Library. Other copies are owned by the Worcester Museum of Art in Massachusetts. The copy at Edinburgh contains an illustration of Yunus and the whale. On the left, Yunus sits beneath the shade of the gourd, while to the right, the enormous fish is depicted staring out from the sea back at the prophet on shore.

David Talbot Rice, in his work *Islamic Art*, speaks of these several copies of "The Universal History," where he writes:

> The most important examples of the style are some volumes of Rashid al-Din's "Universal History" (*Jami al-Tanarikh*) and one of the finest of them is at Edinburgh and dates about 1306. Another volume in the same style, done seven years later, is in possession of the Royal Asiatic Society in London, and another copy is in Istanbul.[39]

Rice continues his analysis:

> The book was actually in four volumes and it is said that Rashid al-Din had two copies of the book written and illustrated each year, one with the text in Arabic, the other in Persian.[40]

---

37. Ibid.

38. *Jami-at-Tawarikh* by Rashid ad-Din. (New York: Metropolitan Museum of Art.)

39. David Talbot Rice, *Islamic Art*. (New York: Praeger Press, 1965.) p. 117.

40. Ibid.

Rashid al-Din (1247–1318) was a Persian physician and historian. "The Universal History" was commissioned by Mahmud Ghazan. It was initially intended as a history of the Mongols and their conquests, but gradually it grew to become a history of the entire human history from the time of Adam to the 14th century. The work is believed to have been completed some time between 1307 and 1316, and it came to its present state during the time of Muhammad Khodabanddeh. The work was finished at the elaborate scriptorium Rabi' i-Rashidi at Qazvin, where a large number of calligraphers and illustrators were employed on lavishly and brightly colored, illustrated books.

A similar image is owned by the British Museum in London. It is a 16th century Turkish miniature from Ishaq al-Nishapuri's *Qisas-al-Anbiya*. In the lower register of the miniature, a nude Yunus emerges from the mouth of the great fish. The fish is accompanied by a host of other aquatic animals, all of whom seem to be singing the praises of Allah. In the middle of the image an angel hovers above the prophet and the fish. The angel has enormous wings, and again he offers the prophet some clothing. In the upper register, various animals and plants also seem to be singing the praises of Allah. In the upper right corner of the illustration, groups of grapes are descending from the heavens.[41]

Al-Shaykh Al-Mufid, a 10th and 11th century Shiite theologian, in his work, *Kitab Al-Irshad* (*The Book of Guidance*) tells the tale concerning the waters near the city of Kufa. Mufid's account goes like this:

> The waters of the Euphrates overflowed and grew so big that the people of Kufa became anxious about drowning. They resorted to the Commander of the Faith. He rode out on the mule of the Apostle of God until he reached the banks of the Euphrates. He dismounted and performed a ritual ablution and prayed alone by himself while others watched. Then he called on Allah with prayers that most of them heard. Then he went toward the Euphrates, leaning on a stick which was in his hand. He struck the surface of the water with the stick and said, "Abate with Allah's permission and His will."[42]

41. Ishaq al-Nishapuri, *Qisas al-Anbiya*, fol. 87r. (London: British Museum.) Ms. 18576.

42. Quoted in Zaynab Al-Fatah Al-Abidin's "Of Fish, Prophets, and Miracles." *Victory News Magazine.* May 6, 2006, p. 4. Abidin's source is Shaykh Mufid, *KitabAl-Irshad* (London: Balagha and Muhammadi Trust, 1981.)

Mufid continues:

> The waters sank so that the fish at the bottom of the flood appeared. Many of them greeted him with the title 'Commander of the Faithful.' However, some of the fish did not speak. They were eels, a scaleless fish (*marmaliq*) and a mudfish (*zumar*). The people were amazed at this and they asked for the reason that some spoke and some did not. And He said, "Allah made those fish that are ritually pure to speak and he kept those silent towards me which were forbidden, impure and worse."[43]

These observations of Shaykh Mufid are consistent with the view that in the waters of the Euphrates near the city of Kufa, the fish are said to sing the praises of Allah. This notion of fish singing Allah's praises is repeated in many of the accounts of the prophet Yunus, as well as other accounts of fish in other contexts. One example comes from Zaynab El-Fatah El-Abidin's article, "Of Fish Prophets, and Miracles." Abidin gives us this story:

> The story of the fish began when Mr. George Wehbi, a Christian Lebanese, was practicing his hobby of fishing, in Dakar, Senegal. He caught many fish. When he went home his wife saw among them a strange fish about 50 cm in length with some Arabic writing on it. He took it to Sheikh Al-Zein, who read clearly what was written in a natural way that could not have been done by a human being, but rather a Godly creation which the fish was born with. He read: "God's servant" on its belly and "Muhammad" near its head, and "His messenger" on its tail.[44]

In his article, published in *Victory News Magazine*, Abidin even provides a picture of the fish in question. What to make of this example is not clear, but there is a long tradition, going all the way back to the 16th century Persian theologian, Ishaq AL-Nishapuri's *Qisas-AlAnbiya*, and continuing into contemporary Islamic life.

In some Moslem accounts of the story of Yunus, it is said that fish, whales, and even seaweed, and all the creatures that lived in the sea, heard the voice of Jonah praying, heard the celebration of Allah's praises issuing from the great fish's stomach. All the sea creatures gathered around the

---

43. Ibid., p. 4.
44. Ibid., p. 5.

great fish and also began to sing the praises of Allah, in their own turn, and in their own ways and languages.

Another 16th century Turkish image of the prophet Yunus is owned by the Archive/Museum of Turkish and Islamic Arts in Istanbul. The manuscript was produced around 1583 and comes from the text entitled *The Fine Flower of Histories*. In the upper register, Yunus has been deposited on the shores of Nineveh. Below the surface of the water, the giant fish can still be seen. The fish is surrounded by a number of other smaller fish, all of whom seem to be singing the praises of Allah.

In the upper left of this Turkish image, Yunus sits beneath the tree being provided for his shade. In the lower register, Jonah sits in the center, looking saintly and serene. To the left is a saddled horse. On the right is what appears to be a temple of some sort, or perhaps Yunus' new residence. At the top of the lower register, in the sky above the scene, gifts from heaven are descending to the prophet.[45]

In addition to these Islamic paintings of Yunus, there was also constructed in the 13th century a Mosque of Nabi Yunus (Mosque of Prophet Jonah). The building is composed of a mosque and a *maqam* or tomb. The structure is two stories. The ground level contains the remains of an Ayyubid Mosque, while beneath it, at the basement level, is said to be the Maqam Yunus, the Tomb of the Prophet Jonah. The tomb is accessed from inside the Mosque via the ground floor entrance.

The tomb itself is a wooden structure with the burial chamber beneath it in an underground room below the Mosque. The tomb is not open to the public. Local residents of the area associate the site with miracles. Indeed, it forms a center for local religious heritage and devotion in the region.[46]

The Mosque was erected over an Assyrian Temple that was converted to a Sassanian fire-temple, then a monastery, and finally a church. In the room with the tomb of Yunus there are also some whale bones. Near the Mosque is a well that Yunus was said to have bathed in after being released from the whale. Iraqi excavations in the 1970s at Nabi Yunus revealed walls and winged bulls at entrances of a huge palace at Esarhaddon.

Another tradition says that the tomb of Yunus is in the village of Halmol about ten miles from the city of Hebron, in the center of the West

45. *The Fine Flowers of History*. (Istanbul: Museum of Islamic and Turkish Art.)

46. Richard Ettinghausen, *Islamic Art and Architecture 650–1250*. (New Haven: Yale University Press, 2003.) p. 362.

Bank, along the eponymous Mount Hebron. It is located in the Biblical region of Judea. The Tomb of Yunus is part of a site known as "The Cave of the Patriarchs." In Islam, Ibrahim is said to have purchased the land, and a number of the biblical patriarchs, or prophets, are said to be buried there.

The tomb of Yunus at the village of Halmol is mentioned in the *Martyrlogium Romanum*, a Latin text promulgated by Pope Gregory XIII and confirmed by Popes Urban VIII and Clement X. It was revised by Pope Benedict XIV in 1749. The text mentions the death place of the Prophet Jonah in the village of Halmol. The Jews, on the other hand, ascribe the tomb to the prophet Gad or the prophet Nathan.[47]

A third tomb of the Prophet Yunus is venerated in el Meschhed about seven kilometers north of the city of Nazareth. Meschhed is the ancient site of Gath-Hepher, said to be the birth place of Jonah/Yunus, so it comes as no surprise that he is also thought to be buried there. Contemporary Judaism identifies Geth-Hepher with the place called Geth near Lydda.

The *Ethiopian Synazarium* contains an account of the death of Yunus. It says that the prophet died on the 25th day of Mashsram. The text tells us, "This holy man was the son of the widow of Beth-Sarapta of Sidon, whom the prophet Elijah raised from the dead. And he followed the prophet and ministered to him."[48] W. M. Thomson's *The Land and the Book* also makes the same claim.[49] Thomson also describes the Shrine of Nabi Yunus, on the southern Lebanese coast. "North of the shrine is a khan, and to the south is a mausoleum that is venerated by Moslems and Druses."[50]

In an article written by David Sagiv called "The Influence of the Proverb on Arab and Hebrew Culture," published by the *Israel Ministry of Foreign Affairs*, Sagiv gives a 1600 image from Baghdad of the prophet Yunus and the big fish. In the image, Yunus has just been spewed up from the belly of the fish. He lies naked on the shore, while above him an angel brings clothes and some other gifts.[51]

47. *Germania Sacra Neue Folge Band 43*. (Berlin: Walter de Gruyter, 2006.) pp. 397–409.

48. E. A. W. Budge, *The Ethiopian Book of Life* (London, 1905) Vol. 1, p. 361.

49. W. M. Thomson, *The Land and the Book* (New York: Harper Brothers, 1860.) Vol. II., p. 419.

50. Ibid.

51. David Sagiv, "The Influence of the Proverb on Arab and Hebrew Culture," *Israeli Ministry of Foreign Affairs*. (Jerusalem, 2006.)

The Armenian Monastery at Kaymakh, an early 10th century ruin, contained a Palace and a monastery. On the exterior walls are still in good condition and decorated with recognizable and realistic reliefs. Many of these images are of Bible stories including Adam and Eve with the serpent, David and Goliath, and a set of three images of Jonah and the whale. Although these are Christian images, the depictions of Jonah look very much like the Turkish and Persian images of Yunus mentioned above.

More contemporary art work on the prophet Yunus can be seen in the calligraphy of Ana Naveed. One of her pieces is an 8.5 by 22 inch depiction of Yunus' prayer inside the fish. On the piece is blazoned in Arabic:

> La illaha illa Subhanaka inni mina-zwalalymin.[52]

A rough English translation of this line is the following:

> There is no Lord but Allah, glory be to You, I was one of the transgressors.[53]

Another contemporary illustration of the Book of Jonah is text and illustrations called *The Story of Yunus* by Moazzam Zaman published in 2006 by the Leyton Business Center in London. On the cover of the book, a large whale has been thrown up on a yellow colored beach. Its enormous mouth is wide open and stretched to its limits. In the promotional materials for the book it tells us it is part of "a series of 15 delightful rhyming storybooks for younger readers."[54] It also says, "A wonderful introduction for impressionable minds to get to know and love the major prophets mentioned in the Qur'an."[55]

Another set of contemporary images of the Prophet Yunus can be found on an Islamic site for children called Play and Learn.org. The site contains four images concerning the Prophet Yunus. In the first of these, a huge cloud is forming over the entire city of Nineveh, which has been plunged into darkness. This is clearly a depiction of what happened to the occupants of the city before they made supplication and after they refused to heed Yunus' warning.

---

52. Arabic transliteration by the author.

53. Arabic translation by the author.

54. Moazzam Zaman, *The Story of Yunus*. (London: Leyton Business Center, 2006.) From the back cover.

55. Ibid.

In the second image of Yunus Jonah is thrown overboard by two of the sailors on their way to Tarshish. The image features a ship with a large square sail. The two sailors are in the process of throwing Yunus overboard. In the third illustration of Jonah, a huge fish apparently has just spewed out the prophet, while off in the distance another whale can be seen. In the final image of these depictions of Yunus, the prophet lies prostrate on a sand beach. Off in the distance, in the water, can be seen the great fish/whale that had deposited the prophet there.

Contemporary Moslem writer, S. M. H. Shamsi, in his 1994 book, *The Prophets of Islam: Biographical Sketches According to the Qur'an*, gives a lengthy account of the Prophet Yunus. Shamsi says that Yunus lived in Northern Iraq. Shamsi tells us:

> Yunus son of Amittai in the clan of Judah was appointed a prophet by Allah toward the people of Ninewah (Nineveh). These people were head strong and obstinate. They refused to listen to his teachings. He got disgusted and disappointed with the lack of progress with his people. He prayed to Allah to punish the people for defying him, and decided to take the river ferry to another territory.

Shamsi continues the story:

> While crossing the river, great swells engulfed the ferry. When it appeared that the boat would sink with the next swell, the captain of the boat addressed the passengers and said that there must be someone among them who has run away from his master. He should give himself up and come forward, so that he might be tossed overboard to save the rest. No one moved for a while. When the next swell struck the boat and it was evident that the end was near, they decided to toss a coin, and it fell for Yunus, so that he was thrown in the river. The storm subsided immediately and all on board the ferry were saved.

Shamsi provides the following commentary on the tale:

> As for Yunus a large fish swallowed him and carried him to the banks of the river, where he was ejected on dry land. His skin was eroded from the digestive juices of the fish. He suffered great pain and disappointment because of the flies and the sun. He sought forgiveness from Allah from having abandoned his mission. Allah made a plant come up by his side, and he convalesced under its shadow by the river bank, and reflected over the extraordinary experience.

Shamsi finishes his analysis:

> In the meantime, his people had realized the error. They repented
> for their sins and ventured out in search of Yunus. They found him
> and rejoiced seeing him alive. They took him back and promised
> to live by his teachings. He lived among this people to a long and
> ripe age. When he died, he was buried near the same place where
> the great fish had ejected him. Many devout followers started to
> build their homes in this location and it soon developed into a
> bustling city. The city of Kufa is located in the same historic site,
> and the grave of Yunus is located on the bank of the river.

A number of the comments made by Shamsi show some of the common beliefs of historical and contemporary Islamic thinkers about the Prophet Yunus. In the Shiite tradition, the city of Kufa is a place in modern Iraq about 170 km south of Baghdad. The city is located on one of the banks of the Euphrates River. Kufa has a population of about 150,000. Along with Samarra, Karbala, and Najaf, Kufa is one of the four sites sacred to Shiite Islam. Locals believed that Yunus was buried on the banks of the Euphrates.

Shamsi's comments also call to mind a number of other traditional judgments about the Prophet Yunus. One of these is that, in general, the Islamic believer is of the view that Yunus was not only picked to minister to the people of Nineveh, he is also one of them.

A final contemporary example of the depiction of the Prophet Yunus can be seen in Noura Durkee's *Yunus and the Whale: Tales From the Qur'an.*[56] On the cover of the book is a large whale disappearing into the sea. There are a number of other illustrations throughout the book, all related to the theme of Yunus and the whale.

In addition to the pieces of art mentioned above, Rachel Milstein, Karin Ruhrdanz, and Barbara Schmitz have catalogued a number of other images on the figure of Yunus in the Islamic tradition. Altogether, they describe 15 other examples of the Jonah and the Fish narrative.[57]

---

56. Noura Durkee, *Yunus and the Whale: Tales From the Qur'an.* (Karachi: Tahrike Tarsile Qur'an, 2000.)

57. Rachel Mistein, Karin Ruhrdanz, and Barbara Schmitz, *Stories of the Prophets* Costa Meza, California: Mazda Publications, 1999.) Among the images they describe are the following:

SOME CONCLUSIONS

In the Islamic faith the Prophet Yunus (Jonah) is numbered among the greatest of Moslem heroes. He is particularly well-known for his moral character, and is often seen as a model of repentance. The Islamic faith sees Yunus as a man whose repentance brought him great rewards, particularly the miracle of his survival in the belly of a great fish for three days.

The Islamic account of Jonah differs considerably from the tale in the Hebrew Bible. The latter says nothing of Jonah's moral character, particularly his moral perfection. The Hebrew version also says nothing of a great

1. "Yunus Coming Out of the Belly of the Fish." (Berlin Staatsbiliotek, 1577.) Text by Naysaburi. Fol. 142b.

2. "Yunus Emerging From the Belly of the Fish," (New York: Columbia University Rare Book and Manuscript Library, Smith Collection.) Ms. X 829.8 Q1/Q. Folio 104b. (1574–1575)

3. "Yunus Emerging From the Belly of the Fish," (Dublin: Chester Beatty Library.) Persian ms. 231. Folio 156a.

4. "Yunus Emerging From the Belly of the Fish," (Istanbul: Beyazuit Devlet Kutuphanesi.) Ms. 5275; folio 184b.

5. "A Sheep Approaching Yunus to Give Him Milk." (Cambridge: Harvard University Art Museum.) Ms. 1985.275. Fol. 169b.

6. "Yunus Emerging From the Belly of the Fish." (Istanbul: Suleymaniye Kutuphanesi, H. 980.) Text by Naysaburi. Folio 98b.

7. "Yunus Seated Under a Tree Having Emerged From the Belly of the Fish." (London: Keir Collection. Text by Nayasaburi. Scribe: Muhammad Zaman. Folio 274a.

8. "Yunus Coming Out of the Belly of the Fish." (London: British Library. Add.18576. Fol. 87a.

9. "Yunus Coming Out of the Belly of the Fish." (New York: New York Public Library. Spencer Collection, Persian ms. 1. (1577.) Folio 114a.

10. "Yunus Coming Out of the Belly of the Fish." (Paris: Bibliotheque Nationale de France.) persan, ms. 54. (1581) Folio 108b.

11. "Yunus Emerging From the Belly of the Fish." (Sofia: Cyril and Methodius National Library.) OP 130. folio 175 b. (1576)

12. "Yunus Emerging From the Belly of the Fish." (Istanbul: Topkapi Sarayi Muzesi.) B.250. folio 157b. (1575–1576.)

13. "Yunus Emerging From the Belly of the Fish." (Istanbul: Topkapi Sarayi Muzesi.) H.1226. Folio 140a.

14. "Yunus Emerging From the Fish." (Istanbul: Topkapi Sarayi Muzesi.) H. 1227., folio 122b. (1575–1576.)

15. "Yunus in the Fish." Ms. Auctioned at Sotheby's May 3, 1977. (London: Sotheby's sales catalogue. Lot. 169., p. 47.

16. "Jonah and the Fish," (Jerusalem: The Israel Museum.) Ms. 903.69. *Rawdat al-Saf'a.*

storm that darkened the skies over Nineveh after the people there refused to worship God/Allah. The Hebrew account of Jonah also says little about the religious beliefs of the people of Nineveh before their encounter with Jonah. In the Islamic version, they practice polytheism, and have been for many generations. In the Moslem account of Yunus this is the motivation for the people of Nineveh to refuse the worship of Allah. In the Islamic account of Jonah, the people of Nineveh only begin to worship Allah when the latter causes the great cloud, along with thunder and lightning, appear in the skies over the Assyrian city. The Old Testament account of Jonah says nothing of the prophet becoming sick from the experience in the belly of the fish, while the Islamic version suggests that Yunus was sick due to the acids in the animal's stomach.

Another major difference in the interpretations of Jonah in the Judeo-Christian tradition and Yunus in Islam has to do with the Prophet's patrimony. The Hebrew text says that Jonah is the "son of Amittai of Gath-hepher." In Judaism, Jonah is a prophet who predicted the restoration of the ancient boundaries of the Kingdom of Israel (II Kings 14:25–27). In the Islamic tradition, Yunus is called "the son of Matta," in the Qur'an, as well as in a number of major hadith. What to make of this difference is not clear, but it is hardly a difference of any real importance.

Perhaps the most important differences between the treatments of Yunus and Jonah in the Hebrew Bible and the Qur'an is what is not included in the latter text. The cities of Tarshish and Nineveh, which play prominent roles in the Hebrew account, are omitted from the Arabic narrative. There is also no mention made in the Qur'an of the storm that led the prophet to be thrown overboard, though the condemnation by lots is included in the Arabic account.

Finally, the Hebrew account says nothing of the prophet Jonah being cast up naked from the belly of the great fish. In Islamic depictions of the Prophet Yunus, he is always shown without clothes. Indeed, in the Moslem depictions angels usually appear to Yunus with clothes for the prophet in hand.

5

Islam and Other Hebrew Bible Figures

Islam, like Judaism and Christianity, is a prophetic religion. It too emphasizes God's relationship to humanity and reveals God's will through the medium of prophets.

—Vartan Gregorian, *Islam: A Mosaic, Not a Monolith*

Muhammed had not come to cancel the old religions, to contradict their prophets or to start a new faith. His message is the same as that of Abraham, Moses, David, Solomon, or Jesus.

—Karen Armstrong, *Islam: A Short History*

Then Allah said to Adam, "Convey to them their names." And when he had told them, Allah said, "Did I not tell you that I know the secrets of the Heavens and the Earth?"

—Qur'an 2:33

INTRODUCTION

Altogether there are twenty-five major prophets of Biblical literature mentioned in the Qur'an. Each of these prophets is believed to have been assigned a special mission by Allah to guide human beings to fulfill certain purposes assigned to each of them. In the previous chapters of this study, we carefully have looked at the purposes that Islam believes Ibrahim Yunus and Musa were given. In the present chapter, we explore the role played by several other Old Testament prophets in the Islamic tradition.

Among the other Old Testament patriarchs we shall discuss in this chapter are Adam, Enoch, Noah, Lot, Jacob, Jethro, David, Solomon, Elijah, Elisha, and Jonah. As we shall see, the Islamic tradition has many commonalities with the views of Judaism and Christianity on these figures; but Islam also sometimes differs considerably from these earlier points of view on these patriarchs.

The main task of this chapter is to explore the roles of these figures in the Qur'an, as well as in later Islam. We will begin our analysis, with a discussion of the figure of Adam in the Qur'an, then we shall move to the other patriarchs mentioned above.

ADAM IN THE QUR'AN

The figure of Adam is mentioned in four principal places in the Qur'an (2:30–39; 5:27; 20:120–121; and 7:19–25). The first of these deals with Adam's birth and the creation of the universe, including the prophet being given dominion over the other creatures of the Earth. The reference in 5:27 is to Cain and Abel, where the Qur'an tells us: "Narrate to them exactly the tale of the two sons of Adam. When each of them offered a sacrifice to Allah that of one was accepted and that of the other was not."[1]

The third mention of Adam in the Qur'an, at 20:120–121, is a description of Satan's temptation of Adam and Eve in the garden. Again, the Holy Book tells us:

> But then Satan tempted him by saying, "Oh Adam, should I show you the tree of immortality, and a kingdom that will never know wane?" And both ate of the fruit, and their hidden parts were exposed to each other. And they patched the leaves of the garden to hide them. Adam disobeyed his Lord and went astray.[2]

The final major mention of Adam in the Qur'an also comes in connection with humanity's parents in the Garden of Eden. Sura 7:19–25 again suggests that Satan deceived Adam and Eve, and attempted to get them to expose their private parts. After eating from the forbidden fruit,

---

1. Qur'an 5:27. Most of the Arabic translations in this chapter are those of the author. I have also used the translation of Ahmed Ali, *Al-Qur'an* (Princeton: Princeton University Press, 1993). Secondary sources I have used include: Andrew Rippin, ed., *Approaches to the History of Interpretation of the Qur'an* (Oxford: Clarendon, 1988); Jacques Jomier, *The Bible and the Qur'an* (San Francisco: Ignatius, 1964); Richard Bell, *Introduction to the Qu'ran* (Edinburgh: University of Edinburgh Press, 1953); H. A. R. Gibb, *Islam: A Historical Survey* (Oxford: Oxford University Press, 1980); and Bernard Lewis, *The World of Islam* (London: Thames and Hudson, 1976).

2. Qur'an 20:120–121.

Allah says to the two, "Did I not forbid you this tree?"[3] The same verse in the Qur'an (7:22) continues: "Did I not tell you that Satan is your open enemy?"[4] This is, of course, a line unconnected to anything in the Hebrew Bible's account of the story of Adam and Eve.

There is nothing in the Hebrew Bible's account that the fall of Adam and Eve in the Garden of Eden was accomplished through the actions of Satan. Genesis three says nothing about the serpent being Satan. In the Islamic tradition, this association is a given. The Evil One in Islam is always identified with the serpent.

In the Qur'an, Adam is portrayed as the first human being, created by Allah but brought to life 40 days after being kept as a dry body. In Islam, this is an early indication that Allah can revive the dead.

Other references to Adam in the Qur'an include angels being commanded to prostrate before Adam at 2:34 and 7:11; that Adam and Eve were banished from the garden (2:36 and 7:24); and that Allah breathed a spirit into him (15:29). In Islam, the only exception to the angels prostrating before Adam was Iblis, or Satan. For the most part, Islamic scholars and interpreters do not believe that Adam and Eve sinned in the garden. Rather, their actions came as the result of trickery by Satan. Islam believes that Adam was forgiven for his mistake.

Other mentions of Adam occur in the Qur'an at 2:30–39; 3:33 and 59; 17:61 and 70; 18:50; 19:58; 40:31; and 41:13–15. The prostration of the angels is mentioned at 18:50, 41:13–15, and 17:61, while 17:70 refers to "honoring the children of Adam,"[5] 19:58 tells us that Adam was among the most favored prophets of Allah; "the people of Noah and Adam" are referred to at 40:31; Adam and Noah being chosen by Allah is mentioned at 3:33, while 3:59 suggests that both Adam and Jesus were made from dust, an indication that Jesus is human.

For the most part, these secondary mentions of Adam in the Qur'an are reflections of materials found in the Old Testament, sometimes taking a new spin on these narratives, like the notion that Adam and Eve did not sin, but simply were tricked by Satan.

The Qur'an suggests that Allah taught Adam the names of everything, and He instructed Adam to tell all of God's creatures these names.

---

3. Ibid, 7:19–25.

4. Ibid, 7:22.

5. Ibid, 17:70.

After making Adam and Eve, Allah instructed the angels to bow down to Adam and his wife, but they refused because they were made from clay (Qur'an 2:30 and 3:59).

At times the Qur'an's view of Adam and Eve seems consistent with the first chapter of Genesis, where humans were made *ish* (male) and *ishah* (female), while at other times it seems more in tune with chapters two and three of Genesis, where Eve is made from Adam's rib.

ADAM IN LATER ISLAM

There are also a number of references to Adam in Medieval Islamic commentators. Abu Haraira suggests that when Allah created Adam, He mixed the clay for some time and then left it for a while until it was sticky like mud. After which, He formed Adam for a great purpose. After that, Allah breathed a spirit into Adam. The spirit passed Adam's eyes and then his nose, causing Adam to sneeze.

Abdullah ibn Umar, seventh-century collector of hadith and prominent authority on Islamic law, tells us that the *Djinns* (the angels) had existed for about 2,000 years before the creation of Adam and Eve. Umar tells us that the *Djinn* came down to earth and shed blood. Subsequently, Umar tells us, Allah sent an army of angels led by Michael and they banished the bad angels to the sea. Similar comments can be found in the commentary of Ibn Abi Hatim, an eighth-century commentator.

Abi Musa al Sha'arai tells us that when Allah made Adam, He took a handful of dust from a variety of lands, thus we have an explanation for white, brown, black, and red races. Bin Masud, one of the companions of Muhammed, suggests that Allah sent Gabriel to Earth to retrieve some clay to make the first people. Ibn Jarir, a prominent ninth-century exegete, reports that Adam was not the first to reason. Instead, he gives that ability to Iblis.

Muhammed Ibn Ishaaq relates that Eve was created while Adam was asleep. Ibn Abbas, one of Muhammed's cousins, makes the same claim and adds that Eve was created from Adam's rib. Abu Haraira tells us that Allah, after creating Eve from the rib, left a part crooked. "If you try to straighten it," Allah said, "it will break. If you leave it, it will remain crooked, so take care of the woman."

Abdul Rahman Ibn Amru, another companion of Muhammed, says that Adam spent one hundred years weeping in Paradise as punishment for eating the fruit of the garden. Other commentators, like Ibn Asaker, seventh-century Iraqi commentator, reports that Adam wept for sixty years in Paradise, and seventy years for his mistake. Asaker also says that because of Adam's mistake, Gabriel stripped Adam of his crown.

In Medieval Islam, Adam is often seen as someone who has made a mistake, a mistake for which he ought to be punished. Nowhere in Islam is this mistake called a sin. For the most part, Adam's mistake is seen as the result of the trickery of Iblis or Shaytan, and not a moral deficiency on the part of the first man.

IDRIS (ENOCH), NUH (NOAH), AND HUD (EBER)
IN THE QUR'AN

The figure of Idris (Enoch) is important in Islam for several reasons. It is said that Idris lived during a period of drought by Allah to punish the people of the Earth who had forgotten Him. Through his supplications, Idris brings rain and an end to the suffering. Idris is also important in Islam because he is thought to have brought writing, astronomy, and mathematics to humankind.

Idris is mentioned in two principal passages in the Qur'an, at 19:56–57 and 21:85. In sura 21, Allah tells us, "Remember Ishmael, Idris, and Dhu-Kafl, they were men of fortitude."[6] Idris is called a "truthful person and a prophet" in sura 19, "and he was raised to an exalted station."[7]

The prophet Nuh (Noah) is mentioned in the Qur'an more often than any other Old Testament prophets but Ibrahim and Musa. All tolled, Nuh is mentioned in 39 different suras of the Holy Book. Like in Judiasm and Christianity, Nuh is known best for the story of the flood. In the Islamic tradition, Nuh was a believer in monotheism, and his faith in Allah led to his selection to build the Ark. In the Islamic faith, there is some disagreement over whether the flood was global or localized, another major difference with Judaism and Christianity, where it was global. One other major difference on Islam and Nuh is that in some early Moslem commentators one of Nuh's sons died along with most of the rest of humanity—a tradition not seen in either Judaism or Christianity; in the Qur'an, Allah argues that the man that drowned along with the others was not member of Nuh's family. Allah tells Nuh: "Oh Noah, truly he is of your family. He is

6. Ibid, 21:85.
7. Ibid, 19:56–57.

surely the outcome of an unrighteous act. Don't ask Me about things you know nothing about. I warn you, don't be one of the ignorant."[8]

The prophet Hud (Eber) plays a role in Islam not unlike that of Nuh. Like Nuh, Hud survived a great flood after warning the people to heed Allah's call. Sura 11 of the Qur'an is named after Hud. The Qur'an tells us that the deluge was sent as a warning to the people of *Ad*. The recently discovered city of Ubar, mentioned in the Qur'an as Iram, is thought by some scholars to be the capital of Ad.

Some accounts of the Hud story in Islam seem to combine the stories of Noah and Moses. In these accounts, the reason for the flood is that Hud's people worshipped idols made of stone. Despite Hud's admonitions, the people persisted in their *shirk* (Arabic for idolatry). To punish them, Allah brings a drought. Even after the drought, the people would not relent, so he brought the flood, saving only Hud and a few other believers.

The prophet Hud is mentioned dozens of times in the Qur'an. Most of the major references to Hud are in connection to the story of the flood, like this reference in 26:120, "We delivered him (Hud) and those who were with him in the laden Ark, and overwhelmed the others with the flood."[9]

Some Islamic accounts suggest that the storm that caused the flood related to Hud lasted seven days and seven nights. Hud is said to be a fourth generation descendant of Nuh's. According to Moslem tradition, Hud is buried in Hadhramaut, in the southern part of the Arabian Peninsula. In the Islamic tradition, then, there were two great floods in the days of the patriarchs. Both Nuh (Noah) and Hud (Heber) build arks in which to survive the floods.

A number of ahadith of later Islam mention these floods. Ibn Abbas, Ibn Kathir, and Muhammed Asad, for examples, refer to them. Ibn Kathir seems to suggest the flood of Nuh was global, not local. The same view was held by Asad and Abbas, though many other hadith argue that the flood was a local one.

One other interesting element about Noah in the Qur'an concerns his wife. Both the wives of Noah and Lot are seen in the Qur'an as morally imperfect creatures. The Qur'an tells us: "Allah gave the examples of Noah's wife and the wife of Lot for those who do not believe. They were

---

8. Ibid, 11:46.
9. Ibid, 11:1–24.

married to two of our most devoted followers and they were unfaithful to them."[10]

This is followed with a description of what happens to non-believers: "Enter Hell with those who are condemned to enter it."[11]

The wives of Noah and Lot are contrasted with the Pharaoh's wife about whom is said, "Allah presents the example of Pharaoh's wife for those who believe."[12]

Throughout the Qur'an, the Pharaoh's wife is exalted because Moslems believe that she aided Moses and his migration of the people out of Egypt.

SALEH (SHELAH), AND LUT (LOT) IN ISLAM

The Qur'an tells us that Saleh was born nine generations after Nuh (Noah) and the flood. He lived in the area between Palestine and the Hijaz, which may have been the ancient city of Petra in Jordan. Saleh's people are described as living in stone houses carved in the mountains. His people tried to worship idols also made from stone. Saleh tried to persuade his people toward Islam, but they refused.

Saleh's people asked for a miracle from Allah. The prophet responded by fashioning a she-camel out of a big rock. Allah ordered the people to milk and feed the camel or the people would be killed. So Saleh left his people, and because they did not believe, Allah brought them a massive earthquake. Another Qur'anic account has it that the prophet Saleh was commanded by Allah to leave behind his people after disobeying Allah's orders to take care of a special camel, but Saleh killed the camel instead. Because of Saleh's actions, Allah brought a great earthquake to his people. Saleh is mentioned in the Qur'an at 7:73–79; 11:61–68; and 26:141–159. The story of the camel is told at 7:73–79 and at 11:61–68. The latter passage also tells us that Saleh's people had been worshipping idols, suggesting a second reason for the earthquake. In Sura 26:141–159, Saleh's people ask for a sign that Allah is the only God. Saleh gives them a she-camel that was to drink water before any of the people; but the camel drank up all the

---

10. The Holy Qur'an 66:11 (author's translation).

11. Ibid., 66:10.

12. Ibid., 66:11.

water, leaving the people thirsty. Saleh's people saw this as a sign that Allah is the one and only God.[13]

The prophet Lut (Lot) plays a special role in Islam. Lut is said to be the nephew of Ibrahim in Islam. He accompanied his uncle to Egypt, and then traveled on to the city of Sadum (Sodom), on the western shore of the Dead Sea. The city, Islam has it, was filled with evil. Its residents were robbers and thieves. They also engaged in illicit sexual activities. These acts were practiced unabashedly. It was at the height of these acts, the tradition holds, that Allah called Lut to preach to the people of Sadum.

Even after Lut's preaching, the people insisted in their immoral behavior. They were so deaf to Lut's teaching that they ignored the prophet's warnings that they will be punished. As a consequence, Allah brought the destruction of Sadum and its sister city, Gomorrah. In Islam, Allah saves Lut and his family, bringing destruction to the rest, with the exception of one elderly woman, Lut's wife. Islam believes that Lut continued to preach to the people, to little avail. Even his own family began to waver, his wife becoming the principal one.

Islam sees both Noah's wife and the wife of Lot to be nonbelievers. The Qur'an says that both women betrayed their husbands. As sura 66:10 tells us, "Allah advanced the examples of Noah's wife and the wife of Lot, for those who do not believe. They were married to two pious devotees, but they were unfaithful to them."[14]

Another Moslem tradition about Lut suggests that the prophet was visited by three angels. The first to see them enter the city was Lut's daughter, who was sitting by the river filling her jug with water. When she lifted her face, she saw three men of magnificent beauty. One of the men asked her "Oh maiden, is there a place for us to rest?" The daughter told the three to stay put, and she ran home to tell her father. When Lut returns to the river, he asks the men who they are. They did not answer the question, instead they ask if they could stay with Lut and his family.

Islam suggests that Lut was embarrassed and did not want the men to know what went on in the city. He asks them to wait until midnight, so that no one would see them, and so the men did not see what went on in the city. When Lut finally brought the guests home, his wife slipped out of the house and told the people of the presence of the three men. The

13. Ibid, 26:141–143.
14. Ibid, 66:10.

people of the city rushed toward Lut's house, and he wondered who could have told them. When Lut saw a mob approaching his house, he locked the doors. The people banged on the doors, but Lut urged them to go home to have sex with their wives, as Allah had intended.

Blinded by passion, the men of the city broke down the door. Lut was angry, but he was unable to prevent the violations of his guests. He stood firm and continued to plead with the mob. Lut prayed that he had the power to save his guests, but one of the men said to him, "Do not be afraid Lut, we are angels, and these people will not harm you." When the mob heard these words, they fled Lut's home, hurling insults at the prophet as they did. One of the angels tells Lut to leave his house before sunrise, and take with him his entire family, except his wife. A short time after they had left the city, the earthquake came.

The Islamic tradition also tells the story of what happened to Lut after he left Sadum. Afterward, Lut is said to have visited Ibrahim. After telling him the story of the destruction of the city, Lut was surprised to find out that Ibrahim already knew. So Lut continued to preach the word of Allah, as did Ibrahim, and the two remained firm in their missions.

In Islam, Lut became the patron saint of fornicators because it is believed that he raped his own daughters while he was drunk. From that moment on, Lut's purpose became that he is to preach to those with little control of their bodily passions. In some accounts of Hell in Islam, the prophet Lut is to be found in the lowest circle of the damned.

ISHMAEL, ISAAC, AND JACOB IN THE QUR'AN

In the chapter on Abraham, we already have explored the role of Ishmael in Islam. There we have suggested that it was Ishmael, Abraham's first son, who was nearly sacrificed by his father. We also suggested that Moslems see Ishmael as the father of Islam. Finally, we have also shown that Ishmael and his mother found the Zam Zam, and that Ishmael and his father built the Ka'ba.

The figure of Ishaq (Isaac) plays a subordinate role to that of his older brother in Islam. Among the Moslems, Ishaq became a prophet in the land of Canaan. He also carried out with his brother the preaching of their father. The figure of Ishaq plays such a subordinate role in Islam, that he only appears in three main passages of the Qur'an. These three are 6:48, 21:72, and 37:112–113. At sura 6:84, we get a reference to Allah guiding Ishaq, as He did Jacob "and of their descendents, David and Solomon, and Job, and Moses, and Aaron."[15]

The Qur'an of 21:72 refers to Allah "bestowing" Ibrahiim with Ishaq, and Yaqub (Jacob) as an additional gift.[16] Similarly, 37:112–113 speaks of "giving Ibrahim" the "good news of Ishaq, an apostle who was among the righteous." It also speaks of "blessing" Ibrahim and Ishaq—"among their descendents, there are some who do good, but some who bring wrong to themselves."[17]

The name for Jacob in the Qur'an is Yaqub. Like his ancestors, he was committed to worshipping only a single God, Allah. Yaqub is called by the Qur'an one "of the company of the Elect and the Good."[18] He is also said to have attained "a high and true renown."[19] The Qur'an also suggests that Esau and Yaqub were born when Ishaq was sixty years old.

The Qur'an also tells us that Yaqub served his uncle Laban for seven years in return for marrying Rachel. The Holy Book tells us that later Yaqub married three other women, and went on to have four wives and twelve sons. These twelve sons became the progenitors of Israel's twelve tribes in the Islamic tradition. The Qur'an also speaks of a report that Yaqub's other wives hatched a plot to separate the prophet Yusuf (Joseph) from his father. They took him out on the lame excuse of tending sheep, and then threw him in a waterless well. When they returned home shedding tears for Yusuf, they tell Yaqub that Yusuf has been devoured by a wolf.

The prophet Yaqub suspected foul play on the part of his sons. Jacob is said to have died at the age of 140, and he was buried in Hebron. When Yaqub was dying, the Qur'an tells us, the prophet called his sons. The Qur'an tells us:

> The same did Ibrahim enjoin upon his sons, and also Yaqub saying, "Allah has chosen for you the true religion, but what will you worship when I am gone?" They said, "We shall worship your God,

15. Ibid, 6:84.
16. Ibid, 21:72.
17. Ibid, 37:112–113.
18. Ibid, 38:48.
19. Ibid, 19:49–50.

the God of your fathers, Ibrahim, Ishmail, Ishaq, one God, and under him we have surrendered.[20]

YUSUF (JOSEPH) IN ISLAM

The prophet Yusuf is mentioned in a number of passages in the Qur'an. Chief among these are: 6:84; 12:4–101; and 40:34, where Yusuf is included in a section that treats the tale where Yusuf comes before Musa with clear divine messages that were, nevertheless, doubted by the people. The Qur'an's 4:34 tells us: "Joseph had indeed come to you before with clear proofs, but you did not cease to doubt what he had brought until he died when you said, 'God will not send another prophet after him.'"[21]

These same people thought that Allah would not send another prophet after him. In 6:84, Yusuf is mentioned along with many of the other prophets: "And We gave him Isaac and Jacob and guided them, as We had guided Noah before them, and of his descendents David and Solomon, and Job and Joseph and Moses and Aaron. Thus We reward those who are upright and who do the good."[22]

All other Qur'anic references to Yusuf come in sura 12, which contains 111 verses on the Joseph narrative. Indeed, it is the longest narrative on a single individual in the Qur'an. It is of some interest to point out that the Yusuf narrative of the Qur'an has some affinities to the tale of Bellerophon of the Iliad, as well as the pre-biblical Egyptian tale of "The Two Brothers."

Sura twelve begins with a description of Yusuf having a dream with "eleven stars and the sun and the moon prostrating themselves to me" (12:4).[23] When Yusuf tells the story to his father, the father's face lit up, he saw that Yusuf would be the one through whom Ibrahim's mission would be fulfilled. Yusuf's father was very aware of the jealousy of his brothers, so he told his son not to tell them about the dream (Quran 12:5–6).

---

20. Ibid, 12:4. For more on Islam's treatment of Joseph, see John Kaltner, *Inquiry of Joseph: Getting to Know a Biblical Character through the Qur'an* (Collegeville, MN: Liturgical, 2003). W. Lee Humphreys, *Joseph and His Family: A Literary Study* (Columbia: University of South Carolina Press, 1988); and M. S. Stern, "Mohammed and Joseph: A Study of Koranic Narrative," *Journal of Near Eastern Studies* 44 (1985) 193–204.

21. The Holy Qur'an 4:34 (author's translation).

22. The Holy Qur'an 6:84 (author's translation).

23. Ibid, 12:4.

Yusuf heeded his father's advice, and did not tell his brothers of the dream. But his brothers plot against Yusuf. The Qur'an tells us:

> Truly Yusuf and his brother Benjamin are loved more by our father than we are. But we are *Usbah* (a strong group). Our father is simply wrong. Let us kill Yusuf or cast him out to some other land, so that the favor of our father may be given to you alone. And after that, you will be righteous folk, by intending repentance before committing the sin.[24]

The Qur'an tells us that one of the brothers said, "Don't kill Yusuf, throw him down to the bottom of a well, he will be picked up by some caravan travelers" (12:8–10). Another of the brothers asks, "Why does father love Yusuf so much?" One said it was because of his beauty, others offered other answers. Finally, Judah, the oldest of Yusuf's brother's decided the plan to put him in a well and distance him to a far land was the right one.

The Quranic account of Yusuf in sura 12 then shifts to Yaqub who is asked by the others sons, "Why do you not trust us with Yusuf? Send him with us tomorrow and we will take care of him." Yaqub responds, "It saddens me that you should take him away. I am afraid that a wolf will eat him, while you are careless with him." They respond, "If a wolf eats him while we are strong, then we will be the losers" (12:11–14).[25]

So the brothers take Yusuf away, the Qur'an tells us, and take him directly to a well. The brothers cast him in, while Yusuf protests. At this point, Allah reveals to Yusuf that he is safe and will not be harmed. Allah also tells Yusuf that he will meet his brothers again some day to remind them of what they have done. There was water in the well, which buoyed Yusuf's body. He sat lonely in the water, then clings to a rock ledge overhead that he crawls upon.

Meanwhile, the brothers have killed a sheep, and they soaked Yusuf's shirt in its blood. One brother says that they should swear to keep what they had done a secret. And all of them took an oath, and they return home weeping in the early part of the evening (12:16). The sons tell Yaqub that a wolf has eaten Yusuf (12:17). They brought the blood-stained shirt to show their father (12:18). But deep in his heart, Yaqub knew that Yusuf

---

24. Ibid, 12:7–9.
25. Ibid, 12:11–14.

was still alive (12:18). The father quizzed his sons, and prayed for patience in dealing with his sons.

Meanwhile, back in the well where Yusuf is kept, dark thoughts begin to enter his mind. Why did his brothers turn against him? Does his father know what happened to him? The image of a smile on his face appears in his mind, and Yusuf's mind gradually begins to subside. The text tells us at this point that Allah was testing the young man in order to bring about in him a spirit of patience and courage.

The next scene in sura 12 shows the wide desert. At the horizon is a long line of camels, horses, and men, a caravan on its way to Egypt. They stop at the well, but when a man from the caravan lowers his bucket, but before it hits the water, Yusuf grabs it. As the man began to pull up the bucket, he felt it was unusually heavy. When he took a peep in the well, he saw Yusuf, and shouted to his companions, "Come give me a hand. I have found a real treasure in this well."

All over Egypt news began to spread that an unusually handsome young man was on sale as a slave. The chief minister of Egypt, Aziz, outbid all the others and took Yusuf home to his estate. Aziz says to his wife, "Make his stay comfortable. We will either sell him or adopt him as our own" (12:19–21).[26] The Qur'an tells us that Yusuf grows to his full maturity, and Allah gave him "wisdom and knowledge" and he became a prophet (12:22).[27] Aziz honored Yusuf, treated him as a son, and put him in charge of his household. Aziz's wife becomes infatuated with Yusuf. Indeed, she falls madly in love with the boy. The Qur'an tells us that she tries to seduce Yusuf. But Yusuf responds by saying that he seeks refuge in Allah. The Qur'an tells us, "Surely he is one of Our chosen servants" (12:23–24).[28]

Yusuf pulls away from the wife who had ripped the shirt off his back; but when Yusuf opens the door to escape, Aziz was standing there. The sly woman immediately changes her tone to anger, and says to her husband, "What is the penalty for one who has evil designs against your wife?" (12:25).[29] Yusuf tells Aziz it was the other way around, "it was she that seduced me!" (12:26). The wise Aziz apologizes to Yusuf for his wife's indecency. He also tells his wife to apologize as well (12:26–29).

26. Ibid, 12:19–11.
27. Ibid, 12:22.
28. Ibid, 12:23–24.
29. Ibid, 12:25.

In the next scene of the Qur'an's account of Yusuf, the master Aziz has a banquet and invites only women to attend. All the women's eyes are focused on Yusuf. Some said he could not be human he is so beautiful. Another exclaimed "This is a noble angel!" Aziz's wife stands up at the feast and confesses. She says, "I have tempted him, and if he does not do what I want, he shall be imprisoned." Aziz's wife convinces her husband that the only way to save her honor is to put Yusuf in prison. As a result of being mesmerized by Yusuf, the guests cut off their fingers with knives given to them by Aziz's wife.

In Islam, this is Yusuf's third test. During his time in prison, the Qur'an tells us, Yusuf was given by Allah the ability to interpret dreams. While his time in prison, Yusuf had two cell-mates, one was a cup-bearer of the king and the other a cook. Both cell-mates have dreams, which they ask Yusuf to interpret. The cook dreamed he stood in a place with bread on his head, and two birds began eating the bread. The cupbearer dreamed that he was serving wine to the king. Before he interpreted their dreams, Yusuf called the two men to Allah. Then he told the cook that he would be crucified until he died; and he told the cup-bearer that he will return to the service of the king. He also told the cup-bearer that when he did, he should remind the king that he has an innocent man in prison—Yusuf. When the servant returned to the service of the king, he forgot to mention Yusuf. In Islam, this is because Satan/Iblis had tempted the servant not to mention the prophet's name.

The scene shifts again in the Qur'an's account of Yusuf to the bedroom of the king, where the ruler has a dream. He sees himself on the banks of the Nile. The water recedes before him, becoming mud. Seven fat cows come out of the river, followed by seven lean cows. The seven lean cows eat the fat cows. The king is terrified. Seven ears of green grain grow on the riverbank and disappear in the mud. The king awoke and called for his sorcerers to interpret the dream.

The sorcerers said, "This is a mixed up dream. How can this make sense, it is a nightmare." One priest said, "Maybe you had a heavy supper." The Chief Minister says, "Maybe you were not covered at night, and you caught cold." But the king's jester said, 'His majesty is beginning to grow old, and thus his dream is confused." They unanimously agreed it was a nightmare.[30]

---

30. Ibid, 12:36–42.

When the news reaches the cup-bearer, he ran to the king to tell him about Yusuf's ability in interpreting dreams. The king sent the cup-bearer to ask Yusuf about the dream. Yusuf told the cup-bearer, "You will have seven years of abundance, where your crops will have great harvests. You should store the surplus because seven years of famine will follow the abundance."[31] He also told them that during the famine they should save some grain to be used as seed for the following harvest. Then, Yusuf added: after the drought, there will come a year where water will be plentiful. If the water is used properly, there will be abundance of grape vines and olive trees.

The cupbearer returned to the king who was fascinated by Yusuf's interpretation. The king was so impressed, he ordered Yusuf to be released from prison, but the prophet refused to leave, unless his innocence was established. The king ordered that Aziz's wife, and the guests at the feast, be summoned. The king felt that Yusuf had been mistreated, but he did not know how. After hearing from the women, the king orders Yusuf to be released.[32]

Meanwhile, Jacob sent ten of his sons, all except Benjamin, to Egypt to purchase provisions. Yusuf hears of the ten brothers who could not speak the language of the Egyptians. When they call on Yusuf to make their purchases, their brother immediately recognizes them, but they did not recognize him. Yusuf asks about the brothers, and they tell him "We are eleven brothers, the sons of a great prophet. Our other brother is at home, tending to our aging father." Upon hearing this, Yusuf began to weep, a longing for home welled up in him, as well as a desire for his parents and brother Benjamin. Yusuf asks the brothers if they are truthful people. They respond by saying, "What makes you think we are not?" Yusuf responds by saying, "if you bring me your brother as proof, I will give you double provisions" (12:58–62).[33]

The scene in Egypt dims, and rises again in Canaan. The brothers retuned to Jacob, but before they could unload the provisions, they say to their father, "We were cheated out of some provisions because you would not let Benjamin go with us." Jacob tells them he would not entrust Benjamin to the brothers. He has allowed Yusuf to accompany them

---

31. Ibid, 12:43–49.

32. Ibid, 12:50–57.

33. Ibid, 12:58–62.

earlier, but Jacob refused to send Benjamin. Later, when the brothers had opened the grain sacks, they discovered the money they had given to Yusuf for the grain.[34]

After some time, they ran out again, and Jacob sent them back to Egypt for more. They reminded their father that if they want double grain, they have to bring Benjamin with them. Jacob agrees to allow Benjamin to accompany them, only if they promise that he will be returned safely. Jacob also called on Allah to witness the pledge. Jacob also advised his sons to enter the Egyptian city by using several different gates.[35]

Yusuf welcomed his brothers and suppressed his desire to embrace Benjamin. Yusuf prepared a feast for them and arranged to seat them in pairs. Benjamin, of course, is paired with Yusuf. Benjamin begins to weep saying, "If my brother Yusuf were alive, he would be sitting next to me." That night when Yusuf and Benjamin were alone, he asks Benjamin if he would accept him as a brother. Benjamin tells Yusuf that he is a wonderful man but can never take the place of his brother, Yusuf. Finally, Yusuf breaks down in tears and tells Benjamin who he is. Yusuf says, "Fate has brought us together after all these years of separation."[36]

The following day, when they were loading the grain, Yusuf tells one of his servants to put the gold cup that the king used for measuring grain into Benjamin's saddle bag. When the brothers were set to return home the gates were locked, and one of the Egyptian soldiers yelled, "You are thieves!" The brothers ask, "What have you lost?" Another soldier said, "The king's golden cup." Yusuf's officer said, "What punishment should we choose for the thieves?" The brothers respond, "According to our law, whoever steals is made a slave of the one stolen from." The guard agreed, and said, "We shall apply your law, rather than Egyptian law."[37]

The soldiers began to check the bags of the brothers. They followed Yusuf's instruction that they should leave Benjamin's bag until last. When all the bags but Benjamin's had been searched, the brothers were relieved. Then Yusuf turned to them and said, "Don't check the bag of this man (pointing to Benjamin), he does not look like a thief." The brothers say, "We will not move an inch unless his bag is examined too. We are not

---

34. Ibid, 12:58–68.
35. Ibid, 12:67.
36. Ibid, 12:74–75.
37. Ibid, 12:76–77.

thieves, we are the sons of a nobleman." The soldiers reach into Benjamin's bag and find the golden cup.[38]

The brothers react with resentment toward Benjamin. Then they remember the oath they had taken about Benjamin. The brothers depart for home. They leave enough provisions behind for Judah who stays in a tavern, awaiting the outcome of Benjamin's situation. In the meantime, Yusuf keeps Benjamin at his house as a guest. He tells his brother about the plan to hide the cup in his bag.[39]

The Moslem tradition generally says that Yusuf's plan to send back the other brothers was a test of their sincerity—to see if they would come back for the two brothers left behind. When the brothers return home, they say to Jacob, "Oh father, your son has been stolen." Jacob is overwhelmed by the news. He prays, "Patience be with me. Perhaps Allah will return my sons to me."

Jacob rebukes his sons, telling them that only the return of his sons would comfort him. So the sons return to Egypt, they collect Judah and then visit Yusuf. They were hungry and thirsty, so they ask alms of their brother. Then Yusuf began to speak to them in Hebrew. He said, "Do you know what you did with Yusuf and his brother when you were ignorant?" They respond, "Are you Yusuf?" "I am," he said, "and he is Benjamin." The brothers began to tremble in fear, but Yusuf comforts them (12:92). Yusuf embraces them, and they all weep for joy.[40]

As the brothers leave Egypt, the scene shifts back to Canaan. Jacob, now blind, sits in his home, tears coming down his cheek. All of the sudden, he stands up, dresses, and goes out to his son's wives. Then he lifts his face up to the heavens and sniffs the air. "I can smell Yusuf in the air," he says. The wives discuss the old man, saying "he will die from grief over Yusuf." Then the old man wanted a cup of milk to break a fast he had been keeping. The caravan had traveled in the desert with Yusuf's shirt (*qamis*) hidden among the grain. When the shirt was retrieved, they placed it over Jacob's face and his blindness was cured.[41]

The Qur'anic view of Yusuf embodies the chief qualities of a prophet: knowledge, trust, fortitude, and patience. The Qur'an depicts Yusuf as

38. Ibid, 12:80–93.
39. Ibid, 12:94–111.
40. Ibid, 12–92.
41. Ibid, 12:93.

protected from error through its portrayal of the most positive elements of the prophet's character. The Genesis narrative portrays Joseph as a heroic character, while the Qur'an's account is far more didactic.

In post-Qur'anic literature, the figure of Yusuf is largely absent from hadith. The most frequent references to Yusuf beyond the Qur'an are to his extraordinary beauty. Some Islamic commentators forgive Aziz's wife and the ladies at the feast, given the uncontrollable passion toward Yusuf. In the Middle Ages (eighth to thirteenth centuries) Yusuf was seen in Islam as the patron saint of the arts. In post-Qur'anic literature, the tale of Yusuf and Zulayka (the Arabic name for Aziz's wife) was considerably enlarged upon. It undergoes romantic adaptations in prose and in poetry in both Arabic and Farsi.

The very fact that Yusuf's narrative is the only complete tale, with a beginning, a middle, and an end, in Qur'anic literature suggests it has a special place in the history of Islam. One Medieval tradition suggests, "Allah would never send a prophet without telling him the story of Yusuf, just as he told it to the prophet Mohammed."[42]

A number of contemporary Islamic scholars have written a great deal on the prophet Yusuf. Among these are John Kaltner's *Inquiring of Joseph*, Marc Bernstein's *Stories of Joseph: Narrative Migrations Between Judaism and Islam*, and an article written by M. A. Abdel Haleem for *Islam and Christian-Muslim Relations*.[43] For the most part, these and other scholars raise the issue of why the Yusuf narrative in surah 12 is the longest and fullest narrative of any Biblical figure in the Qur'an.

DAUD (DAVID) IN ISLAM

C. T. R. Hewer, in his book, *Understanding Islam: An Introduction*, describes the different views of Judaism and Islam on the figure of David. Hewer points out that "The biblical tradition is capable of living with the

---

42. For more on the role of prophets in Islam, see Suzanne Haneef, *A History of the Prophets of Islam* (London: Kazi, 2003); Chawkat Georges Moucarry, *The Prophet and the Messiah* (Downers Grove, IL: InterVarsity, 2002); Muhammed Saed Abdul-Rahman, *Islam: Questions and Answers: Islamic History and Biography* (London: MSA, 2003); and especially, Imam Imaduddin Abu-Fida, *Stories of the Prophets* (London: MSA, 2003).

43. John Kaltner, *Inquiries of Joseph*; Marc S. Bernstein, *Stories of Joseph: Migration Between Judaism and Islam* (Detroit: Wayne State University Press, 2006); M. A. Abdel-Haleem, "The Story of Joseph in the Qur'an and the Old Testament," *Islam and Christian-Muslim Relations* 1 (1990) 171–91.

sin of characters such as David, who according to the Bible wanted the wife of Uriah the Hittite and so planned for him to be killed in battle so that he could have her" (2 Samuel 11–12).[44]

Hewer continues:

> Such a sinful act is unthinkable in the Islamic tradition. That is not the way that prophets behave. This means that Islam does not accept this biblical account of David's sin. It must have been something that was added into the biblical tradition, as it could not have been an accurate account of David's life.[45]

As we already have seen elsewhere in this study, Islam sometimes deviates considerably from Judeo-Christian views of a number of biblical characters. These deviations also lead to differing views on hermeneutics and the nature of truth in biblical interpretation. More is said about these differences in the final chapter of this study, "Some Conclusions Concerning Islam's View of Biblical Characters." It is enough now to point out that Islam does not accept the claim that Daud sinned in 2 Samuel.

The Qur'an tells us that the Psalms (the *Zabur*) were revealed to David. He is said to have killed *Jalut* (Goliath) with a rock from his slingshot. Daud is also believed to have set the foundations of the Dome of the Rock during his reign as king. Some Islamic accounts suggest that the sacred stone that Ibrahim threw at Iblis in the desert of Mecca is the same stone that Daud used to kill Jalut.

In the Qur'anic account of the David and Goliath story, David becomes King by the killing of the giant: "By the will of Allah they defeated them, and David killed Goliath, and Allah gave him wisdom and kingship, and taught him whatever he pleased."[46]

The Qur'an also tells us that when Daud was a young king he was unjust, so Allah sent his angel *Mikail* (Michael) to mock David, and make him aware of his ill treatment of others. Daud sought solace in the desert, where he prayed for Allah's forgiveness that was eventually granted. The Qur'an tells us that while Daud was in the desert, his son, Abu Salama, rose up against Daud and attempted to seize the throne. But Allah made

---

44. C. T. R. Hewer, *Understanding Islam: An Introduction* (Minneapolis: Fortress, 2006) 17.

45. Ibid.

46. The Holy Qur'an 2:151–152 (author's translation).

an example of the rebellious sons and ordered the angel of death Azrail to kill Abu Salama by hanging him from a tree by his own hair.

The Qur'an tells us that plants, birds, beasts, and even mountains responded to the sweetness of the voice of Daud (38:17). In later Islam, a number of ahadith suggest that Daud fasted every other day. Bukhari suggests that Allah saw this gesture as a great act of kindness. Others, like Abdullah Ibn Amir Al-As tells us that the prophet Daud prayed all night and fasted all day. The Qur'an's 34:10 tells us that Allah made iron pliable for Daud so that he might bend it.

Sura 2:246–252 deviates considerably from the Hebrew Bible's account of Saul, Gideon, David, and Goliath. First Samuel 10 suggests that Israel's first king is Saul, and he has a prophet named Samuel. The Qur'an does not name the prophet, nor does it state the name of Israel's first king. Although the prophet remains anonymous throughout the Qur'an, the king in question is called Talut at 2:247 and 249). The Qu'ran also tells a slightly different version of the disagreements between Saul and David, with David (Daud) being the much more exalted figure in the Moslem Holy Book.

The Qur'an also points out that Daud had extraordinary abilities to discern justice, and that Daud had the voice of a nightingale. Daud's youngest wife, a woman named Nasaja, gave birth to Solomon—a son who matched the wisdom and charisma of his father. The Qur'an says that the light that the baby Solomon exuded was so bright that the Djinns (evil spirits) saw his brightness in the darkness. When Daud died, 40,000 priests are said to have recited the funeral prayers, while the entire nation mourned.

In addition to the prophets mentioned in this chapter, there are also a number of Biblical prophets that are not mentioned in the Qur'an and later Islamic literature. Isaiah, Jeremiah, and Amos, for examples, are unknown in the Islamic Holy Book. Some Islamic scholars point out that the list of prophets in the Qur'an is not exhaustive. There is room in Islam for prophets that may not have been mentioned in the Qur'an but may still be seen as holy messengers of Allah.

CONCLUSIONS

In this chapter, we have explored various Islamic points of view of ten of the 25 major prophets discussed in the Qur'an. We have seen that Islam follows the Genesis narrative about Adam and Eve, with one major difference. Islam, for the most part, does not see our first parents as having sinned in the Garden of Eden. After discussing the figure of Adam, we moved in this chapter to Islamic views of Enoch, Noah, and Eber. We saw that both Enoch and Noah stand as two of the great prophets in Islam.

We also have seen that the story of Hud (Eber) in the Islamic tradition is a curious blending of the narratives of Noah and Moses. Next, we moved to a discussion of Shelah and Lot in Islam. Saleh (Shelah) was used by Allah against Moslems who worshipped idols, while Lut (Lot) has been sent in Islam as a prophet to homosexuals, among other things. Next, we moved in this chapter to a discussion of three prophets: Ismail, Ishaq, and Yaqub (Ishmael, Isaac, and Jacob). In this section we reiterated some ideas we had explored earlier in this chapter on Ibrahim (like the notion that it was Ismail and not Ishaq to be sacrificed), as well as showing that Ishaq plays a subordinate role in Islam.

We brought this chapter to a close with a discussion of Yusuf (Joseph) in the Qur'an and later Islam. As we have seen sura 12, "Yusuf," is the longest complete narrative in the Qur'an. In Islam, the story of Yusuf is a tale of deceit, misinformation, and greed; but we have also seen it is a story of passion, loyalty, patience, and fortitude. In Islam, the figure of Yusuf is admired beyond any, with the exception of Ibrahim, Musa, and Muhammed.

We have also pointed out in this chapter that the figure of Yusuf is largely ignored in post-Qur'anic literature, and that the most frequent references to Yusuf in ahadith are in reference to Joseph's great beauty. Indeed, in Islam the story of Joseph is often used to show the dangers of passion, as well as the efficacy of possessing patience and fortitude.

In the following chapter, we shall explore the roles in Islam of one final Old Testament prophet, the figure of Ayyub, the Arabic name for Job. As we shall see, Islam sees Job in some very different ways than those of Judaism and Christianity.

6

The Image of the Biblical Job (Ayyub)
in the Qur'an and Later Islam

The Islamic sources and later traditions extol Job as the pious and righteous servant of Allah. He was the recipient of revelation, as were Abraham, Ishmael, and Isaac and Jacob, Jesus and Jonah, Aaron, David and Solomon (Qur'an 4:161). His righteousness was recompensed, as was that of Abraham, Joseph, Moses, and Aaron, David and Solomon (6:84). When he cried to his Lord ("Thou art most merciful of those who show mercy"), the burden of his woe was lightened (21:83f). "Verily we found him patient!" (38:44).

—Nahum Glatzer, *The Dimensions of Job*

Satan races back and forth from heaven to earth. He resorts to various ruses and disguises. He causes female breasts to grow on Job's chest, and warts the size of sheep's buttocks.

—Abu Jafar Al-Tabari, *Jami Al-bayan 'an ta' wil aya, Al Quran*

INTRODUCTION

I N THIS CHAPTER, WE have three principal goals. First, carefully to look at the four major places that the figure of Ayyub (Job in Arabic) appears in the Qur'an. Second, we will explore the places and roles that the prophet Ayyub has had in Medieval Islamic commentaries on Ayyub and his book. Finally, we make some general conclusions about the figure of Ayyub in Islamic history and theology.

JOB IN THE QUR'AN

There are two kinds of references to the book of Job in the Qur'an. The first is a series of expressions, and allusions that the writers of the Qur'an either borrowed from the Biblical book of Job, or were so much a part of Semitic culture that they can be found in both these works, as well as the New Testament, the Dead Sea Scrolls, or other noncanonical literature of Judaism, Christianity and Islam, originating in the Middle-East.

In some cases, it appears as though the authors of the Qur'an may have been quoting directly from the text as in the Qur'an's 9:119 and Job 16:19, or the Qur'an's mention of the ephemeral nature of a spider web in 29:40, which can also be found in Job 36:9b, or in certain linguistic constructions shared by Hebrew, Aramaic, and Arabic. There are also a number of phrases in the 63rd *sura* of the Qur'an, for example, that look very much like phrases in Job, particularly the speeches of the patriarch.

Some modern interpreters of the Qur'an suggest that several passages in the Qur'an, as well as a couple of verses in the book of Job, are ancient evidence that the writers of Job and Mohammed knew of modern theories on embryology. Other Islamic sources debate whether these passages were plagiarized from Aristotle's view of human embryonic development.

In other instances, the similarity between the Biblical book of Job and the Qur'an is probably a function of a shared Semitic culture rather than philology. In Job 10:11–12, for example, the text waxes poetically about the miracle of conception from a single drop of semen. Mohammed, with equally mistaken patriarchal pride, makes the same point in the Qur'an's 22:5; 36:76; and 96:2. In a similar vein, the Islamic sources recompenses Job, depending on the tradition, with as many as twenty-six sons, though a great proliferation of daughters apparently would not have counted as a blessing. Professor George Sale mentions the burying of unwanted female babies in early Islam, and its connection to this verse. Ecclesiasticus 26:10–12 and 42:8–11 also has much to say about the high value placed on sons in the Semitic world, as does the Job Targum found in cave 11 at Qumran whose editors construed the *sibanah* of the Hebrew text as dual and thus doubling the number of sons to 14, while leaving the number of daughters at three. It is clear that the real emphasis at the end of the

Masoretic Job is on the male children,[1] in much the same way as it has been in traditional Islamic culture.

Although Job's daughters are given names and property rights, these should be seen, I think, more as inducements for suitors than as a step in the direction of an ancient brand of feminism among the tribes of Israel or Ancient Islam. The same view of the relative importance of the sons over the daughters is also shared by Islamic interpreters of the book of Job.

In addition to these linguistic and cultural parallels to Job, there are also a number of explicit references in the Qur'an to the man from Uz. In general, it is in the context of a kind of test theodicy, and a Divine Plan point of view that Job is most often mentioned in the Qur'an.

Altogether four references are made to Job in the Qur'an. Since they are relatively brief, it might be helpful to quote all four (4:163; 6:83–84; 21:83–84; and 38:41–44) in their entirety. In the first, 4:163, Job is referred to in connection with those worthies to whom Allah has given his revelation:

> We have sent thee inspiration, as we sent it to Noah and the Messengers after him: we sent inspiration to Abraham, Ishmael, Isaac, Jacob, and the tribes, to Jesus, Job, Jonah, Aaron, and Solomon, and to David We have given the psalms.[2]

In the minds of the writers of the Qur'an, Job is on a moral par with, as well as being privy to the same kind of revelation as, Abraham, Isaac, Jesus, and other patriarchs. But unlike the other holy men, it is not clear what the nature of Job's revelation was. Indeed, if Job were "in the know" in regard to God's ways, the book of Job would not be the same work. In the *Testament of Job* the truth about Satan is vouchsafed to Job, but this is precisely why the central issue of the apocryphal work is one of endurance and patience, and not the larger theological conundrum about why the innocent sometimes suffer. A few more modern theological interpretations take this same view of the Hebrew book of Job: that as P. T. Forsyth has it, Job is not provided with "an answer to a riddle but a victory in a battle."[3]

---

1. *Targum on Job* 42:8–11.

2. Quran 4:163. Translations on this text vary. Some mention Job in this list of patriarchs, and some do not.

3. Ibid. 6:84. Again, translations of this verse vary. N. J. Dawood's translation of 6:84 is very different from that of Abdullah Yusef Ali. See note 4.

No less a literary figure than American president, Calvin Coolidge in the midst of the Depression wrote a magazine article to the effect that in Job we have the archetypal hero of thrift, proper diet, and above all patience, who overcame adversity like a brave soldier in battle, securing in the end twice as much as he had before.[4] A similar kind of view is taken by the writers of the Qur'an in this first reference to the man from Uz.[5]

The second reference to Job in the Qur'an occurs in a similar context of patience as the ultimate answer to the problem of innocent suffering. Again, in 6:84 God speaks: "We gave him Isaac and Jacob: all three We guided: and before him, we guided Noah, and among his progeny, David, Solomon, Job, Joseph, Moses and Aaron. Those do we regard who do the good."

Allah has revealed himself to Job and others, and he has guided them, for He rewards those who do the good, though it is not clear in the Qur'an whether God's guidance is responsible for their goodness, or if Allah, in his infinite wisdom, knows before hand that the prophets will be good and thus guides them because of their original moral character. What is clear is that, Allah ultimately has a plan for recompensing men of Job's moral worth.

The third reference to Job in the Qur'an occurs in the context of questions about the proper attitude of good Moslems who are facing suffering:

> And remember Job when he cried to his Lord, Truly distress has seized me, but Thou art the Most Merciful of those who are merciful. So we listen to him. We removed the distress that was on him, and we restored his people to him, and doubled their number—as a grace from Ourselves, and a thing of commemoration, for all who will serve.

Here again the premium is on fortitude and patience, which replace the larger question about why Allah would allow such worthies to suffer in the first place. The final mention of Job in the Qur'an makes this point about patience even more explicitly:

> Commemorate Our Servant Job.
> Behold he cried to his Lord:

4. Ibid. 21:84. Again, Dawood's translation varies considerably from Yusaf Ali's on this sura.

5. Fig. 1.

"The Evil One has afflicted me with distress and suffering."

The Command was given:
Strike with your foot:

Here is water wherein to wash, cool and refreshing and water to drink.

And We gave him back his people, and doubled their number as a Grace from Ourselves, and a thing for commemoration, for all who have Understanding.
And take in thy hand a little grass and strike therewith, and break not thy oath."

Truly we have found him full of patience and constancy.
How excellent in our service?
Ever did he turn to us.[6]

Here Ayyub appeals to Allah, and Allah conceives of Job's suffering as a kind of test which he passed with flying colors, which he knew Job would pass before the test even began. But the source of Job's afflictions is not Allah, it is the Evil One, *Iblis*. Indeed, nothing at all is said in the Qur'an about Satan needing permission from God to inflict suffering on Job. Nor does it say in the Hebrew text that Job knows it is Satan testing him.

Thus, an important difference between the Hebrew Bible's treatment of Job and the Qur'an's treatment of Ayyub is that in the former the patriarch is unaware that the source of his suffering is Satan, while in the latter, Ayyub knows from the beginning that his suffering comes from Iblis. Indeed, in several places in the Qur'an, the text speaks of Shaytan/Iblis being an enemy of Allah and humans, so this is a given in the Qur'anic treatment of the prophet.

What all four references to Job in the Qur'an have in common is their adherence to what we earlier have called the "Saint Job" motif. As in the traditions about Job in the first few centuries of Christianity, in the Qur'an, the Job of the Hebrew poetry, as opposed to the Job of the prose, is nowhere to be found. All the emphasis on the Islamic Job is on the fortitude and the ability to combat *Iblis*. In the Hebrew tradition it is abundantly clear that Job at times sees his real enemy as God, while in the early Islamic tradition, as in the early Church fathers, it is as if Job has

---

6. Naphatali Apt, "Die Hiobserzählung in der arabischen Literateur," Ph.D. dissertation, University of Heidelberg, 1913.

been let in on the heavenly wager between God and *Shaytan*—something not present in the Hebrew text.

JOB IN MEDIEVAL ISLAMIC COMMENTARIES

Later Islamic tradition added other elements of the Saint Job point of view to the Job story. These new particulars were gleaned from the Jewish *haggadah*, as well as from the Jewish and Christian apocryphal writings. A number of other elements seem to have been borrowed from the early Christian canon (the Epistle of James), and from the church fathers of the first six centuries, particularly Clement of Rome, Augustine, Ambrose and Jerome.

As early as the eighth century, Ka'b al-ahbar and Wahb, two Yemenite Jews converted to Islam, went so far as to describe Job's appearance: a tall man with a big head and crisp hair, beautiful eyes, a short neck, and long limbs.[7] In fact, most artistic depictions of Job in the Moslem tradition portray him as a much younger man than in Christian iconography. Perhaps the major reason for this discrepancy is that Medieval Islamic artists tend to portray Job after his health and riches have been restored, while the Christian iconographers more often depict the man from Uz in the midst of his illness. In a 1913 dissertation written at the University of Heidelberg, Naftali Apt traced a number of these Arabic literary and artistic uses of Job in Medieval Moslem literature.[8]

As in Jewish literature, various opinions are put forward in the Islamic Medieval tradition about Job's origins and the period in which he lived. The question found among the ancient rabbis about whether Job loved God out of devotion or out of fear is never raised in the Islamic commentaries. Indeed, the interesting question about the possibility of Job's self-interested goodness never occurs to the Islamic commentators.

Some Islamic sources suggest that Job was a Rumi, an Edomite, who lived during the time of the Hebrew patriarchs. Other sources say that Job's son, Bishr, succeeded him as a prophet and was known by the name Dhu al-Kifl.[9] Still other sources identify Job as living in the time of Lot, Abraham or Noah. In later Islamic tradition from the eleventh and twelfth

---

7. J. Horovitz' *Koranische Untersuchungen* (Berlin, 1926) 100–101, mentions several medieval commentaries that take this view.

8. Ibid.

9. Ibid.

centuries, Job is generally depicted as being a descendant of Essau (as he was in the Babylonian Talmud and the *Testament of Job*). Another more modern Islamic tradition identifies Ayyub as, "the grandson of Issac, and Ibrahim was his great grandfather." In the eleventh century, Tha'Labi, in his *Stories of the Prophets*, refers to Job's wife as Rahma, the daughter of Ephraim; others call her Dinah, Leah and Mahkir, the daughters of Manassas or Jacob. Still other Islamic traditions identify Dina, probably a variant of Dinah, as Job's second wife, the bearer of twenty-six new sons.[10]

If Medieval Islamic exegetes were interested in Job's provenance, they seem decidedly disinterested in whether Job worshipped God out of fear or love. Most later Medieval Islamic exegetes took for granted the notion that Job was innocent of any wrong-doing. Job was put to the test by *Iblis* because the Evil One was jealous of Job. Other sources suggest that *Shaytan* was angry at human beings because they had refused to worship him. In either case, they attempted to link Job with Adam—one who withstood the temptations of *Iblis*, and one who did not.

The fourteenth-century scholar Ibn Kathir called Job the "ultimate exemplar of patience and fortitude whose outcome of endurance is relief."[11] Ibn Asakir, a twelfth-century anecdotal historian of the patriarchs and prophets, suggests that the exemplary Job will be held up to the sick as a role model on the day of judgment.[12] Asakir thought the source of Job's great patience was his foreknowledge that all his goods would be restored,[13] a tradition that may have its roots in the *Testament of Job*.

Al-Tabari suggested that only the most loved by God are able to withstand such torture as Job's.[14] Al-Zamakhshari in his paraphrase of the book of Job says to his wife: "I am ashamed before God to call upon him when the length of my tribulations has not reached that of my property."[15]

This emphasis in the Islamic tradition on Job's extraordinary piety and patience moved various Medieval Moslem scholars to speculate on

10. Quoted in ibid., 103.

11. Ibid.

12. Ibid., 105.

13. Apt mentions this tradition was very popular in philosophical circles of Islam in the tenth to fourteenth centuries ("Die Hiobserzählung," 100–101).

14. Cf. the appendix D on medicine in this volume.

15. Fig. 2.

just how long Job remained on his ash-heap. Al-Maqdisi thought Job sat for seven years, seven months, seven days, seven hours, and seven seconds, while Ibn Kathir thought the patriarch's suffering lasted eighteen years.[16] Ibn Asaker tells us that

> Ayyub was a man with much wealth of all kinds: beasts, slaves, sheep, vast lands of Hauran, and many children. All these favors were taken from him, and he was physically afflicted as well. Never a single organ was sound except his heart and tongue, with both of which he glorified Allah, the Almighty, all the time, day and night. His disease lasted for a long time until his visitors felt disgusted with him. His friends kept away from him and people abstained from visiting him. No one felt sympathy for him, except his wife. She took good care of him, knowing his former charity and pity for her.[17]

Abu Huraira had a similar judgment about the character of Ayyub:

> While Ayyub was naked taking a bath, a swarm of gold locusts fell on him, and he started collecting them in his garment. His Lord called him: "Oh Ayyub, have I not made you too rich to need what you see?" He said: "Yes, Lord. But I cannot shun your blessings."[18]

The ninth-century interpreter of the Qur'an, Abu Jafar Al-Tabari, gives us this account of Ayyub's troubles: "Satan rushed back and forth from heaven to earth. He resorts to various ruses and disguises. He caused female breasts to grow on Ayyub's chest, and warts the size of sheep's buttocks."[19]

Other Medieval Islamic sources go to great lengths to describe the series of calamities that befell Ayyub's body. In all these accounts, Iblis is shown to be responsible for inflicting the prophet with these symptoms. Some Islamic accounts suggest that Allah gives Iblis full power over Ayyub, except his heart and tongue. A number of Moslem accounts have Iblis blowing in Ayyub's nostrils, causing an inflammation of the body and filling it with worms. In these accounts, Ayyub's body becomes so defiled,

---

16. Apt., "Die Hiobserzählung," 105.
17. Abdul Wahid Hamid, *Companion to the Prophets* (London: Nelson, 1967) 164.
18. Ibid., 165.
19. Ibid.

he is forced to leave and find refuge atop a dungheap.[20] Some say this was a sign of patience, while others say it was a signal of his repentance.

In almost all Medieval Islamic commentaries on Job we find what is considered by the commentators to be an important moral distinction between committing evil and allowing it. God permits the evil *Shaytan* to tempt Job, but it is *Shaytan* who is morally blameworthy. This, of course, is an important philosophical move in laying the groundwork for the moral qualities, or test theodicy. If Allah can be let off the moral hook, then the character testing of Job can take place without any objections that the testing violates the notion of God's omnibenevolence.

Allah gives *Iblis* full power over Job, except his tongue, which Allah continued to make free (again, a tradition most likely borrowed from the *Testament of Job*).[21] *Iblis* blew into Job's nostrils, causing an inflammation of the body and filling it with worms. His body became so defiled he was forced to leave and find refuge atop a dungheap. In the ancient Hebrew traditions rabbis were divided over the meaning of the dungheap. Some said that he sat on the dungheap as a sign of repentance; others argued that he was ostracized because he suffered from a communicable disease. In the Islamic tradition, the latter reason is always given by Medieval exegetes.

Throughout the later Middle Ages, the patient Job remained the standard view among Islamic exegetes. Al-Baydawi, a thirteenth-century commentator, held a view of Job practically indistinguishable from Christian proponents of the Saint Job motif from the Epistle of James to the work of Gregory's epitomizers. In commenting on the Qur'an's 21:83, Al-Baydawi advises that the followers of Allah "ought to be patient like Job was patient, for they will be rewarded the way Job was rewarded."[22]

Later Al-Baydawi suggests, as the Septuagint and the *Testament of Job* do, that Job's reward consists not just in double recompense and a long life, but also in eternal bliss in Paradise, something not offered by the writers of the Hebrew book of Job. For Al-Baydawi, Job's survival after death will take the form of immortality of the soul, not the resurrection

20. Ibid. Also see Stephen Vicchio, "The Image of Ayyub (Job) in the Qur'an and Later Islam," *The Bible and Interpretation* (August, 2005) 1–11.

21. For a fuller discussion of this point, see the appendix on "Job and Geography," in *The Image of the Biblical Job*, vol. 3.

22. Cf. the comments of the work of Baydawa on sura 21:83; and Masudi on the Murudj 1:91; in Horowitz, 100–101.

of the body suggested by the Septuagint, nor that strange amalgam of the two traditions talked about in the *Testament of Job*.

Mohammed Ali, another late Medieval commentator, suggested that Job's suffering is meant by Allah to remind us of his later prophet, Mohammed. Indeed, in keeping with this spirit, Ali describes the Qur'an 38:42–45, as an "account of Job's flight from one place to another." In the same way that Christian scholars turned Job into a Christ figure, Ali makes the man from Uz a "Mohammed figure."

One interesting facet of the Medieval Moslem commentaries on Job is the treatment of his wife, usually called Rahma. In a note on Islamic commentaries on the Qur'an's 21:83, George Sale points to a fundamental ambivalence about Job's wife in the minds of Medieval exegetes:

> his wife, however, (whom some call Rama, the daughter of Ephriam the son of Joseph, and the others Makhir the daughter of Mannasses), attended him with great patience, supporting him by what she earned by her labor; but that the devil appeared to her one day, after having reminded her of her passed prosperity, promised her that if she would worship him, he would restore all they had lost; whereupon she asked her husband's consent, who was so angry at the proposal, that he swore, if he recovered to give his wife a hundred lashes.[23]

In a similar context, Sale mentions the Medieval scholar's view of the end of Job's woes:

> God sent Gabriel, who taking him by the hand raised him up; and at the same time a fountain sprang up at his feet, of which, having drunk, the worms fell off his body, and washing therein he recovered his former health and beauty; that God then restored all to him double; his wife also became young and handsome again, and bearing him twenty-six sons; and that Job, to satisfy his oath, was directed by God to strike her one blow with a palm tree branch having one hundred leaves.[24]

---

23. Cf. appendix on "Job in Art," in *The Image of the Biblical Job*, vol. 1.

24. Cf. The various maps in the appendix on "Job and Geography." Stephen Vicchio, *Job in the Modern World*. (Eugene: Wipf and Stock, 2006.) pp. 197–212. For further discussion of these geographical points also see Hanna Kohlberg's *De tijding van Job in de Bijbel en in de Koran* (The Hague: Voorhoeve, 1981). This book, which is yet unavailable in English, is an invaluable reference for Islamic attitudes about the biblical Job. H. Zafrani's "Une Historie de Job en Judeo-arabe du Maroc," *Revue Etudes Islam* 36 (1987) 279–315, provides a very helpful overview of Islam's preoccupation with Job. T.

Unlike Christian Medieval depictions of Job's wife extending food on the end of the stick to her husband, lest she have defiling contact with him, the Medieval Islamic tradition, following the *Testament of Job*, have his wife attend to him "with great patience." Also like the *Testament of Job*, in the Islamic commentators of the Middle Ages Job's wife is naïve and impressionable, unwittingly falling into *Ibis'* carefully laid trap. The ambiguity about Job's wife arises in the Islamic tradition, not because of her suspect moral character, but rather the dichotomy between her good moral character and her womanly tendency to get into trouble simply because she is not wise enough to do otherwise.

This view, of course, is a far cry from Augustine's view that Job's wife was the *diablo adultrix*. In the Islamic tradition, Rahma shares Job's glory because she nearly rivaled his patience. In the end Allah holds Job to his oath of lashing Rahma with strokes, but the letter of the law is met with Job's single use of a benign palm branch with 100 leaves.[25]

ISLAM AND THE LAND OF UZ

Among Islamic scholars is some confusion about where the land of Uz is to be found. Early Jewish tradition and subsequent Byzantine and Arabic cultures thought Ayyub's land of Uz was to be found in Hauran. In Islam, the land of Ayyub has also been identified around Nawa and Sheikh Miskin, on the high road that cuts across Trachonitis. The name "Ausis" found in the appendix of the Septuagint's version of the book of Job (42:17d) suggests the land of Uz is to be identified with Dhuneibeh, between Sheikh Miskin and Ezra.

Etheria, a Christian piligrim in the fourth and fifth centuries, identifies the land of Job with Carneas and Dennaba, a city south of Nawa. Thus, a series of Christian and early Islamic sources place the land of Uz firmly in Trachonitis. Indeed, in that region can still be found the *Deir Ayyub*, the monastery of Job.

At the end of the nineteenth century, German biblical scholar J. G. Weitzstein (1815–1905) traveled to this monastery near Damascus, where he also found Ayyub's tomb, his well, and a stone on which he is said to

---

W. Arnold's *The Old and New Testament in Muslim Religious Art*, Schweich Lectures of the British Academy (1928); and R. Gottheil, "An Illustrated Copy of the Koran," in the *Revue des Etudes Islamiques* (1931) 1:21–24, provide pictorial evidence for the Saint Job tradition in Islam.

25. Kohlberg, *De tijding*, 27.

have sat. He also found several petrified rocks about which he tells us this:

> While these people were offering up their Aur [afternoon prayer] in this place, Sayed brought me a handful of small round stones which tradition declares to be the worms that fell to the ground from Job's sores, petrified. "Take them with you," he said, "as a remembrance of this place. Let them to teach you not to forget Allah in prosperity, and in misfortune not to contend with him."[26]

Weitzstein goes on to quote a poem authored by a Medieval Haurian Christian that speaks about the petrified worms. Charles Clermont-Ganneau, a French scholar at the end of the nineteenth century, also speaks of a number of stories associated with the prophet Ayyub, including his petrified worms. Thus, in Islam there are two competing claims about the location of the land of Uz, one south of Israel and the Negev, and the other north of Israel near Damascus.

AYYUB AND THE SACRED WATER

One other striking parallel between the *Testament of Job* and the Medieval Islamic understanding of the man from Uz is the manner in which Job is healed of his sickness. The Masoretic text and the Septuagint leave the process to our imaginations, while the *Testament of Job* and the Islamic commentators make specific reference to his healing through sacred water. Indeed, in Tha'Labi's *Stories of Prophets*, Iblis appears to Rahma in the guise of a physician who offers to cure Job's illness. Job wisely sees through Iblis' subterfuge and refuses medical treatment. The same polemic against physicians can be seen at the end of the *Testament of Job* where, ultimately it is only God who cures disease. As we have seen in our discussion of the Job targumim at Qumran, a similar critical view of physicians may have been a fairly common view among religious people of the ancient Near East.[27]

The theme of Job's healing through a sacred stream was popular among Medieval Moslem commentators, and it was also the most popular extant image in late Medieval Islamic art. The most common depiction

26. Falzan Rahman, *Major Themes of the Qur'an* (Chicago: University of Chicago Press, 1980) 179.

27. See chapter on Job in the Dead Sea Scrolls in Stephen Vicchio's *Job in the Ancient World*, pp. 177–96..

of Job in the twelfth to fifteenth centuries shows the patriarch as a young man wearing Medieval Islamic dress. Ayyub is usually visited by the Angel Gabriel who hands Job a flower. Between the two figures runs a sacred stream.

One of the most beautiful and interesting of fifteenth-century Islamic artistic depictions of Job is an illustrated manuscript (ms. 414, fol. 82) owned by the Chester Beatty Library in Dublin. The healed Job is accompanied by Gabriel who presents the patriarch with a rose. The legend read, "Job was healed with the aid of those waters, and he died at the age of 93."[28] Several other commentators mention this as the age of Job's demise. The origin of this figure is unclear. It bears no resemblance to the considerably more robust 140 years he is given in the Masoretic text or the 170 and 240 years suggested by various manuscripts of the Septuagint. Professor Apt quotes one other source that suggests that Job's troubles lasted 80 years, corresponding to his eight decades of happiness.

This view of Job as a saint and a healer of diseases continues in the Western tradition through the Renaissance. "The Legends of the Prophets," a sixteenth-century text, is owned by the New York Public Library (MS 456f. 109). Job is shown standing in a spring that flows around the patriarch's feet, suggesting the Quranic tradition that Job was healed by holy waters. Indeed, all extant Islamic depictions of Job from the twelfth to sixteenth centuries tend toward the depiction of Job in his restored state. In Islamic manuscripts the patriarch is most often depicted accompanied by the angel Jibrail (Gabriel), and attended to by his faithful wife, whose Arabic name is Rahman.

Unlike Christian Medieval artistic depictions of Job that invariably portray a suffering Job accompanied by his wife and three friends, Islamic art usually shows a triumphant Job, a Job accompanied by a heavenly messenger and healed by the magic waters of Allah.[29]

This association of Job with healing waters also gave rise in Islamic popular culture to a tradition of Job's well or Job's stream, a kind of fountain of youth, which, according to legend and story was variously located outside Jerusalem, in the Transjordan in Hauran, and in or around Damascus.[30]

28. Chester Beatty Library, Dublin. Ms. 414, fol. 82.

29. See Arnold and Gottheil, 24; also chapters 2 and 3 of Apt.

30. Vicchio, *Job in the Modern World*, pp. 204–5.

The origin of this tradition of associating Job with curing waters is not clear. Again it most likely owes its life to the *Testament of Job*, or to the Qur'an where Allah tells Ayyub to tap on the ground with his foot. Beneath the foot forms a healing stream.

There is, of course throughout the Middle East myths and stories about the curative power of that rare commodity, water. Perhaps the simplest and clearest answer to the association of this water tradition with Job is a single verse from a speech of Zophar's (11:16 of the Masoretic text), where the comforter suggests that Job's troubles eventually will be washed away like water. Although Job is sometimes referred to in the Christian tradition as the patron saint of lepers and sufferers of other diseases, his curative powers were not related to water in that tradition.[31]

THE ROLE OF PROPHETS AND AYYUB IN MODERN ISLAM

In modern Islam (sixteenth century to the present) Allah is thought to have sent messengers to all nations. It is believed that from the beginning of time, Allah sent over 125,000 prophets and messengers. These messengers and prophets are human beings who were born into the nations to which they were to minister. They were not angels or supernatural beings. These prophets and messengers were to set their lives as examples for others to emulate.

Each prophet or messenger, it is believed in the Moslem tradition, was given a book, a piece of scripture that was the word of Allah. The lives of the prophets and these pieces of scripture became the norms for the Moslem community.

Ayyub (Iyov) is the Arabic name of Job. Some modern traditions suggest he was the grandson of Issac, and the great-grandson of Abraham. This tradition also suggests Ayyub's wife was the granddaughter of Joseph.[32] Other modern Islamic traditions argue that Ayyub was the son of Abu Ayyub, a close companion to Mohammed.[33] Still another modern source has it that Ayyub was "one of the descendents of the prophet Ibraham (Abraham), and a nephew of the prophet Ya'quib (Jacob).[34] This source

---

31. See appendix on Job in Medicine.

32. E. Dhorme, *A Commentary on the Book of Job* (London: Nelson, 1967) ccxx.

33. Ibid., ccxx.

34. Abdul Wahid Hamid, *Companions of the Prophet* (London: MELS, 1967) 1:233.

suggests that Ayyub was sent to minister to those who lived in the desert in the north-eastern corner of Palestine.

In all modern Moslem accounts, Ayyub is seen as a prosperous man with a firm faith in Allah. He is said to have possessed vast farms, enormous wealth, and many cattle and valuable property. But these things did not make Ayyub arrogant.

In modern Islam, Ayyub was an example of humility and patience. He suffered from a number of calamities. His farms were attacked by thieves. They killed many of his servants, and his children, and carried away his cattle. But through all of this, Ayyub remained faithful.

After a few years, modern Islam has it, Ayyub suffered from a skin disease. His entire body was covered by loathsome sores. Those sores were full of worms, fell from the wounds and praised Allah. All of Ayyub's friends and family deserted him, except his faithful wife, Rahma. She grew tired of her husband in the long run and prayed for his death. She cursed her husband who retained her faith in Allah.

Ayyub turned to Allah with mercy. Ayyub was commanded to strike the earth with his foot. He complied with the order and water gushed forth. He bathed in the water and his disease was cured. After this, Ayyub was restored to prosperity. The prophet is said to have kneeled and prayed, expressing a deep sense of gratitude to Allah. As one modern tradition has it, "The prophet Ayyub was one of the celebrated prophets. His example illustrates that those who remain patient, under the stress of all circumstances, are never deprived of higher rewards."[35]

Another modern account gives a different story of Ayyub. This tradition suggests that upon seeing Ayyub's prosperity, Shaytan decided to lead Ayyub astray. Since he was dealing with a prophet, Shaytan/Iblis requested permission from Allah to test Ayyub.

Shaytan came down to earth and stole Ayyub's property and children. The Shaytan gave Ayyub a loathsome disease. Later, Shaytan decided he would test Job through his wife, Rahma, who supported her husband by doing odd jobs outside the home. One day, Shaytan appeared to Rahma and told her he knew a way to cure Ayyub's disease. He told her to take a sheep and kill it in his name, rather than in the name of Allah. Shaytan claimed that the meat would cure Ayyub's illness.

---

35. *An Introduction to the Prophets of Islam*, na, nd.

When Rahma approached Ayyub with the plan, he immediately knew about the ruse. Ayyub says, "Has the enemy of my Lord misled you?" Ayyub adds, "If I am relieved with my afflictions, I will flog you with a hundred lashes." Ayyub then told his wife to go away and leave him alone. Finally, Ayyub appealed to Allah, who cured him of all of his troubles, and restored his prosperity.[36]

There is also another modern version of Job's wife. When there was no food in the house, the wife sought a loaf of bread for Ayyub. A man attracted by her lovely hair agreed to give her food in exchange for a lock of her hair. She gave the man her hair, and received food in return. In those days the hair of a woman was cut and removed if she was guilty of fornication. It pained Ayyub to see his wife without her hair, so he swore to punish her with 100 lashes.[37]

The account was clearly borrowed from the *Testament of Job's* version of Job's wife. It also agrees with the account that Ayyub was the son-in-law of Joseph, that Ayyub's disease lasted for seven years, that Ayyub saw Shaytan's ruse working with his wife, and that Ayyub punished his wife with a hundred lashes.

One other important aspect of this account of Ayyub is that it suggests, as many Medieval Christian sources do, that Ayyub was the prophet of skin diseases and ailments. When he was asked why he did not heal himself he said, "I have enjoyed Allah's grace and blessing for 80 years, and it would be ingratitude if I grumble when I have been made to taste distress."[38]

A third modern account of Ayyub suggests that angels of Allah were discussing the conditions of mankind and Allah points out Ayyub's exemplary character. Shaytan takes on the job of testing Ayyub, and Shaytan was unsuccessful in getting Ayyub to give up his faith. Eventually, in this third account, Ayyub's prosperity is restored.[39]

Among the major holidays in Islam is a day of fasting called Ashura which celebrates and commemorates a number of things, including the day Noah started his life after the flood, and the day that the prophet Ayyub was released from his suffering.

36. Syed Maududi, *Commentary on the Qur'an* (London: 1887) 163.

37. Hamid, *Companions*, 234.

38. Nasir Ahmed Comp, *The Fundamental Teachings of the QUR'AN* (Karachi: Jamiyat, 1969) 89–90.

39. Ibid., 91.

The figure of Ayyub is also identified with the B'hai feast of Rivdan, the holiest of B'hai festivals. Rivdan occurs in the spring and lasts for twelve days and commemorates the birth of the Bab, the founder of the movement.

Associated with the feast of Rivdan is the *Lawh i Ayyub*, the tablet of Job, also known as *Suriya i Sabr* (the city of patience). The tablet of Job, written in Arabic, celebrates the life of Ayyub, particularly his patience, during the festival.

In summary, all modern Islamic accounts of Job share the following points:

1. Job is a prophet from Allah.

2. He is known for his humility and patience.

3. Shaytan, with Allah's permission was the agent of the dissolution of Ayyub's property and family.

4. Shaytan may have acted through Rahma, Ayyub's wife.

5. Ayyub's former life is restored by Allah.

It should also be clear that most of the modern Islamic materials have borrowed from the Hebrew text of Job, the *Testament of Job*, and the early, Judeo-Christian accounts of the patient, saintly Job of the prose. Like the early Christian tradition, there is no evidence in Islamic accounts of Ayyub that the prophet is also angry and iconoclastic.[40]

It should be clear that most of this modern Islamic material on Ayyub borrows heavily from various sources: the Hebrew text of Job, the apocryphal Testament of Job, earlier Islamic accounts of Ayyub, the Qur'an, as well as the early Judeo-Christian account of Job as the patent, saintly Ayyub of the prose. Like early Christian accounts there is no evidence of Islam of the Ayyub of the poetry, the angry iconoclast.

CONCLUSIONS

As we have seen in this chapter, the Qur'an's view of Job is essentially patterned after three major sources: the Hebrew Bible, the apocryphal *Testament of Job*, and the early church father's view of the patient, saintly Job. Early on in Islam, scholars realized that the standard answer given to the problem of evil in the first generations of Islam—retributive justice—

40. Ibid., 92.

would not hold up under scrutiny when applied to the biblical figure of Job. Rather than make Job guilty of something. Islamic commentators chose instead to shift the ground of the problem of innocent suffering away from retributive justice and towards a kind of moral testing theodicy, something found in many of the early Christian exegetes. The principal effect of all of this was that the Job of early Islam like the Job of early Christianity, was essentially the patient, saintly Job of the prose, not the iconoclastic, often complaining, impatient Job of the poetry. Subsequent Islamic perspectives on Job were a good deal more complicated, borrowing elements from the Talmud and the Midrash, as well as from the early Christian sources.

From early Islam on, the Medieval Islamic exegetes inherited the preoccupation with questions about Job's pedigree, particularly interest in his bloodlines and the specific time of the patriarchal period in which he lived. Answers found in Islamic literature and exegeses to these questions are as varied as the sources from which they have borrowed. Islamic sources, like their Jewish predecessors, have Job living from Edom to southern Israel, from the time of Abraham to the period of Jewish kingship. Questions about Job's moral motivation, however, a very popular theme among the ancient rabbis, are never mentioned among Medieval Muslim interpreters.

Islamic biblical interpreters of the late Middle Ages seem to have taken for granted the goodness of Job. In fact, they ranked him among the holiest men of the Hebrew Bible. Unlike the Talmud or the Midrash where fierce debates raged over whether Job loved God out of fear or from devotion, the Islamic tradition tacitly assumed the latter view was the proper one.

Medieval Moslem interpreters continue the view of Job as a perfect example of patience and fortitude, while adding the more pedestrian concerns about his origins. Above all, they saw Job as a man well rewarded for his great virtues, recompensed both here and beyond the grave. In the Medieval Jewish tradition Job's moral virtues are on par with those of Abraham or any of the other Jewish patriarchs. There is also very little discussion in the Moslem traditions of whether Job was a Jew or a Gentile. The Qur'an suggests he was a Jew, while later commentators thought him a Gentile.

The depth of the commitment on the part of the later Islamic exegetes to the Saint Job motif can be seen clearly in Islamic religious art from the eleventh to the fifteenth centuries. There a "Job Triumphant" was portrayed. In late Medieval Islamic iconography Job is always depicted as a young, saintly Job, visited by the angel Gabriel and healed of his afflictions by Allah's magic waters. As we have suggested these portrayals of Job in Medieval Islamic art were part of a tradition in popular culture that expressed belief in the existence of Job's well or Job's stream, a kind of fountain of youth, somewhere in the deserts of the ancient near-east.

The Medieval Islamic attitude toward Job's wife also came from the same sources, though the Muslim view is more complicated than either ancient or rabbinic views that hardly mention her at all, or the early Christian tradition that is preoccupied with Job's wife as an agent of the devil. Like her husband, she is given a variety of pedigrees and at least five different names in the Medieval Islamic tradition. In regard to Job's wife there are, however, two elements on which the Muslim scholars agreed.

First, Job's wife is seen as a virtuous and patient, and second, as gullible. Although she falls prey to Iblis' temptations, the fall is more the function of her lack of capacity than it is some moral failing. The most likely source for this ambivalent view of Job's wife is the *Testament of Job*, where the wife Sitidos, supports her husband by working out of the house and by selling her hair, while easily falling prey to the beguiling Satan. In the Islamic tradition Job's wife falls not because she is bad, but because she lacks intelligence to understand she is Satan's pawn.

We have also seen that the role of Ayyub in modern Islam is very much in consort with earlier Islamic accounts. In modern Islam, Ayyub continued to be seen as a prophet of Allah, a man of patience and fortitude. The major questions in modern Muslim about Ayyub are his pedigree, the nature of Rahma's involvement, and the identity and role played by Shaytan/Iblis in the Ayyub tale.

One interesting fact about commentaries on Job written in Arabic in the Middle Ages is that one of the longest and the best was written by a Jew, Saadia Gaon, in the tenth century. His commentary featured an extraordinary combination of literary ability and knowledge of philology. It shows a thorough knowledge of rabbinic and Islamic traditions on Job, as well as an impressive grasp of both the logic and the metaphysics of Aristotle.

One final point about Job and Islam is in order. Among the versions of the book of Job derived from the Septuagint is an Arabic version of the text. There is also an Arabic version in Walton's polyglot that seems to derive from the Peshitta.

It appears to have been Saadia Gaon (ca. 942) that assumed the task of translating the entire Hebrew Bible into Arabic. Saadia's Arabic text is transcribed in Hebrew characters without vowels. He also uses the names Allah and Shatain as the participants in the bet. Saadia's Arabic version is the second oldest text of Job. E. Dhorme, in his commentary, writes, "Saadia's Arabic interpretation of the Hebrew would make the subject of an interesting study." It was not until recently that L. E. Goodman completed that study.

In 1870 Graf Baudissin edited an Arabic translation of the book of Job made from an Egyptian manuscript discovered by Tischendorf in the sixteenth century, which was later acquired by the British Museum, where it is cataloged as (Add. 26, 166). This manuscript, which probably dates from the ninth century, contains an Arabic version of the book of Job. This is the oldest extant Arabic translation of Job. It has become the standard Arabic translation in the English speaking world.

The Image of Jesus in the Qur'an and Later Islam

The human characteristics of Jesus, as the Qur'an describes them, are manifold. Jesus and Mary, his mother, are spoken of as being of exceptional purity.

—Jacques Jomier, *The Bible and The Qur'an*

The Qur'an gives a greater number of honorable titles to Jesus than any figure from the past.

—Geoffrey Parrinder, *Jesus in the Qur'an*

Oh you who believe be helpers of Allah, as Isa, son of Maryam, said to his disciples, "Who will help me in the way of Allah." And they answered, "We are the helpers of God." Then a section among the children of Israel believed, but another section among them did not.

—Qur'an 61:14

INTRODUCTION

In this chapter, and the three following it, we shall look at the various perspectives of Islam on the figure of Jesus, as well as other New Testament characters, including Mary, Joseph, Iblis (Satan), John the Baptist, and the Djaal, the Arabic word for the Anti-Christ. As we shall see, Islam sometimes shares the views of Judaism and Christianity on these figures, and sometimes significantly diverges from them.

In this chapter, we carefully look at the image of Jesus, called Isa in Arabic, in the Qur'an and later Islam. For Mohammed, Isa was among the most holy of humans. Although Mohammed and later Islam did/do not believe that Isa is the son of God, he is, nevertheless, offered as one of the chief moral exemplars in the Moslem faith. We move now to a section on Isa in the Qur'an.[1]

ISA IN THE QUR'AN

All tolled there are ninety-three references to Jesus in the Qur'an. In 5:46–47, Jesus is affirmed as a prophet in a long line of prophets sent by God to human beings throughout the ages. In Qur'an 43:57–59 tells us that Jesus led an exemplary life, and that he was no more than "a servant of God." This comment was voiced, no doubt, to contradict the Christian notion that Jesus is the son of God, or a member of the Divine Trinity. Indeed, at several places in the Qur'an the Holy Book argues against Jesus as a member of the Trinity.

The Qur'an's 5:73 makes it clear when it says, "Say not of God that he is one of three." The Qur'an's 42:11 also makes the same claim of the Oneness of Allah, where the text tells us that Allah was "the Originator of the heavens and the earth."[2] Islam stresses the singular nature of this passage. In general, when Moslems hear Christians speak of the trinity, they understand them as comments on three gods which, of course, is utterly condemned by the Qur'an.

The birth of Jesus and his early years are discussed in two principal passages of the Qur'an: (3:35–47 and 19:16–35). Both of these passages describe an angel that appears to Mary to announce that she will conceive

---

1. Most of the Arabic translation in this chapter are those of the author. The primary edition of the Qur'an I have used in this chapter is the translation by Ahmed Ali (Princeton: Princeton University Press, 1993). I have also consulted the translations of A.J. Arberry, *The Koran Interpreted* (London: Allen and Unwin, 1995), and M. M. Pickthall, *The Meaning of the Glorious Qur'an* (New York: Meridian, 1997). Secondary sources I have relied on in this chapter include the following: Jacques Jomier, *The Bible and the Qur'an* (San Francisco: Ignatiuis, 1964); Richard Bell, *Introduction to the Qur'an* (Edinburgh, 1953); Geoffrey Parrinder, *Jesus in the Qur'an* (London: Faber, 1965); H. Kennedy, *The Prophets and the Age of the Caliphs* (London: Longmans, 1986); and Andrew Rippin, *Approaches to the History of Interpretations of the Qur'an* (Oxford: Clarendon, 1988).

I have also consulted the following articles in preparing this chapter: Amar Djaballah, "Jesus in Islam," *The Southern Baptist Theological Journal* 8 (2004); Norman L. Geisler, "Jesus and Mohammed in the Qur'an: A Comparison and Contrast," *The Southern Baptist Theological Journal* 8 (2004); Kevin Bywater, "Islam: The End of Christianity," *Christian Research Journal* 25 (2003); Raj Kripalani, "The Doctrine of Jesus and Jihad," *Conservative Theological Journal* 6 (2002); and Clete Hux, "Jesus vs. Muhammed," *Areopagus Journal* 2 (2002).

2. *The Holy Qur'an* 42:11, author's translation.

and bear a son who would become a prophet. In the Islamic view, Mary was a virgin and was made pregnant without any human intervention but simple by the command of Allah. In Islam, this is much like how Allah created the universe by commands out of nothing.

The figure of Isa (Jesus) is referred to in fifteen different suras of the Qur'an, where ninety-three verses are related to the character.[3] Islam's basic view of Christology is garnered from these verses, as well as from the gospels, both canonical and not canonical, and from other Christian literature. Isa has a variety of names in the Qur'an, including *Nabi* (prophet), *Rasul* (messenger), and *ibn Maryam* (son of Mary). The latter term appears more frequently than the others. In fact, "son of Mary" appears 33 times in the Qur'an, not counting the 16 time where "Mary mother of Isa" is used.

A number of scenes from the life of Jesus are reflected in the Qur'an, including the Annunciation, the Conception, and the birth of Jesus. There are many features about these elements that clearly reflect the gospel narratives. Other than the denial of the divinity of Jesus, P. Hayek, in his *Le Christ de l'Islam*, goes so far to say, "apart from the dogma that Mary is the mother of God, rejected by Muslims since they formally deny the divinity of Jesus, all other dogmas defined by the Church, or transmitted by its traditions of worship, find support in the Koran."[4]

The longest version of the Annunciation to Mary is in sura 19 of the Qur'an, verses 16 to 21. One translation of the Arabic text goes like this:

> Commemorate Mary in the Book. When she withdrew from her family to a place in the East. And took cover from them. We sent a spirit of ours to her who appeared to her in the physical form of a man. "I seek refuge in the Merciful from you, if you fear Him," she said. "I am a messenger from you Lord, sent to bestow a good son on you." "How can; I have a son?" she asked, "when no man has touched me, nor am I sinful." He said, "Thus, it will be. Your Lord said 'It is easy for Me,' and that: 'we shall make a sign for men and a blessing for Us.' This is the thing already decreed."[5]

3. Qur'an 2:87; 2:136; 2:253; 3:45; 3:52; 3:55; 3:59; 3:84; 4:157; 4:163; 4:171; 4:172; 5:17; 5:46; 5:72; 5:78; 5:110; 5:112; 5:114; 5:116; 6:85; 9:30; 9:31; 19:34; 21:91; 23:50; 33:7; 42:13; 43:57; 43:63; 57:27; 61:6; and 61:14.

4. P. Hayek, *Le Christ de l'Islam* (Paris, 1959), quoted in the article on "Isa," in *The Encyclopedia of Islam* (Leiden: Brill, 1978) 4:81.

5. Qur'an 19:16–21 (author's translation).

A second account of the Annunciation also can be found in sura 3:37–47: "Recall when the angel said, 'Oh Mary, God has chosen you and purified you, and chosen you above the women of the world.'"[6] And "Oh Mary, be obedient to your Lord, prostrate yourself, and bow to those who bow."[7] And a little later in sura 3: "Remember when the angel said, 'God gave you tidings of a word from himself whose name is Messiah, Jesus, son of Mary, a famous one in this world and the next. One of those brought near to God.'"[8] In the same sura, there are a number of other verses related to Mary and Jesus: "And he will speak to the people in the cradle, and as a grown man. One of the righteous shall he be."[9] And a few verses later:

> She said, "My Lord, how shall I have a child, seeing that no man has touched me?" He said, "So shall it be. God creates what He wills. When he decides on something, He simply says, 'Be!' and it is."[10]

In addition to these passages, references to Mary are made at 21:91 and 66:12. Both passages refer to remembering the woman "in whom We preserved her chastity, so We could breathe a new life into her."[11]

A number of conclusions can be made from these passages of the Qur'an on the Annunciation. First, early Islam saw Mary as a virgin before the announcement. Second, the angel that appears to Mary in the Qur'an does not have a name. Later commentators in Islam have assumed that the messenger was Jibril (Gabriel), since he appears in several other passages in the Qur'an where he is the angel of revelation. Third, the Qur'an seems to imply that Isa could speak with people, and give them advice, when he was in the cradle, as 3:46 seems to say. Whether this is to show the supernatural powers of the baby Jesus, or whether it was for some other purpose, we do not know. What we do know is that in later Islam, the messenger to Mary was often seen as Jibril (Gabriel). Tabari in his commentary identifies the messenger with Jibril. He says, "He was sent to Mary, so that he might blow in her sleeve and conceive."[12] Baydawi,

---

6. Qur'an 3:35 (author's translation).

7. Qur'an 3:43 (author's translation).

8. Ibid, 3:39.

9. Ibid, 3:46.

10. Ibid, 3:47.

11. Ibid, 21:91 and 66:12.

12. Tabari, quoted in Article on "Isa," in *Encyclopedia of Islam*, 4:86.

a twelfth century writer of hadith, repeats this story of blowing air into Mary's chemise, so that he might give her the breathe of life.[13]

The child "speaking in the cradle" is mentioned in two other places in the Qur'an, at 5:110 and 19:30. Sura 5 says: "Remember the favors I bestowed on you and your mother, and reinforced you with divine grace, that you spoke to men while in the cradle, and when in the prime of life."[14]

In the Qur'an the distinction between the Annunciation and the conception of Jesus is not always clear. The gospel of Luke 1:26–28 seems to say that the angel that makes the announcement is distinct from the Holy Spirit who performs the miracle. Whereas, the Qur'an seems to unite these two ideas. In fact, in 19:17 there is mention of an angel that appears to Mary in the form of a mortal, in two other texts (66:12 and 21:9) there is reference to "Our Spirit," but no mention of an angel at all. At any rate, some later commentators refer to Jibril as "the father of Isa."[15]

The Qur'an gives an account of the birth of Isa at 19:22–34. There the text tells us:

> When she conceived him she went away to a distant place. The birth pangs led her to the trunk of a date-palm tree. "If only I had died before all this," she said, "and have become a thing forgotten and not remembered." Then a voice called to her from below. "Don't grieve. The Lord has made a little river gush forth just below you, and it will give you ripe dates. Shake the trunk of the tree, and it will bring you dates. Eat and drink, and be at peace. And if you see any man, tell him, "I have vowed a fast to Ar-Rahman and I cannot speak to anyone today."[16]

Ar-Rahman is one of the favorite pre-Qur'anic names for God. It occurs 55 other times in the Qur'an. The narrative continues:

> Then she brought the child to her people. They yelled, "Oh Mary, you have done an amazing thing. Oh sister of Aaron, your father was not a wicked man, nor was your mother sinful." But she pointed to him and said, "How can we talk to one who is only an infant in the cradle?" "I am a servant of God," he answered. "He has given

---

13. Ibid.

14. Qur'an 5:110 (author's translation).

15. Ibid, 66:12 and 21:9.

16. Ibid, 19:22–26.

me a Book and made me a prophet, and blesses me wherever I go and gave me worship and alms for as long as I live."[17]

This is followed by a mention of the birth of Jesus:

"And be dutiful to my mother. He has not made me haughty or rebellious. There was peace on me the day I was born, and will be the day I die and on the day I will be raised from the dead." This was Jesus, son of Mary a true account they contend about.[18]

One final comment regarding the birth of Jesus. Islam, by and large, does not believe in the doctrine of original sin; but there is a tradition found in later Islam, particularly in al-Bukhari, that suggests that both Maryam and Isa were granted reprieves from having any contact with Iblis during the moment of birth. As Bukhari puts it, "Every son of Adam when born is touched by Satan, except for the son of Mary and his mother."[19]

Mary is seen by Islam as having been pure before the Annunciation, and Jesus is also understood in Islam as being born without sin. Thus, Islam for the most part rejects the doctrine of original sin, though it speaks specifically of the purity of both Mary and Jesus.

THE MISSION OF ISA

Isa is described as both a *nabi* (prophet) and as a *rasul* (messenger). Like all prophets, he has a mission to fulfill. Isa is thought to have a special mission in Islam, and as proof it offers several examples. One mentioned above is to speak to adults from the cradle. A second piece of proof (*bayyinat*, in Arabic) is an incident described in the Qur'an in which he makes models of small birds from clay and then breathes life into them and they become "a bird by the leave of Allah." This same tale is told in the second chapter of the apocryphal Gospel of Thomas, as well as in "The Gospel of the Childhood," an Arabic text.

A third piece of evidence in Islam that Isa has a special mission can be seen in the various miracles, or "signs" that he performs throughout the Qur'an. He cures a man blind from birth and a leper (5:110). He raises the dead, but always with Allah's permission (3:43). As a request from the

---

17. Ibid, 19:27–31.
18. Ibid, 19:32–34.
19. Bukhari, quoted in *Encyclopedia of Islam*, 4:82.

apostles, he made a prepared meal come down from the heavens (5:111–114). The Qur'an tells us this about the final bit of evidence:

> When the disciples said, "Oh Jesus, son of Mary, could the Lord send us down a table laid out with food?" "Fear Allah, if you really believe." They said, "We should like to eat of it to reassure our hearts and to know that what you told us is the truth, and that we shall be witnesses to it." Then Jesus, son of Mary said: "Oh God, our Lord, send down a table well laid out with food from the sky, so that today we may have a feast for both the earlier among us and the later."[20]

A few verses later, the text tells us: "And Allah said, 'I shall send it down to you; but if any of you disbelieve after this, I shall bring such punishment on him that has never been inflicted to any other man.'"[21]

The Qur'an suggests that Isa has come to declare the truth that has been given in the Torah (3:44). The gospels are accepted by Islam because they "fill the hearts of those who follow them with meekness" (5:82). Isa is referred to in the Qur'an as the *Misih*, the Arabic word of Messiah. The word is used eleven times in the Qur'an, all reference to Isa. In Islam, Jesus is the Messiah, but debates about the Misih in Islam are often about another question: could Allah kill the Misih? Some verses of the Qur'an suggest Allah could kill the Messiah, while others disagree.

Jesus is sometimes called an *Abd* of Allah. Abd is the word for "slave" in Arabic, but it also sometimes means "servant" or "creature," as opposed to Creator. At 4:170 of the Qur'an, angels are referred to as Abd. Above and beyond these descriptions what must be remembered is that the Qur'an insists that Isa is simply another of Allah's creatures. This is said explicitly at 43:59. Islam also reacts instantly to any suggestion that Isa is God, or that Maryam gave birth to the son of God (3:52 and 73).

Indeed, the Qur'an repeatedly asserts that Jesus was nothing more than a man, like this passage from 3:59: "For Allah the likeness of Jesus is as that of Adam whom He fashioned out of dust and said, 'Be!' And he was."[22] The Qur'an makes the same conclusion at 5:57: "The Christ, son of Mary, was but an apostle, and many apostles had come and gone before

---

20. Qur'an 5:111–114 (author's translation).

21. Ibid, 5:114–115.

22. Qur'an 3:59 (author's translation).

him; and his mother was a woman of truth. They both ate the same food as men."[23]

Throughout the Qur'an, Jesus is discussed as being nothing more than a human being, made from the soil, as Adam was. Consequently, the Qur'an also says in several places that Jesus is not the son of God and Mary is not the mother of God.

The Qur'an at times also suggests that the God of Jesus and the God of Muhammed may not be the same God, such as this passage from 43:57–59:

> When the example of Mary's son is quoted before them, your people cry out for it and say, "Are our Gods better than his?" They say this only for disputing. Surely they are a contentious people. Jesus was only a creature whom We favored and made an example for the children of Israel.[24]

ISA AND MOHAMMED

An important verse at 41:6 of the Qur'an has a great bearing on the relationship between Isa and Mohammed. According to this verse, Jesus announced that someone would be coming after him. Although there is some debate over the meaning of this verse, many commentators, both Medieval and Modern, suggest that it refers to the coming of the prophet Mohammed.

As to Muslim interpretation of the "Word" coming from Allah to Isa, four different interpretations can be distinguished. The first view says that Isa is the fulfillment of uttered at the moment of his conception (4:169 and 9:30). A second view says that Isa is a prophet announced the word of God, received and preached by earlier messengers. A third view of Isa in the Qur'an says that Jesus is the word of Allah because he speaks on behalf of Him, and thus leads people in the right way. And a final view says that Isa is the word of God because he speaks of himself as being "good tidings." All four of these views can be found in the Qur'an. Most later interpreters of Isa do not find them contradictory. Rather, they each give a description of a holy man who has been a mouthpiece for Allah on Earth.

23. Ibid., 5:57.
24. Qur'an 43:57–58.

In one passage of the Qur'an (3:40) Isa is mentioned as being among the "close" to the Lord. This status of being "close to Allah" is shared by the angels (4:170). Despite how close Jesus and the angels are to God, the Qur'an repeats the view that Allah is a unity. In 3:52–55, the unity of God, and the denial of the divinity of Jesus, are made very explicit. Thus, Mohammed rejected the Christian doctrine of the trinity. He also rejected any suggestion that he is divine. Mohammed insists on the human nature only in the person of Jesus in 5:19–21.

One passage of the Qur'an at 61:6 tells us that Jesus foretold the coming of a messenger after him, whose name would be Ahmad, a form of the name Muhammed. Many Islamic scholars make the obvious connections. They also tie references in John's Gospels at 14:26, 15:26, and 16:8 and 13–15, Jesus' references to the sending of a *Paracletos* after him, as linking Isa and Muhammed.

ISLAM ON THE CRUCIFIXION

C. T. R. Hewer sums up the Qur'anic view of Jesus' crucifixion: "The Qur'an refers to the end of the earthly life of Jesus in Qur'an 4:157–159. Here we read that the Jews did not crucify Jesus or kill him but it only appeared that way. Jesus was actually 'taken up' to God."[25] This one section of the Qur'an has led to a long history of Moslems believing that Jesus was not crucified. The passage in question is 4:157 that reads this way:

> And for saying, "We killed the Christ, Jesus, son of Mary, who was an apostle of God," but they neither killed nor crucified him, but it appeared that way to them. Those who disagree on the matter, are only lost in doubt. They have no knowledge of it but conjecture, but surely they did not kill him.[26]

This verse seems to suggest that Jesus was neither crucified nor killed on the cross, but it appears that way. The Arabic for this verse is *Wa maa qataluhuu wa maa salabuhuu wa laakin shubbiha lahum.*[27] Unfortunately, this is the only verse in the Qur'an that refers to the crucifixion of Jesus. One modern critic, E. E. Elder, has this to say about 4:157:

25. C. T. R. Hewer, *Understanding Islam: An Introduction* (Minneapolis: Fortress, 2006) 184.

26. *Encyclopedia of Islam*, 4:157.

27. From the Arabic text by Ahmed Ali.

In the first place, it does not say that Jesus was not killed, nor was he crucified. It nearly states that they (the Jews) did not kill or crucify him. This is true historically, although the responsibility was theirs, the Roman soldiers actually did the work.[28]

Elder's argument is quoted with approval in Geoffrey Parrinder's *Jesus in the Qur'an*, where he writes:

Since the hidden pronoun could, remotely, be some other agent, it has been suggested that the intention is to indicate a non-Jewish subject of the verb, probably the Romans, or, as just noted above, even God himself. This makes havoc both of the Arabic construction and of the evident sense. If the context intended to substitute "the Romans," it would surely have to say "It was not they, the Jews, who killed Him. It was the Romans." There is no such construction here, nor could it tally, if there were, with the rest of the passage. We have no opinion but to read for "they" the Jews. We cannot escape the negation of crucifying by confusion as to the agent.[29]

The clause that has led to real confusion on this matter is *wa laakin shubbiha lahum*, "and so it was made to appear to them." This clause had led to incredible speculation. Various theories have arisen in Islam to make sense of the Qur'an 4:157. Around the year 1000, Abd Al-Jabbar suggests that when Judas went to identify Jesus he pointed out the wrong man. Thus, Simon of Cyrene, one of Jesus' disciples, or a Roman soldier have all been suggested in Islamic sources for the identity of the one crucified. Elder quotes the view of Tabari, ninth century Moslem historian and collector of hadith:

Tabari, although he treats the subject very fully and gives a great number of traditions, does not seem to have known the story of a Jew who was crucified. As to Judas, he states that some of the Christians assert that he was the one made in the likeness of Isa and crucified. Tabari realizes that constantly the confusion in the different contradictory statements current even in his time, and after venturing the above remark, says that Allah knows best how it was.[30]

Contemporary exegete, Guilio Basetti-Sani, in his book, *The Koran in the Light of Christ*, sums up the substitution theory, when he writes:

28. E. E. Elder, "The Crucifixion in the Koran," *The Muslim World* (1923) 256.

29. Parrinder, quoted in Kenneth Cragg, *Jesus and the Muslim*, 170.

30. Elder, "The Crucifixion in the Koran," 246.

"God miraculously put a 'double' in his place. Because of this interpreta-tion, all Christ apologists were firm in concluding that the Koran could not possibly be of divine origin. This error was too blatant."[31]

Modern critic, M. A. M. Daryabadi, in his commentary on the *Qur'an* is also an adherent to this substitution theory. Dayabadi writes: "It was not Jesus who was executed but another, who was miraculously substituted (how and in what way is another question, and it is not touched upon in the Koran) for him."[32]

This first theory we shall call the "Substitution Theory;" but modern Islam offers a number of other explanations of the meaning of 4:157. A second theory is offered by S. A. A. Maudidi in his *Meaning of the Qur'an*, he tells us this about 4:157: "After this, Allah, who can do anything He wills, raised Isa to Himself and rescued him from crucifixion, and the one who was Crucified afterwards was somehow or other taken for Christ."[33]

Maudidi seems to combine the Substitution Theory with a second one—that Allah brought Isa bodily into heaven.[34] He seems to base this conclusion solely on the fact that Allah is omnipotent. Yusuf Ali (1872–1953) suggests: "The Qur'anic teaching is that Christ was not crucified nor killed by the Jews, notwithstanding certain apparent circumstances which produced that illusion in the minds of some of his enemies."[35]

In the nineteenth century, William St. Clair-Tisdall (1859–1928), in his *Religion of the Crescent* suggests that Mohammed was aware of the Nestorian heresy, with its denial that Jesus was human. Tisdall writes:

> But in teaching his followers that Christ was not really crucified by the Jews, but miraculously delivered from their hands, someone being substituted in his stead, Mohammed was merely following in the footsteps of Basilides, the Valentinians, the Manicheans and other heretics of early times.[36]

In another work of Tisdall, the British scholar suggests the same theory:

---

31. Giulio Basetti-Sani, *The Koran in the Light of Christ* (Chicago: Franciscan Herald, 1977) 163.

32. M. A. M. Daryabadi, *The Holy Qur'an with English Translation* (Karachi, 1975).

33. S. A. A. Maudidi, *The Meaning of the Koran* (Lahore, 1991) 390.

34. Ibid.

35. Yusuf Ali, *The Holy Qur'an*, 230.

36. William St. Clair-Tisdall, *Religion of the Crescent* (London: SPCK, 1910) 168.

Irenaeus tells us with reference to the teaching of the Gnostic heretic Basilides, who flourished about A.D. 120, that in speaking about Jesus, He taught his deluded followers "That he has not suffered; and that a certain Simon of Cyrene has been compelled to carry his cross for him; and that this man was crucified through error and ignorance. Having been changed in form by Him, so that it would be thought that it was Jesus himself. This language coincides very closely with that of the Qur'an on this matter.[37]

There are a number of moral difficulties in believing the Substitution Theory. For one thing, why would Allah allow the appearance of a bystander to look like Isa so that the Jews and Romans could crucify him instead? Also, if the Moslem prophets are truly men of righteousness, why would Isa allow a double to stand in for him? Contemporary exegete Kenneth Cragg, in his *The Call of the Minaret* raises the same objectives:

What are we to say of the nature of a God Who behaves in this way or of the character of a Christ who permits another—even if a Judas—to suffer the consequences of an antagonism his own teaching has aroused against himself? Is this kind of victory the worthiest in prophets of God?[38]

Cragg goes on to point out that in the substitution theory, one by-product of that point of view is the killing, indeed the crucifying, of an innocent man. Any theory that makes this suggestion, it goes without saying, is not a satisfactory moral point of view. Of course, if the substitution theory is the best explanation of Qur'an 4:157, then the crucifixion of Jesus becomes the greatest hoax in the history of the human race. It also raises the question of how Islamic thinkers can simultaneously say that the gospels are authoritative, while at the same time we should not believe what is written about Jesus' death. The Bible clearly testifies to the trial, death, and resurrection of Jesus, while at the same time Moslem thinkers say the death never happened.

Other Islamic commentators suggest other theories. Another point of view we shall call the "Swooning Theory." It is believed by followers of the Ahmadiyya Movement, which was founded by Mirza Ghulam Ahmad in 1889 in Punjab, India. The Ahmadiyya Movement teaches that Jesus was indeed crucified, but that he survived the cross, was taken

37. W. S. C. Tisdall, *The Original Sources of the Qur'an* (London: SPCK, 1899) 183.
38. Keneth Cragg, *The Call of the Minaret* (London: One World, 2000) 296.

down in a swoon, and presumed to be dead. The story goes on that Jesus recovered from his injuries, went to India, and lived to be 120 years old. The Movement also suggests that Jesus died in Srinagar, where he is also buried.

The tomb of one particular ascetic, named Yus Asaf, has become the tomb of Jesus in India. The "Swoon Theory" is also held by a number of other contemporary Islamic thinkers. Two good examples of this view are Deedat and Sheard.[39] Both Ahmed Deedat, in his *Crucifixion or Cruci-Fiction?*, as well as W. J. Sheard in his book, *The Myth of the Crucified Saviour*, both adhere to the view that Jesus did not die on the cross. Rather, they say, he was brought up to heaven by Allah.

The Swooning Theory, some Muslim commentators argue, is also supported by another line in the Qur'an, 3:55. Allah speaks directly to Isa: "Oh Isa! I will take you and raise you up to Myself and clear you of the lies from those who speak blasphemy of you; I will make those who follow you superior to those who reject the faith, to the Day of the Resurrection."[40]

The Swooning Theory does not seem to be a better explanation of Qur'an 4:157 than the substitution theory. Although it is consistent with the Qur'anic view, it nevertheless flies in the face of the four gospel narratives that present the crucifixion of Jesus as an historical fact.

Some Christian scholars have pointed out what they see as an affinity between the Qur'an 4:157, and several passages in the New Testament that speak of God sending his son in "the likeness of sinful flesh," (Romans 8:3), and Hebrews 2:17, where it says that Jesus was "born in the likeness of men." Some Christian scholars point out that these passages may well be where Mohammed got the idea that Jesus was not crucified. Others point out that theories that Jesus' body was stolen from the cross or the tomb already were in circulation in the first century, where one of the gospels suggests the theory. Matthew 28:11–15 tells us:

> When they were going, some of the guards went into the city and told the chief priests everything that had happened. After the priests had assembled with the elders, they devised a plan to give a large sum of money to the soldiers, telling them you must say, "His disciples came by night and stole him away while we were asleep." If this comes to the governor's ears, we will satisfy him and keep you out of trouble. So they took the money and did as they

39. Qur'an 3:55 (author's translation).
40. Ibid.

were directed. And this is still the story told among the Jews to this day.[41]

Some Christian thinkers suggest that this may be the source of the Qur'anic view that Jesus was not crucified nor killed; but again, there may be other pre-Qur'anic sources that are the origins of the view. At this point in the scholarship on the matter few clear conclusions can be made on the matter.

Whatever we make of the Islamic view of the crucifixion, it is clear that contemporary exegete Ernest Hahn, in his book, *Jesus in Islam* is certainly correct, when he writes: "Yet, regardless of these varying interpretations the vast majority of Muslims continue to agree that Jesus escaped crucifixion and death on the cross, that he was soon taken alive in his body to heaven and that he will return to earth in the future."[42]

The future to which Hahn refers is a reference to another Islamic theory about the crucifixion of Isa. We shall call this point of view the "Resurrection Theory," which says that Isa will only die, or assumed into heaven after the resurrection of the dead. This view, of course, is directly at odds with the gospel accounts of Jesus' death and resurrection, where there is no evidence for the substitution theory, the swooning theory, or the resurrection point of view.

Hewer sums up these Islamic views of the Crucifixion when he writes:

> The Qur'an refers to the end of the earthly life of Jesus in Q4:157–159. Here we read that the Jews did not crucify Jesus or kill him but it only appeared that way. Jesus was actually "take up" to God. Muslim scholars have interpreted this verse in different ways. Some held that Jesus was not put to the cross at all but that someone else was substituted and was crucified in his place. Others have held that he was indeed put upon the cross but was not crucified to death; instead he was taken down in a faint, revived, and then "taken up" to God. Still others have seen this as a rejection that the Jews killed Jesus, and that whatever happened was an act of God alone.[43]

---

41. Matthew 28:11–15. The other three gospels say nothing about this narrative.

42. Ernest Hahn, *Jesus in Islam*, 22.

43. C. T. R. Hewer, *Understanding Islam: An Introduction* (Minneapolis: Fortress, 2006) 184–85.

Hewer continues:

> A minority of scholars have held that God's "taking up" of Jesus
> actually referred to his death as an act of God; in this case, God
> "taking him up" would be a euphemism, a bit like we might de-
> scribe someone's death as falling asleep. Whatever the verse may
> mean, scholars do not interpret it as Jesus' death and resurrection
> to eternal life.[44]

ISA IN LATER ISLAM

In later Islam some interpreters, like al-Baydawi for example, suggest that
Isa, upon returning to earth will descend on the white arcade of the eastern gate of Damascus, or, in another tradition, on a hill in the Holy Land
which is called *Afik*. This view says Isa will be clothed in two *musarra*.
His head will be anointed, and he will have a spear in his right hand with
which he will kill the *Djaal*, the Anti-Christ. This tradition continues by
saying that Isa will then travel to Jerusalem at the time the dawn prayer
is being said. Led by an *Imam*. Isa will put the Imam in front of him and
will pray with the Imam to fulfill the prophecy of Mohammed. After this,
Isa will kill all the pigs, will break the cross, and destroy all the synagogues
and churches. Finally, Isa will kill all people who do not believe in Allah;
and there will be only one community—that of Islam.[45]

Another late tradition of Islam says that when Isa was "taken up" by
Allah, it was in the middle of the night. This tradition also suggests that
when Isa went to heaven, he met Ibrahim and Musa.

In later Islam there is also a good bit of discussion among mystical writers in the Islamic tradition. These writers tend to focus on Isa
and Mary's poverty, his detachment from the world, and his devotion to
prayer. Mystical tales associated with the life of Isa can be seen in the work
of Abu Nu'aym, al-Tirmidhi, and especially in Al-Ghazali. When *Sufis*,
(Moslem mystics) came into contact with the gospels, they took from
them elements that corresponded to their own asceticism. Ibn Arabi, seventh-century collector of hadith, even went a bit farther. He says the Isa
"merits the Seal of Universal Holiness," because he possesses the quality of
amana, faith above all others. Arabi tells us, "Know that without doubt Isa
will descend and will be our judge, according to the law of Mohammed."

44. Ibid, 185.
45. Suggested in the anonymous article on Isa in the *Encyclopedia of Islam* 4:86.

Among Al-Zamakh-shari, al-Baydawi and al-Firuzabadi there was a prolonged discussion of the meaning of the word *Masih* (Messiah) in relation to Jesus. Zamakh-shari and Baydawi say that it is a foreign word, and Firuzbadi provides a list of nearly fifty meanings of the word. Some other Moslem exegetes suggest the word is related to the verb *masaha*, "to rub one's hands," or to anoint. Other thinkers say the word may be related to the verb *saha*, which is used to describe traveling on a pilgrimage. The *Sufis* often suggest this latter view, who sometimes call Isa "the model of all pilgrims," as well as "the *Imam* of wanderers." The commentary of Mohammed al-Alusi, a nineteenth-century Ottoman scholar, is a good example of this view.

Two other modern works written by Islamic scholars are also worth mentioning. The first is a book published in Cairo in 1952 by Abbas Mahmud al-Akkad. It is entitled, *The Spirit of the Messiah.*[46] In this book the writer approaches the figure of Isa with great respect, but he makes a distinction between the teachings of Isa and the historical figure, not unlike what Thomas Jefferson did in his version of the gospels.

The other modern book, entitled *An Iniquitous City*, was written by an Egyptian physician named Kamil Husayn.[47] The book is a kind of meditation on the trial and the condemnation of Isa; but the author leaves the topic of the crucifixion in the background. He does not state that Isa was crucified, nor does he say that he was not. He simply repeats a line from the Qur'an: "Allah has raised Isa to Himself." This leaves open the possibility for either a Christian or an Islamic interpretation.

Much of post-Quranic Islamic comments on the figure of Isa deal with his character. Eighth century exegete, Hammam ibn Munabbih, tells the tale of Isa seeing a man steal. Isa said, "Did you commit theft?" The man answered, "Never. I swear by Him than Whom there is none worthier of worship." Isa answered, "I believe Allah, and falsify my eyes."[48]

Ahmad ibn Hanbal, ninth century collector of hadith, tells the tale of a man who asked Isa how he could walk on water. He replied, "Through the surety of my faith." The man said, "We too have faith." Then Isa answered,

---

46. Abbas Mahmud al-Akkad, *The Spirit of the Messiah* (Cairo, 1952).

47. Kamil Husayn, *An Iniquitous City* (Cairo, 1954).

48. Hamman ibn Munabbih, *Sahifat Hammam b. Munabbih.* Edited by Muhammed Hammidullah (Damascus: Al-Majma al-Ilmi al-Arabi, 1953) 99.

"Do you believe that stones, mud, and gold are all equal in your sight?" "No," the man replied. Isa said, "They are all the same in my sight."[49]

Similar comments about the virtues of Isa are made in a number of other Medieval Islamic commentators. Abdallah ibn Qutayba, another ninth-century collector of hadith, suggests that Isa said to his followers, "If people appoint you as their heads, then be like their tails."[50] Qutayba tells another tale about Isa meeting a man and he asks him, "What are you doing?" "I am devoting myself to Allah," the man replied. Then Isa asked, "Who is caring for you?" "My brother," replied the man. Then Isa said, "Your brother is more devoted to Allah than you are."[51] Qutayba also quotes Isa as saying, "Blessed are he who sees with his head but whose head is not in what he sees."[52]

Other comments about Isa's character are made by Abu Bakr ibn Abi al-Dunya, a ninth century commentator. Abu Bakr tells us that a pig passes by Isa and Isa said, "Pass in peace." The pig replied, "Spirit of Allah, how can you say this to a pig?" Isa responded, "I hate to accustom my tongue to evil."[53]

Ibn Abd Rabbihi, tenth century collector of hadith, reports that Isa once asked who his teacher was. "No one," he replied. "I saw the ugliness of ignorance and avoided it."[54] For the most part, Medieval Islamic exegetes on Jesus see him as one of the greatest of Moslem's prophets, as a man who is possessed of the greatest of moral virtues among Allah's people. Abu al-Layth al-Samarqandi, tenth century collector of hadith and author of *Tanbih al-Ghafilin*, tells us that Isa spoke to the Israelites and said, "Do not reward a wrongdoer with wrongdoing, for this will nullify your virtue in the sight of Allah."[55] For the most part, all other Medieval Moslem views of Jesus express similar views about the prophet's virtue.

49. Ahmad ibn Hanbal, *Kitab al-Wara*, edited by Muhammed Zaghlul (Beirut: Dar Al-Kitab al-Arabi, 1988) 79.

50. Abdallah ibn Qutayba, *Kitab Ulyan al-Akhbar* (Cairo: Dar Al-Kutub al-Missriyya, 1925–1930) 1:143.

51. Ibid.

52. Ibid.

53. Abu Bakkar, *Jamharat Nasab Qursysh*, edited by M. M. Shakir (Cairo, 1962) 1:17–18.

54. Ibn Abd Rabbihi, *Al-Iqd al-Farid* (Cairo: Lajnat al-Talif wa al-Tarjama wa al-Nashr, 1940–1953) 1:126.

55. Abu al-Layth al-Samsrqandi, *Tanbih al-Ghafilin* (Cairo: Al-Matba al-Yusufiyya, n.d.) 58.

ISA IN ISLAMIC ART

Islamic art of biblical figures has a long history. Part of that history was a prohibition against the depictions of holy figures or representations in Islamic art. The Qur'an has nothing to say about the matter. Of all the visual arts, calligraphy is the most highly regarded. The Arabic script, in combination with arabesque ornamentation, became the most prized decoration for architecture, and other functional works related to furniture, textiles, and vessels.

Much of Islamic art related to the Bible originated in Persia. One of the most richly illustrated manuscripts of the sixteenth century is the Zubdat-al-Tawarikh in the Museum of Turkish and Islamic Art in Istanbul.[56] The Museum was dedicated to Sultan Murad III in 1583. The manuscript contains forty miniatures, reflecting the mature Ottoman court style.

The author of the manuscript in question was named Seyyid Loqman Ashuri, the prolific historiographer of the court of Murad III. In addition to the copy at the Museum of Turkish and Islamic Art in Istanbul, there are two other copies of the manuscript in the Topkap Saray Museum Library (H1321), dated 1586, and the other in the Chester Beatty Library (number 414) in Dublin.[57]

All three versions of this manuscript are illuminated. There are ninety-one folios and forty miniatures. Many of these miniatures are of Biblical figures, like Adam and Eve, Joseph and Jacob, Jonah and his fish, and Samson and Delilah. Another figure is a representation of the Ascension of Isa. The text by Loqman Ashuri that accompanies the image tells us that a man named Feltianus was chosen by the Romans and the Jews to be executed in Isa's stead. In the meantime, Christ ascended to heaven, brought by angels. In the image, Isa is lifted by two angels in the upper register, while in the right of the lower register the figure of an identical Jesus in the person of Feltianus is shown, caught by Jews.

This image of the Ascension of Isa is accompanied by a miniature of the *Miraj*, "the Ascension of the Prophet Mohammed." The prophet is shown sitting in a mosque with Ali, Hasan, Huseyin, and other friends. A

56. "The Ascension of Isa," manuscript illustrating a sixteenth-century manuscript owned by the Museum of Turkish and Islamic Art in Istanbul.

57. Tokap Saray Museum Library (ms. H1321) and Chester Beatty Library (ms. 414) in Dublin.

flaming halo crowns Mohammed. A descending Jibril has come to take the prophet on his journey.

Contemporary depictions of Isa in Islamic art also tend to be Persian. The illustrations that accompany the portrait of Isa by contemporary Persian writer, Shin Parto's book, *Haft cehre*, are good examples. In one of these images Isa is shown traveling to heaven with the aid of the angel Jibril (Gabriel). Like the earlier Persian depictions, a second image that looks like the ascending Isa is present in the image. These images, of course, are predicated with the conviction that Isa was not crucified, nor did he die. He was simply ascended into heaven, like Mohammed was, accompanied by the angel of revelation, Jibril, or someone was substituted for him. These images seem to be consistent with this observation from Yusuf Ali: "The Qur'anic teaching is that Christ was not crucified nor killed by the Jews, notwithstanding certain apparent circumstances which produced that illusion in the minds of some of his enemies."[58]

ISA AS THE SON OF GOD

The Qur'an's 9:30 speaks of the Jews calling Ezra a son of God and of Christians calling Jesus the son of God. The Qur'an puts the matter this way:

> The Jews say, "Ezra is the son of God;" the Christians say: "Christ is the son of God." That is what they say with their tongues, following assertions made by unbelievers before them. May they be damned by God? How perverse they are.[59]

Verse 31 of sura nine continues this thought:

> They consider their rabbis and monks and the Christ, the son of Mary, to be gods apart from Allah, even though they had been told to worship only one god, for there is no God but He. Too holy is He for what they ascribe to Him.[60]

This section, 9:30–31, must be read alongside sura 112, which makes it clear that God is One, unique, eternal, and like no other. Sura 112 tells us that Allah "begets but is not begotten." These two passages are bolstered

---

58. Yusuf Ali, *The Holy Qur'an*, 230.

59. Qur'an 9:30 (author's translation).

60. Ibid, 9:31.

by 4:171, which says that Allah is One and "far exalted above having a son."[61] Thus, the Qur'an explicitly states that there is only one God.

In several other places, the Qur'an tells us that: Allah has no wife or consort (72:3); Allah has no son (2:116, 10:58; and 19:91–92); that Allah has no daughters (6:100 and 37:149–153); and that the angels are not the children of Allah (17:40 and 16:40).

The Qur'an explicitly states in several places that Jesus is simply a human being. Two representative examples are 3:59 and 5:75. The first of these tells us: "For Allah the likeness of Isa is like that of Adam whom He fashioned out of dust."[62] The same conclusion can be derived from 5:75:

> The Christ, son of Mary, was but an apostle; and many apostles had come after him and gone before him; and his mother was a woman of truth. They both ate the same food as men. Behold how we show men clear signs, and behold how they wander astray.[63]

From all these passages, it should be clear that the Qur'an does not believe that either Ezra or Jesus is the son of God. Although Jesus is seen in the Qur'an as one of the greatest of Islamic prophets, and as a man of extraordinary goodness, the Holy Book also speaks of Jesus as a man like the rest of us, another one of Allah's human creatures.

Subsequent Moslem writers continued this tradition of denying both the divinity of Jesus, as well as the claim that Maryam (Mary) is the mother of God. Much more about the nature of the place of Maryam in Islam is said in the next chapter. It is enough now, however, to point out that Islam does not see her as the mother of God.

COMPARISON OF ISLAMIC AND CHRISTIAN VIEWS OF JESUS

The Islamic tradition believes that Jesus was a messenger of Allah (Qur'an 5:75). It also believes that Jesus was born of a virgin (Qur'an 19:16–21). Muslims believe that Jesus had a miraculous birth (Qur'an 3:57), and that Jesus was able to speak to adults from the cradle (Qur'an 19:29–30). The Islam faith also teaches that Jesus performed miracles (Qur'an 5:110).

---

61. Ibid, 4:171.
62. Qur'an 3:59 (author's translation).
63. Qur'an 5:75.

On the other hand, Islamic beliefs do not attest to the trinity (Qur'an 4:171), nor do they believe that Jesus was God (Qur'an 112:1–4); nor, for the most part, does Islam believe that Jesus was crucified on the cross (Qur'an 4:157). And Islam does not believe that Jesus was resurrected from the dead. Rather, he was assumed into heaven and will reappear at the end of time. Some other Islamic accounts about Jesus suggest that a substitute was crucified in Jesus' stead. It may have been a Roman soldier, Joseph of Arimethea, or some other proxy. Whoever the substitute might have been, the Islamic tradition does not believe that Jesus was crucified, nor that he resurrected from the dead three days later.

Of course, over and against these views, Christians assent to Jesus' miraculous birth, being born of a virgin, the performing of miracles, belief in the trinity, belief that Jesus is the son of God, that Jesus was crucified and died on the cross, and that he resurrected from the dead three days after his death. But Christians do not, by and large, believe that Jesus could speak to adults from the cradle.

Despite the fact that Islam does not think that Jesus is God or the son of God, He is nevertheless, seen as one of the greatest of Islam's prophets—a man worthy of moral admiration, an exemplar of the nature of a good and pure Moslem life. In Islam, Jesus is among the greatest of the prophets. Very few have a status in Islam above that of the prophet Isa.

CONCLUSIONS

In this chapter, we have attempted to describe and discuss several points of view about Jesus in the Islamic tradition. We began the chapter by discussing at some length the many references to Isa in the Qur'an, where Jesus is seen as a patient and faithful prophet. More specifically, we described and discussed the Annunciation, the Nativity, and the life of the prophet.

In the second section of this chapter, we have explored what the Qur'an has to say about the mission of Jesus, and what made his mission unique. We also discussed a number of pieces of evidence for Moslems believing that Jesus has a special status, including his ability to perform miracles, as well as his ability to speak to adults from the cradle.

The relationship of Jesus to the prophet Mohammed was the subject of a third section in this chapter. We have shown that in addition to both being among Allah's greatest prophets, both figures ascended into heaven accompanied by the angel Gabriel. In a major section of this chapter, we have explored the meaning that Islamic thinkers have for the understanding of a reference in the Qur'an that Jesus was not crucified, nor killed.

In this section of the chapter entitled, "Islam on the Crucifixion," we have suggested and explored a number of theories about just what the Qur'an means with respect to Jesus' death. As we have seen, there are three principal theories that Islam has employed to explain what the text meant at 4:159 that Jesus was neither crucified, nor killed.

We have also explored in this chapter a number of observations about Isa in later commentaries on the Qur'an, as well as other Islamic works that mention Jesus. And finally, we have seen in this chapter a number of observations about Jesus in Islamic art that, for the most part, are reflections of traditional Islamic theology. Among the chief images of the figure of Isa in Islamic art, as we have shown, is the Ascension of Isa, as well as the substitution of a bystander for the actual prophet.

In the next chapter, we shall make a number of observations about how three other New Testament figures are seen in the Islamic tradition. As we shall see, the figures of Isa's mother, called Maryam, John the Baptist (Yahya), as well as the father of Isa, called *Imran* in the Qur'an, are often considerably different from the views of traditional Christianity. Following the next chapter are two other chapters on figures in the New Testament, one on Satan, or Iblis as he is sometimes called in Islam, and a chapter on the figure of the Djaal, the Arabic word for the Anti-Christ.[64]

64. For more on the role of Jesus in Islam, see the following: Mark A. Gabriel, *Jesus and Muhammed: Profound Differences and Surprising Similarities* (Phoenix: Charisma, 2004); Muhammed Ata Ur Rahim, *Jesus: Prophet of Islam* (Lahore: Tahrike Tarsile Qur'an, 1992); Robert Allen Lee, *Representations of Jesus in Islam* (London: ProQuest/ UMI, 2006); and *The Jesus of Islam: Christians Have More in Common with Muslims Than They Realize* (Palo Alto, CA: Gale, 2005).

8

The Images of Mary, Joseph, and John the Baptist
in Islam

The Koran, which is the Bible of the Moslems, has many passages concerning the Blessed Virgin. The Koran believes in her Immaculate Conception and also in her Virgin Birth. The third chapter of the Koran places the history of Mary's family in a genealogy that goes back through Abraham, Noah, and Adam.

—Fulton Sheen, "Mary and the Moslems"

Mary, the mother of Jesus, is the only woman called by her proper name in the Qur'an.

—Geoffrey Parrinder, *Jesus in the Qur'an*

Commemorate Mary in the Book. When she withdrew from her family to a place in the East.

—Qur'an 19:16

INTRODUCTION

IN THIS CHAPTER, WE shall describe and discuss various Islamic perspectives on the figures of Mary, the mother of Jesus, who is called Maryam in the Qur'an, Joseph, her husband, called Imran in the Qur'an, and John the Baptist, who goes by the name Yah Yah in the Holy Book. As we shall see, all three figures play significant roles in the history of Islam. In the opening section of this chapter, we shall explore what the Qur'an has to say about these three characters. In a second section of this chapter, we shall explore how these three personages were discussed in post-Qur'anic Islam. In the end of this chapter, we shall make some general conclusions about Mary, Joseph, and John the Baptist in the Islamic faith.

152

MARY, JOSEPH, AND JOHN THE BAPTIST IN THE QUR'AN

Maryam receives more treatment in the Qur'an than any other woman. She is among only eight people who have a chapter named after her in the Holy Book, Sura 19. The third Sura is named after her father Imran. Suras 3 and 19 are among the most beautiful chapters of the Qur'an, or in Arabic literature in general.

The name Mary (Maryam) appears 34 times in the Qur'an. In twenty-three instances, it comes after the name of Isa, and in eleven cases it describes Mary's own experiences. She is described as one of the two "examples" among women who believe (Qur'an 66:11–12). Those who have uttered words of slander against her were condemned by setting a seal on their hearts for blasphemy (4:156). Maryam is described as having been born on the prayer of her mother, who is called the "woman of Imran," and she is believed to have been a descendent of Musa (Moses).

The most common mentions of Maryam in the Qur'an is the expression, *Isa ibn* Mary, "Jesus, the son of Mary."[1] Indeed, the Qur'an uses the name Mary more times than the New Testament does (34 more times in the Qur'an, only 19 in the Gospels). Parrinder opens his chapter on the image of Mary this way: "Mary and Jesus are 'a sign to the world,' (21:91). But, as in the gospel, the importance of Mary in the Qur'an is in being the mother of Jesus. She has no role to play apart from that."[2]

This notion of Maryam being a "sign to the world" is repeated in 23:52: "And We made the son of Mary and his mother a sign."[3]

This same verse suggests that both Maryam and Isa have an exalted status in Islam. "And we made them reside in an elevated abode, full of

1. Most of the Arabic translations in this chapter are those of the author. The primary edition of the Qur'an I have used in this chapter is *Al-Qur'an*, translated and edited by Ahmed Ali (Princeton: Princeton University Press, 1993); I have also consulted A. J. Arberry, *The Koran Interpreted* (London: Allen and Unwin, 1995); Abdullah Yusuf Ali, *The Holy Qur'an* (Brentwood, Maryland: Amana Corporation, 1989); and M. M. Pickthall, *The Meaning of the Glorious Koran* (New York: Meridian, 1997).

Secondary sources I have used in preparing this chapter include: N. Daniel, *Islam and the West* (Oxford: Oneworld Press, 1997); J. L. Esposito, *Voices of Resurgent Islam* (Oxford: Oxford University Press, 1983); H. A. R. Gibb, *Islam: An Historical Survey* (Oxford: Oxford University Press, 1980); Richard Bell, *Introduction to the Qur'an* (Edinburgh: T. & T. Clark, 1953); idem, *The Origin of Islam in its Christian Environment* (London, 1926); Geoffrey Parrinder, *Jesus in the Qur'an* (London: Faber, 1965); and Jacques Jomier, *The Bible and the Koran* (San Francisco: Ignatius, 1964).

2. Parrinder, *Jesus in the Qur'an*, 60.

3. Qur'an 23:52 (author's translation).

quiet and watered springs."[4] The nature of this exalted status for Maryam in the Qur'an is alluded to at 19:20, which tells us, "How can I have a son when no man has touched me?" The writers of the Qur'an were firm believers in the Virgin Birth. In sura 66:12, the conception of Isa in the womb of Maryam is attributed to a "divine spirit," in much the same way it is in Luke 1:34–35. A third mention of the Virgin Birth is seen at 3:37–38, where the Qur'an tells us:

> Her Lord accepted her graciously, and she grew with excellence, and was given into the care of Zachariah. Whenever he came to see her in her chamber, he found her provided with abundant food, and he asks, "Where did you get this food?" "From Allah," she answered, "who gives abundant food to whomever He wishes."[5]

This notion of the purity of Maryam is among the most often expressed attributes of the mother of Jesus in the Qur'an. At 3:42–43, we get another reference to this purity: "The angel said, 'Oh Mary, indeed Allah has favored you and made you immaculate, and chosen you from all the women in the world.'"[6]

Mary's chastity is spoken of again at Qur'an 21:91. The text tells us: "Remember he who preserved her chastity, into whom We breathed a new life from Us, and made her and her son a token for mankind."[7]

Additional references to Maryam's chastity in the Qur'an can be found at 19:16–21 and 32:9. Indeed, this notion of Maryam's purity and chastity is one of the most often made references to the mother of Isa, like this comment in the Qur'an 66:12: "And of Mary, daughter of Imran, who guarded her chastity, so that We breathed into her a new life from Us, and she believed the words of her Lord and His Books, and was among the obedient."[8]

Later commentators remark on the verbs used in these verses, *istafa* (chosen) and *tahara* (pure), further evidence for Maryam's exalted status. In fact, in the Moslem tradition Maryam, the mother of Jesus, is generally

---

4. Ibid.

5. Ibid, 3:37–38.

6. Qur'an 3:42–43 (author's translation).

7. Ibid, 21:91.

8. Ibid, 66:12.

considered one of the four greatest women who ever lived—the others being Fatima, Asiya, and the chief of the women of Paradise.[9]

We already have described the Qur'anic view of the Annunciation in the previous chapter, but we will repeat the general outline here. The angel Jibril (Gabriel) appeared to Maryam in the form of a man, in some traditions a beardless youth with a shining face. The angel announces the birth of a male child. Maryam responds with surprised amazement, but the angel reassures her and she complied with the will of Allah. Thereupon the angel blew his breath into the womb of Maryam and Isa was conceived. Later Islamic traditions suggest that the angel blew into the fold of her shirt, as described in the previous chapter. In this view, after the angel's withdraw, Maryam puts on the shirt and becomes pregnant. Generally, Islamic traditions say that the Annunciation happens in a cave, near a well called Silwan.

Maryam is declared, along with her son Isa, to be an *Ayat Allah*, a sign of Allah at 23:50 of the Qur'an, a woman who has guarded her chastity (66:12). She is called "obedient one" at 66:12, "chosen of the mother and delivered to Allah while still in the womb" (3:36). Maryam is called a "chosen one" at 3:42; a "purified one" at 3:42); a "truthful one" at 5:75; a "fulfillment of prophecy" at 66:12; and Maryam is said to be "exalted above all women of the world" at 3:42.

Some scholars suggest that the Qur'an gives Maryam the status of divinity, and that she and her son were venerated as gods. Some say this is reflected in sura 5:7, while many others disagree with this interpretation. Others say that Isa was an apostle only, who was preceded by other apostles. More specifically, some collectors of hadith point to 4:171 that suggests one should say "nothing but the truth about God,"[10] and a verse later that says "don't call Allah three"[11]—an obvious criticism of the trinity.

Many of the features narrated about Maryam in the Qur'an are reflections of events in the gospels. Sura 23:52 mentions the elevated status of Isa and his mother, which might be an allusion to Luke 1:39, where Mary went up into the mountains to visit Elizabeth. The fullest narratives of Isa's birth are in 19:1–35, a sura named after Maryam, and 3:31–42, which look very much like the account of the birth of Jesus in the gospel

9. Bukhari, *Commentary on the Qur'an*, edited by Ahmad Mujtaba Hasan. (London: Tauris, 2006) 78.

10. Qur'an 4:171 (author's translation).

11. Qur'an 4:172 (author's translation).

of Luke. Sura 19 opens with the story of Maryam and Isa (verses 16–34). Sura 3:31–42 contains the birth of Maryam, the annunciation of Yah Yah (verses 33–36), and then the annunciation of Isa (verses 37–41). If one compares sura 3 with sura 19, one can conclude that Mohammed most likely became familiar with the story of the birth of Maryam later than the story of Yah Yah.

The account of Maryam's birth in the Qur'an is an interesting one. Maryam's father is called Imran in the Qur'an, and Joachim in the Christian tradition. Maryam is called a sister of Harun at 19:29. Miriam is also the name of Moses' sister, and Harun is the younger brother of Abraham; but the Qur'an makes little distinction between the two Maryams. The Qur'an names two families being especially chosen (3:32), the family of Abraham and that of Imran. The family of Imran is important in the Qur'an because that is the one to which Moses, Aaron, Maryam, and Isa belong.

The Qur'an in two different places (3:47 and 16:40) tells us that Maryam became pregnant through Divine command, as 3:47 says, "Allah says 'Be,' and it is"; 16:40 suggests of Allah, "When We will a thing, We have only to say, 'Be,' and it is." This view is parallel to both Matthew 1:18–21 and Luke 1:26–35.

The miraculous account of Maryam's birth, and her exalted status in Islam, are given at Qur'an 3:35–36, where the text tells us:

> Remember, when the wife of Imran prayed, "Oh Lord, I offer what I carry in my womb in dedication to Your service, please accept it, for You hear all and know everything." And when she had given birth to the child, she said, "Oh Lord, I have delivered a girl." But Allah knew better what she had delivered: A boy could not be as that girl was.[12]

The Qur'an says that Jesus' birth was the result of a virgin birth, and that neither Maryam nor her son are divine. Rather, they are described as "honored servants" at 21:26. The Qur'an also says that one of the reasons, among many, for Allah's punishment of "the People of the Book"—"Allah has sealed their hearts" (4:155)—was because of "monstrous lies they told about Maryam" (4:156). This is generally believed to refer to accusations of Maryam's lack of chastity by some Jews when she returned home with her baby. Sura 5:116–119 of the Qur'an includes a prophecy about Judgment Day, where "Jesus, son of Mary" will be questioned by Allah in regards to

12. Qur'an 3:35–36 (author's translation).

those who have worshipped him and Mary, and that Jesus will deny them at the end of time.

Imran's wife, Isa's grandmother, is not mentioned by name in the Qur'an. In both Christianity and Islam, she is called Hannah. In the Qur'an, her genealogy is clearly worked out. She is the daughter of *Fakudh* and the sister of Ishba, the biblical Elizabeth. Thus the Qur'anic genealogy of Mary and Jesus looks something like this:

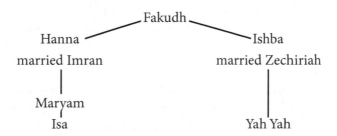

In an alternate genealogy, Ishba and Maryam were sisters, the daughters of Imran and Hanna.[13] This second genealogy is recommended by Al-Masudi and Tabari and looks like this:

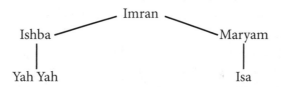

Al-Ya'qubi, ninth century, in his commentary on the Qur'an also gives a genealogy of Mary and Jesus, which follows very closely the accounts of the gospels. Sidney Griffith points out another feature of Ya'qubi's commentary:

> A striking feature of al-Yaqubi's presentation of Jesus in these pages is that he almost always calls him simply "Christ" or the "the Messiah." He never uses his proper name as it appears in the Qur'an, that is, Isa. When he does use Jesus' proper name, he quotes it in the Christian Syriac form, transliterated into the Arabic script as Isu.[14]

13. Tabari, *The History of Al-Tabari* (New York: SUNY Press, 1987) 134.

14. Sidney Griffith, "The Gospel, the Qur'an, and the Presentation of Jesus in the al-Ya'qubi Ta'rikh." John C. Reeves, ed., *Bible and Qur'an* (Atlanta: Society of Biblical Literature, 2003) 154.

What to make of this fact is not clear, but Al-Yaqubi follows the accounts of Mark and John's gospels in regard to the genealogy, and suggests that Yah Yah is a cousin of Isa. Al-Yaqubi also gives a full discussion of the crucifixion of Jesus, following the gospel of John, rejecting the Qur'anic view that Jesus was not crucified.

It was not until the time of Ibn Hasim (994–1064) that an Islamic scholar gives as much attention to the gospels as Al-Yaqubi. Ibn Hasim's view of the gospels was that it was important to show their utter unreliability. Indeed, many Medieval Islamic commentaries frequently hold this view of the gospels, sometime denigrating the figures of Mary and John the Baptist.

Islam speaks of one *Djuraydj* (the Arabic word for "carpenter"), who was betrothed to Maryam. He is the first to recognize her pregnancy, and to be convinced by her of its miraculous nature. This material finds parallels in narratives in some of the canonical and non-canonical gospels, which may indicate a common folklore tradition in Islam. The name for this carpenter is not given in the Qur'an, but later Islam refers to him as Yusuf (Joseph). This is the only mention of Isa's earthly father in the Qur'an. It calls him a "carpenter," but it does not give him a name.

The Qur'an also tells us that before the birth of her son Maryam took herself off to some quiet place before the child was born. During this time, Mary is said in Islam to have been sustained by a stream of pure water and dates that fell from a tree against which Mary rested. Islam tells us that a voice spoke to Maryam and told her to remain silent when she returned to her people with the baby. Some Moslem scholars say this was the voice of Allah, others that it was an angel, particularly Jibril. Still others suggest it was the voice of Jesus himself soothing his mother about her worries about her reputation.

Maryam is defended against attacks by the Jews in Qur'an 4:155–156. She is called a "faithful woman" at 5:75. When she brought her baby home and was suspected of improper behavior, the child himself justified her behavior and said, "I am the servant of Allah" (19:28f). Twice in the Qur'an Maryam is said to have kept her purity, and twice she protests her virginity when the birth is foretold.

The name Yah Yah is mentioned five times in the Qur'an. Many Moslems trace the root of the name to an Arabic verb meaning "to quicken," or "to make alive," possible references to Hanna's barrenness prior to Yah Yah. In the Qur'an 3:39, Yah Yah is spoken of as a noble, chaste, prophet who will witness the truth of the word of Allah. The Qur'an speaks of Yah Yah at 6:85, along with Zechariah, Isa, and Elias as being "of the righteous." The Qur'an's 19:7 describes the giving of Yah Yah to Zechariah, with a note that this name was used for the first time as the name of a prophet. This material has a clear parallel in Luke 1:59–63.

The Qur'an 21:90 explains the birth of Yah Yah as a response to Zechariah's prayer for a son, his wife's infertility being cured in this instance. Although the details of John the Baptist are few in the Qur'an, post-Qur'anic commentators, as we shall see in the next section of the chapter, are elaborated upon to great lengths.

The Qur'an suggests that Allah gave Yah Yah wisdom while still in the womb. It also says that Allah made John sympathetic and merciful toward people, and pure from sins. The Qur'an called Yah Yah righteous and dutiful to his parents, and he was neither arrogant nor disobedient toward Allah or his parents. It suggests that Allah has granted Yah Yah peace "the day he was born, the day he died, and the day he will be raised to life again" (Sura 19:1–12).

YAH YAH IN LATER ISLAM

The idea that Yah Yah was *hasur* (chaste) gave rise to a number of interpretations in later Islam. Tabari suggests that this term with reference to Yah Yah meant that the prophet was incapable of having coitus. Tabari says, "He had a penis no bigger than a piece of straw." Ibn Kathir rejected this theory on the grounds that if a prophet could not have sex, then he would be imperfect. Kathir argues that the reference to being *hasur* was in regard to his thoughts.

Other elaborations on John the Baptist in Islam suggest that Yah Yah was six months older than Isa; that Yah Yah and Isa met in the Jordan River when Isa was 30 years old; and that Yah Yah was killed prior to the ascension of Isa. Other accounts suggest that Yah Yah traveled to Palestine, met and baptized Isa, and departed with 12 disciples to preach the word of Allah.

There is some confusion about John the Baptist, however, because other Islamic accounts have Yah Yah living in the time of Nebuchadnezzar who is said to have attacked Israel because the king Josiah has Yah Yah ibn Zechariah (John the son of Zechariah) killed.

James McAuliffe, in his article, "The Prediction and Prefiguration of Muhammed," writes at length on Tabari and his view of John the Baptist. He points out that the ninth-century Tabari quotes Islamic sources who place John the Baptist's death both before and after the Ascension of Jesus.

A number of post-Quranic collectors of hadith communicate stories about John the Baptist and Maryam. Abu Bakr, ninth-century commentator, tells the tale of Jesus and John the Baptist meeting. The face of John was smiling, while Jesus was gloomy and frowning. Isa said to Yah Yah, "You smile as if you feel secure." Then John said to Jesus, "You frown as if you are in despair." Abu Bakr adds, "Allah revealed, 'What Yah Yah did is dearer to Us.'"[15]

Ahmad ibn Hanbal, ninth-century commentator and author of *Al-Zuhd,* relays another tale of John the Baptist meeting Jesus. In this story, Yah Yah says, "Ask Allah's forgiveness for me, for you are better than me." Isa replied, "You are better than me. I pronounce peace upon myself, whereas Allah pronounced peace upon you." Hanbal adds: Allah recognized the merit of them both.[16] This theme of whether Yah Yah or Isa is more worthy in the mind of Allah is one that is repeated throughout Medieval Islam. The conclusion that is nearly always made in these tales is that both prophets are of great worth in the eyes of their Creator.

JOHN THE BAPTIST AND A PROPHET TO COME

The gospels record an event in the life of John the Baptist where he says "He who comes after me ranks ahead of me because he was before me." This comment in the gospel of John (1:15) has puzzled both Christian and Moslem scholars alike. Some Moslem scholars point out John could not have been speaking of Jesus. Most Christian scholars, of course, think the prophet to come is Jesus, for He was pre-existent in the Gospel of John, and will exist after John's death.

The Islamic tradition sees this remark in an entirely different way. In an anonymous article called "The Bible's Last Prophet," written by a Moslem, the writer tells us this about John 1:15: "John the Baptist rec-

---

15. Abu Al-Bakkar, *Jamharat Nasab Quraysh*, vol. 1, edited by M. M. Shakir. (Cairo: 1962) 17.

16. Ahmad ibn Hanbal, *Kitab al-Zuhd.* Edited by Muhammed Zaghlul. (Beirut: Dar al-Kitab al-Arabi, 1988) 139.

ognizes the Prophet Mohammed as superior and more powerful than himself."[17]

It is clear that the writer of this article published by the *Islamic Review* was of the belief that the prophet to whom John refers in 1:15 is Mohammed. This *Islamic Review* article was written in September of 1928, and both before and since many Moslem thinkers have identified the "one who comes after" John the Baptist as the prophet Mohammed.

Islamic scholars sometimes point to Acts 11:27–28 and 13:1, as well as 15:32, and 21:9–10 as evidence that Christianity will have other prophets and holy men after the time of Jesus. If that is true, they argue, then Jesus cannot be the one referred to in John 1:15. Now if it is not Jesus, they say, then what other prophet comes after the time of Jesus and John the Baptist. The conclusion is obvious: the prophet discussed in John 1:15 is Mohammed.

The writer of the article mentioned above speaks of Ernest Renan's classic work, *La Vie de Jesu,* who identifies the prophet in John 1:15 as Jesus, as most Christian scholars do; but the writer for the *Islamic Review* adds these comments about Renan: "If the learned French writer had the least consideration for the Prophet Mohammed's claim in the world of prophets, I am sure his profound investigations and comments would have led to an entirely different conclusion."[18]

Of course, that different conclusion that the writer had in mind is Mohammed. This conclusion can be found in a number of Moslem writers, both before and since the article in question. Thus, an important difference between Christian and Islamic views of the figure to whom John the Baptist refers in John 1:15 is that Christians believe it refers to Jesus, while many Moslems believe the reference is to the prophet Mohammed.

Some other contemporary Moslem scholars, like Ruqaiyyah Waris Maqsood and Abdul Ahad Dawud, for example, also point to other Old and New Testament passages that they believe are also references to Muhammed. Among these passages are Deuteronomy 18:15 and Matthew 3:11 and Luke 3:16.

In Deuteronomy 18:15, God tells Moses that he "will raise up for them a prophet like you from among their brethren; and I will put my words in his mouth." Many Christians have taken this line to mean Jesus,

17. Anonymous, "The Bible's Last Prophet," *Islamic Review* (September, 1928) 313.
18. Ibid.

but many modern Moslem commentators believe it speaks specifically about the coming of the prophet Muhammed.

Abdul Dawud also points out that both the gospels of Matthew and Luke refer to John the Baptist saying, "one more powerful than I is coming after me," as a parallel passage to John 1:15. Again, although most Christian scholars think that John the Baptist was speaking of Jesus, Dawud and other modern Islamic scholars are convinced these references are to the prophet Muhammed.[19]

THE USE OF THE NAME JOHN IN THE QUR'AN

Another confusion about John the Baptist in Islam arises from a comment in the Qur'an. It comes at 19:7, where Allah says , "Oh Zechariah, We gave you good news of a son named John. To none have We attributed the name before." This line is confusing, for most translations make it look as if no prophet in Islam had the name of John before John the Baptist. In fact, the Old Testament uses the name *Johanan* (John in Hebrew) twenty-seven times.

In some of the uses of Johanan in the Old Testament they appear to have been prophets or leaders among the ancient Jews. Chief among these references are 2 Kings 25:23; 1 Chronicles 3:15 and 24; and Ezra 8:12. In addition, the Hasmonean Dynasty, which ruled Palestine for a century before John the Baptist, included a priest-king whose name was John Hyrcanus. Josephus, in his *Jewish Wars* mentioned a John the Essene who served as a rebel general in Timna. First Maccabees at 2:1–2 and 16:9 also mentions Johns who lived before John the Baptist.

Most translations of the Qur'an, even modern ones, say little or nothing about this comment at 19:7. Thus, most translations seem to render the idea that no one before John the Baptist was named John. One can find this idea in the translations of Pickthall, George Sale, A. J. Arberry, and E. H. Palmer. One other modern translation, that of Yusuf Ali, trans-

---

19. Abdul Dawud, *Muhammed in the Bible* (London: International Islamic Publishers, 1996) 32.

lates the last part of the Qur'an 19:7 this way:[20] "On none by that name have We conferred distinctions before."[21]

Not only does Ali provide this translation, he also provides an explanation in his commentary, where he says, "for we read of a Johanan . . . in 2 Kings 25:23." Ali goes on to point out that the name John had been used before, and thus the verse in the Qur'an cannot be historically correct; or could it be the case that Ali did not take the verse literally. Whatever sense we make of the verse, and what Islam makes of it, it is clear that there were many references to people with the name John prior to the time of John the Baptist.

MARYAM AND THE ROLE OF WOMEN

Certain women are important models of faith for Moslem men, and particularly for Islamic women. The wives of Muhammed, for example, are referred to as the "Mothers of the Believers." The Qur'an's 33:6 tells us: "The prophet is closer to the faithful than they are to themselves; and his wives are as their mothers."[22]

Islam also speaks of four "perfect" or "special" women. These are Khadija, the first wife of Muhammed, Fatima, the prophet's only surviving daughter, Maryam, the mother of Jesus, who is a model of chastity, faith, and devotion (Qur'an 66:12), and a woman named Asiyah, the wife of Pharaoh. The fourth woman is numbered among the greatest of women, for as sura 28:9 tells us that she saved the life of the infant Moses.

Indeed, in the Qur'an, the Pharaoh typifies arrogance and wickedness, while Asiyah had her life focused on Allah. She shunned wrongdoing and sought the life of heaven. The Qur'an's 66:11 tells us: "And Allah presents the example of Pharaoh's wife for those who believe, when she said, 'Oh Allah, build me a house in Paradise, and save me from Pharaoh and his deeds, and save me from wicked people.'"[23]

---

20. George Sale, *Koran Or, Al-Koran of Mohammed: The Bible of the East* (New York: Viking, 1909); E. H. Palmer, *The Koran* (London: Kessinger, 2004); M. W. Pickthall, *The Glorious Qur'an* (Lahore: Tahrike Tarsile Qur'an, 2001); and A. J. Arberry, *The Koran Interpreted* (London: Touchstone, 1996).

21. Abdullah Yusuf Ali, *The Qur'an: Text, Translation, and Commentary* (Lahore: Tahrike Tarsile Qur'an, 1987).

22. Qur'an 33:6 (author's translation).

23. Qur'an 66:11 (author's translation).

Asiyah, of course, was not the follower of any known prophet. Thus, her example is important in showing that the natural tendency in human nature is to be a Moslem, and that we ought to live a life of *taqwa*, even if we are separated from the guidance of Allah's great prophets. In such conditions, our natural inclinations are to do the good and this nature can flourish through reason and reflection.

The laws governing inheritance in Islam are extremely complex. Two thirds of a man's property is distributed after his death according to a set pattern laid out by Islamic law. The remaining third may be disposed of according to the dead man's wishes. Frequently, wives and daughters inherit land and property under the conditions of this final third.

As we have seen, the person of Maryam, the mother of Jesus, also holds a special status in Islam. She stands as an example of purity and obedience to Allah for Islamic women everywhere.

MARYAM IN LATER ISLAM

Later Islamic traditions on Maryam speak of her giving bread to the Magi when they arrive. Masudi's commentary on the Qur'an is a good example of this tradition (IV:79–80). Another tradition suggests that after the death of Isa, Maryam went to Rome to preach to Marut (Emperor Nero). She is said to have been accompanied by John the disciple and Shimun (Peter Simon), who was a coppersmith. This account says that when Peter and *Tadawus* (Thaddaeus) were crucified upside down, Maryam fled with the apostle John. When the two were persecuted, this account says, the earth was opened up and withdrew them from their persecutors. This miracle was the cause, some Moslems say, of Nero's conversion.

Maryam is much venerated in later Islam, often along with Fatima, Mohammed's only surviving daughter. Both women have been taken by Moslem women as examples and as a recourse in times of trouble, sometimes visiting Christian shrines dedicated in her name. Moslems honor Maryam's name at Matariyya, near Cairo. In Jerusalem, is the *Hammam Sitti Maryam* ("the bath of Mary"), near Saint Stephen's gate, where it is believed Mary bathed. The place is visited in the Islamic tradition by women who seek a cure for infertility.

A number of plants have been named after Maryam in the Islamic faith. One of these is said to have acquired its sweet taste after Mary wiped her tears with its leaves. Another plant named after Maryam is shaped like a fist and is used to ward off the evil eye. A similar tradition is held about Fatima who brings protection with what is called the *Kaff Fatima*, if an amulet is worn around the neck. This same plant is also used as a birth charm in modern Arabia.

Other later accounts of Maryam, like that of Bukhari, say "every child that is born is stung by Satan so that it cries, except Maryam and her son." Bukhari, a ninth-century Sunni scholar, also tells us "Many men reach the level of perfection, but no woman reached such a level but Maryam." Al-Nawawi suggests, as does Baydawi, that Isa, Maryam, and the other prophets are *isma* (impeccable). Modern commentator, Mohammed Abduh argues that the privilege of preservation from Satan do not put Mary and Jesus on a higher plane than Mohammed.

Parrinder sums up the Islamic view of Maryam when he writes: "Down the ages the purity of Mary has been cherished. Already Ibn Ishaq spoke of 'Mary the virgin, the good, and the pure.'"[24]

In the Sufi tradition, a female mystic named *Rabi'a* (717–801) was called "a second spotless Mary."[25]

The thirteenth-century collector of hadith, Abdallah ibn Umar Al-Baydawi, in his commentary on the Qur'an, called *The Secrets of Revelation and the Secrets of Interpretation* (Arabic: *Asrur ut-tanzil wa Asrar ut-ta ta'wil*) accepted the name of Maryam's mother as Hanna, and tells a tale about Mary that is found in the apocryphal book of James. The tale goes like this: One day Hanna was sitting under a tree, watching a bird feeding its young. This caused her to lament her infertility. She promised that if Allah would give her a child, she would devote [the child] to the service of Allah in the temple. She made this vow on the assumption she would be given a male child, but she is given a female, Maryam.

Baydawi goes on to say that Maryam was brought up in the Temple, and that the priests drew lots to see who would be her guardian. Other accounts say it is to decide who would have Maryam as a wife. Parrinder sums up the view of Isa by Muhammed:

> The prophet Mohammed had a deep veneration for Mary as mother of Jesus. The oldest historian of Mecca, Azraqi who died in 858, said that the Ka'ba of Mecca, on the column nearest the door, was a picture of Mary with Jesus on her knee. When Mohammed

24. Parrinder, *Jesus in the Qur'an*, 61–62.
25. Ibid., 61.

entered Mecca, he gave orders to destroy the idols of the Ka'ba and its paintings of prophets of angels. But it is said that when the followers began to wash away the images with water from the Zam Zam, Mohammed put his hands on the picture of Mary and Jesus he said, "Wash away everything except what is below my hands." Whether this story is true or not, there is no doubt that the prophet showed the utmost respect for Jesus and his mother.[26]

The theme of Isa communicating from the womb of Maryam is also a popular theme among Medieval Moslem collectors of hadith. Abu al-Qasim ibn Asakir, great twelfth-century scholar of hadith, conveys the tale of Maryam saying, "In the days I was pregnant with Isa, whenever there was someone in my house speaking with me, I would hear Isa inside of me praising Allah. Whenever I was alone and there was no one with me, I would converse with him and he with me, while he was still in my womb."[27]

Similar comments about Isa's ability to communicate from the womb are told in a variety of other Medieval hadith. In nearly all of these descriptions the communication is with Maryam, but in some others Jesus gives advice to others from the womb, including friends of his mother and sometimes even passersby. Nothing like this ability to communicate from the womb of his mother can be found in the Christian tradition, nor are there any instances in the Hebrew Bible where prophets give advice or communicate before birth. It is probably best to see these tales as indications of the degree to which Jesus is revered as a prophet and holy man in Islam. Indeed, he is seen to have supernatural powers in the Moslem faith—even from the womb.

SIMILARITIES OF MARYAM TO FATIMA

Some modern scholars have pointed out a number of similarities between the Islamic view of Mary and that of Muhammed's daughter, Fatima. Both women are considered prophets of Allah. Both have a special status among God and his creatures. Both Fatima and Maryam are related to two of the greatest prophets in Islam: Fatima to Muhammed and Maryam to Jesus.

Muslims regard Fatima Zahra (the "Radiant") as the greatest woman who ever lived, and the leader of all women in Paradise. She is also seen as

26. Ibid., 66.
27. Abu al-Qasim ibn Asakir, *Sirat al-Sayyid al-Masih*, p. 176, number 204.

a paragon of female virtue in much the same way as the Blessed Mother is in the Christian tradition. Fatima was the first wife of the first Shiite Imam, the mother of the second and third, and the ancestor of all succeeding imams. Indeed, the Fatimid Dynasty, which dominated North Africa and the Middle East from 909 to 1171, is named after her.

Fatima is also known in Islam as the Lady of Light, and the popular amulet to ward off evil spirits is said to represent the hand of Fatima. Fatima is also sometimes called "the Virgin," and "the Mother of the Two Jesuses," reflecting the important influence of Christianity on early Islam. In Shiite Islam, both her birthday and her marriage to Ali, the first Imam, are annually celebrated.

In Iran, Fatima's birthday, the 20th of Jumada, is the date for National Women's Day. The homilies on this date frequently include tales about Fatima's virtue. Fatima is said to have been very close to her father Muhammed. In some early hadith the prophet said of his daughter, "She is part of my flesh. Whoever upsets her upsets me."

It should be clear from these comments that there are many parallels between the image of Fatima in Islam and the role of Mary in Christianity. John L. Esposito, in his *Islam: The Straight Path*, point to some other parallels of Maryam to Fatima. He points out that Fatima was Muhammed's only surviving child, just as Jesus was Maryam's only son. Fatima is the primal mother figure in Islam in the same way that Mary is in Christianity. Both women, Esposito argues, are objects of prayer petitions. But more fundamentally than all this, Esposito concludes: "Like the Virgin Mary in the Christian tradition, Fatima is portrayed as a woman of sorrow, symbolizing the rejection disinheritance, and martyrdom of her husband and sons."[28]

In the same way that Jesus has become a martyr in the Christian faith, Fatima's son, Husayn is seen as a martyr to be venerated in the Islamic faith. Both women's sons died by execution, and both women express great sorrow over the innocent sacrifice of their sons; and both held a special place in the family of a prophet. Like Mary in Christianity, Fatima is known for her purity. Indeed, one of Fatima's principal names in Islam is *Maryam al-Kurba* or "The Greater Mary."

---

28. John L. Esposito, *Islam: The Straight Path*, 3rd ed. (New York: Oxford University Press, 1998) 112.

MARY AND JOHN THE BAPTIST IN CONTEMPORARY ISLAM

The figure of Maryam has undergone a radical transformation in Islamic scholarship from the twentieth century. The main transformation has involved the raising of the status of Fatima, while at the same time lowering the status of Maryam. In contemporary Islamic scholarship, and in the popular imagination, stories are told about Fatima that used to be uttered about Maryam. Included in these narratives are tales about Fatima's purity, goodness, and righteousness.

In the contemporary Islamic view of Fatima, Mohammed's only surviving daughter has taken the place of the mother of Isa; and concomitant with this shift is a devaluing of the importance of the figure of Mary in Islam. Indeed, like many other issues involving Moslems on Christian figures, the importance of Maryam, as well as the truth of the gospels, and the role of John the Baptist in Islam, have been denigrated.

In much of contemporary Islam, Fatima is seen as a perfect model of the values and teachings that are revealed in the Holy Qur'an. The Holy Book tells us that Fatima is among the infallibles in Islam (33:33). Fatima is said to have championed the rights of women when she was denied her inheritance. Since that time, she has been seen as a morally righteous figure. As Bukhari says, "Fatima is a part of me, and he who makes her angry makes me angry." In another place, Bukhari identifies Fatima as "the leader of all the ladies in Paradise."

In more recent scholarship and in the popular imagination, Fatima has become the hero of women's rights, as well as a moral exemplar. And in the process, the role of Maryam in Islam has been lowered. While Maryam was called "the greatest woman in the world who has ever lived" (3:42), rarely is this thought expressed in popular Islamic culture.

Fulton J. Sheen, writing in 1952, already began to see this trend of elevating Fatima, while lowering the status of Maryam. Sheen writes: "The Moslems should be prepared to acknowledge that, if Fatima must give way in honor to the Blessed Mother, it is because she is different from all other mothers of the world, and without Christ, she would be nothing."[29]

Sheen seems to be suggesting that if we honor the place of Fatima above that of Maryam, then we dishonor a woman that is "different from all other women in the world," and that the qualities contemporary

---

29. Fulton J. Sheen, "Mary and the Muslims," in Jomier, ed., *The Bible and the Qur'an*, 121–26.

Moslem women who admire Fatima are precisely the characteristics that Christian women admire about the Blessed Mother.

Whether this elevation of Fatima and the concomitant demotion of Maryam in contemporary Islamic culture is a product of current or past animosities toward Christianity, or the result of not allowing any woman to the status of those in Mohammed's own family is not clear. Nevertheless, there is much more discussion in modern Islam about Fatima than there is about Maryam, the mother of Isa.

Most contemporary mentions of John the Baptist in today's Islamic scholarship comes in connection with earlier Qur'anic commentaries by people like Tabari, Kathir, Baydawi, and Bukhari. Ibn Kathir, a fourteenth-century Syrian scholar of hadith, comments on Zechariah asking for a son. He says that the letters *Kaf, Ha, Ya, Ain, Sad* are one of the miracles of the Qur'an known by Allah alone. These letters spell Yah Yah (John), which are a sign that Allah brought a miracle. Kathir says that Zechariah says, "Oh Allah, my bones have grown feeble and grey hair has spread on my head, and I have never been unfaithful to you . . . My wife is barren, so give me an heir."

Kathir says that Allah responded this way: "Oh Zechariah, We give you the glad tidings of a son. His name shall be Yah Yah. We have given that name to none before him."[30]

Kathir says that Zechariah answered, "My Lord, how can I have a son, when my wife is barren, and I have reached such an old age?" Allah responds, "It is easy for Me. I created you out of nothing, why not another?" Then Zechariah asks for a sign. Allah answered, "Your sign is that you should not speak to mankind for three nights, while having no bodily defect." Then Zechariah returned to his people from Al-Mihrab (a place for prayer) and he told them to glorify Allah and praise him in the mornings and in the afternoons.

The tenth-century Persian commentator also gives a similar account of John the Baptist about which many contemporary Islamic scholars write. Tabari holds a view of Yah Yah not unlike that of Kathir, and puts great emphasis on the miraculous story of Zechariah.

Al-Yaqubi, a ninth and tenth-century Moslem scholar, wrote a two volume commentary on biblical narratives. A version of the text was published in 1883. Yaqubi gives an extensive treatment of Yah Yah, again con-

---

30. Kathir, *The Words of Ibn Kathir*, edited by S. S. R. Mubarakpuri (London, 1998) 167.

centrating on the divine aspect of Yah Yah's birth. Other later treatments of John the Baptist commented on by contemporary scholars includes works by Tabari (839–923), Persian collector of hadith, Tabari's commentary is called *The Annals of the Apostles and the Kings*; and thirteenth-century commentator Abdullah ibn Umar ibn Baydawi, whose two volume commentary on the Qur'an called *The Secrets of Revelation and Interpretation*, a version of which was edited by H. O. Fleischer and published in 1846–1848 in Leipzig, also contains a discussion on the figure of Yah Yah.[31]

Almost all contemporary Islamic scholars who write about John the Baptist do it by commenting on these Medieval hadith. Three good examples of this scholarship are three collections of essays commenting on the Islamic views of New Testament figures. The first of these books is edited by John C. Reeves and is called, *Bible and Qur'an: Essays in Scriptural Intertextuality*. This volume includes essays by Reuvan Firestone, Vernon Robbins, Brannon Wheeler, Sidney Griffith, and Kathryn Kueny.[32]

The second volume is entitled, *Approaches to the History of the Interpretation of the Qur'an*, edited by Andrew Rippin, a prominent British scholar of Islam. This book, which is published by Clarendon, has a number of essays that explore the relationship between the New Testament and other pre-Qur'anic traditions in the history of Islam. Among the most important essays in this volume are those by Jane McAuliffe, David Powers, and Fred Leemhuis.

The third volume is edited by J. L. Esposito and is entitled, *Voices of Resurgent Islam*, which was published by Oxford University Press in 1983.[33] The volume contains a number of essays on the contemporary relationship between Islam and Christianity.[34] Geoffrey Parrinder's *Jesus in the Qur'an* also has an extensive treatment of both Maryam and Yah Yah, as does J. M. S. Baljon's *Modern Moslem Koran Interpretation*, published in London in 1961.[35] In all of these contemporary works, most of what is said about Maryam and Yah Yah is related to what the Qur'an has to

---

31. Ibn Baydawi, *The Secrets of Revelation and Interpretation*, edited by Z. H. O. Fleischer (Leipzig, 1846–1848).

32. See note 10.

33. See note 1.

34. Ibid.

35. J. M. S. Baljon, *Modern Moslem Koran Interpretation* (Leiden: Brill, 1961).

say about these figures, or there are discussions of these figures in Tabari, Baydawi, Kathir, Yaqubi, and Bukhari.[36]

DIFFERENCES BETWEEN ISLAM AND CHRISTIANITY ON MARY

As we have seen in this chapter, there are some marked similarities, as well as profound differences in the views of Islam and Christianity on Mary. The two traditions agree on the Virgin Birth, the miraculous fact of Mary's birth, that Mary was known for her chastity, and that Mary was chided for becoming pregnant; but the differences between Islam and Christianity on Mary far outweigh the similarities.

The major difference of Islam on Mary is that the Islamic tradition does not believe that Maryam ibn Isa was the mother of God; nor do they believe that Isa was God, nor was he part of a God-head embodied in the Trinity. There are some traditions in Islam that have come close to the deifying of Maryam, but in general that view is not held in Islam.

In both Islam and Christianity, Mary has an exalted status. In both Christianity and Islam Mary is a fine exemplar for the moral life, and in both she is known for her chastity, but she is far better known in this regard in Islam than she is in Christianity. There is also a good bit more discussion of the miraculous birth of Maryam in Islam than there is in Christianity.

Indeed, in some respects the status of Mary in Islam, at times, seems to be even higher than that of Mary in Christianity. Jacques Jomier speaks of this status: "The human characteristics of Jesus, as the Qur'an describes them, are manifold. Jesus and Mary, His mother, are spoken of as being of exceptional purity."[37]

Jomier goes on to argue that it was not an accident that the Qur'an calls Mary's father's name Imran, the same names as that of Moses' father.

36. For more on the role of Maryam in Islam, see Hila Plaza, *Why Do Muslims Honor Jesus and Mary?* (London: Hila Plaza Productions, 2006); Mary Montagu, *L'Islam au peril des femmes* (Paris: La Decouverte, 2001); Fatima Mernissi and Mary Jo Lakeland, *The Forgotten Queens of Islam* (Minneapolis: University of Minnesota Press, 1997); Yvonne Yazbeck Haddad, *Islam, Gender, and Social Change* (Oxford: Oxford University Press, 1997). For more on the role of John the Baptist in Islam, see Mary Blye Howe, *A Baptist Among the Jews* (London: Jossey-Bass, 2003); John Renard, *Seven Doors to Islam* (Los Angeles: University of California Press, 1996); and *Understanding Islam: A Guide for the Judeo-Christian Reader* (Beltsville, Maryland: Amana Publications, 2003).

37. Jacques Jomier, *The Bible and the Koran* (San Francisco: Ignatius, 1964) 65.

Moses' sister's name was Maryam. Thus, the Qur'an seems explicitly to be drawing a parallel between the life of Moses and that of Jesus. This parallel is rarely made so explicitly in Christianity—another important difference between the two faiths.[38]

CONCLUSION

In this chapter we have looked carefully at the images of Mary, Joseph, and John the Baptist in Islamic thought. As we have seen, the only reference to Joseph, Jesus' earthly father in the Qur'an is to the fact that he was a carpenter. It does not mention Joseph by name, though some sources in later Islam refer to Jesus' father as Yusuf.

The references to the image of Mary (Maryam in Islam) are ubiquitous. She appears in thirty-four different suras of the Qur'an. As we have seen, Mary is numbered among the Islamic prophets. She is given a moral status higher than all but a few other women. In Islam, Maryam is primarily known for her chastity, as well as the virgin birth of her son, Isa. The Qur'an gives a version of the Annunciation by the angel Jibril to Maryam, and she is frequently defended in the Qur'an and in later Islam, when she appeared pregnant and is questioned by her family and friends.

The 19th sura of the Qur'an is named after Maryam. It has ninety-eight *ayat* or verses, and is named for the mother of Isa. Sura Maryam is a *Makkan* sura, that is it speaks of the great expanse of Allah. Maryam is venerated as "the Lady of the women of the world," but not as the mother of God. Sura Maryam tells the story of the birth of John the Baptist after his father became desperate for a child. It goes on to say that Allah himself named him and that he was the first prophet of Islam to carry that name. Then sura 19 tells the story of the pregnancy of Maryam and the birth of Isa (Jesus) who is called the Messiah in Islam.

In most contemporary discussions of Maryam in Islam, her status is reduced, while the place of other women in Islam, like Muhammed's daughter Fatima, are elevated. This may be a product of contemporary relations between Islam and Christianity, or it could be that no woman will be seen as higher than those in Muhammed's own family.

Yah Yah is also mentioned among the greatest of Moslem prophets. He is mostly spoken of in contemporary Islam, as we have seen, in relationship to his miraculous birth, which was announced to his father

38. Ibid.

Zechariah before his conception. Both Maryam and Yah Yah are seen as holy saints and people of righteousness.

In the following two chapters, we describe two other New Testament figures in the history of Islam. In chapter seven, we talk about the image of Shaytan (Satan), who is also called Iblis throughout the history of Islam. As we shall see, much of what Islam has to say about this figure is directly related to interpretations of Satan in early Christianity.

In the penultimate chapter of this study, we shall describe and discuss the image of the Djaal, the Arabic word for the Anti-Christ." As we shall see, there are some fundamental similarities to the New Testament's views of the Anti-Christ, as well as some important differences; but first, we shall turn to the image of Satan in the Qur'an and in post-Qur'anic Islam.

9

The Image of Satan, Heaven, and Hell in the Qur'an and Later Islam

One Shiite hadith even goes so far as to suggest that a dangerous substance tests under the fingernails, that which Satan claims.

—Katherine Kueny, "Abraham's Test"

In the words of the final chapter in the Qur'an (114:5), Satan is an insidious whisperer who whispers in the hearts of men.

—Bernard Lewis, *The Middle East*

But Satan tempted them and had them banished from the happy state they were in. And we said, "Go, one of the antagonist of the other, and live on the earth for a time ordained and fend for yourself."

—Qur'an 2:36

INTRODUCTION

IN THIS CHAPTER, WE describe and discuss the role of Satan (called Shaytan and Iblis in Islam). We begin the chapter by examining three incidents in which Iblis is extensively discussed in the Qur'an: Iblis at creation, Iblis in the Garden of Eden, and Iblis in the End Times. We continue the discussion with further references to Iblis in the Qur'an. We also make some general observations in this chapter about Islamic discussion of the nature of Iblis, the nature of the sin of Iblis, as well as the image of Iblis in later Islam.[1]

1. Most of the Arabic translations of this chapter, like those of the previous chapters, are those of the author's. The primary edition of the Qur'an I have used in this chapter is *Al-Qur'an*, translated and edited by Ahmed Ali (Princeton: Princeton University Press,

As we shall see, the image of Iblis in Islam has borrowed much from both the Jewish hagaddah, as well as the early Christian traditions on the Devil; but we also shall show that at times the Islamic view of the demonic deviates considerably from these two earlier traditions. Let us begin the chapter with a discussion of the nature of Iblis in Islam.

THE NATURE OF IBLIS AND IBLIS IN THE QUR'AN

Iblis is mentioned in seven major suras of the Qur'an. These occur at 2:34; 7:11–18; 15:31–44; 17: 61–65; 18:50; 20:116–123; and 38:71–85. The passages in suras 2, 7, 15, 17, 18, 20 and 38 all mention Iblis' refusal to bow down to Adam. Many of these passages also allude to Iblis ruling the land of the damned, humans made of clay and Iblis made of smoke, and suras 20 and 38 speak specifically of Iblis's temptation of Adam and Eve.

The Islamic tradition is not always uniform on the nature of Iblis. Some say he is an angel, while others say he is one of the Djinns. One place in the Qur'an says "All the angels bow together, except Iblis." This seems to imply that Iblis is an angel. On the other hand, some Moslem thinkers say that Iblis is one of the djinns, or even the Lord of the Djinns. Some argue that there are both good djinns and bad djinns, spirits that may be associated with good or evil.

In Islamic mythology the Djinni (plural of Djinn) are fiery spirits, who are comparable to the fallen angels in Christian mythology. The word comes from the Arabic, *junna*, the verb for angry, as well as the verb "to be possessed." The English word, genie comes from the Arabic Djinni. The Qur'an 51:56 tells us that Allah created the Djinn and human beings in order that they might worship Him.

In some Islamic traditions, the Djinn lived on earth before human beings. The Qur'an tells us they were made of "smokeless fire," whereas humans were made from clay. The Djinn are often disruptive, but can

---

1993). I have also consulted A. J. Arberry, *The Koran Interpreted* (London: Allen and Unwin, 1995); Abdullah Yufuf Ali, *The Holy Qur'an* (Brentwood, MD: Amana, 1989); and M. M. Pickhtall, *The Meaning of the Glorious Koran* (New York: Meridian, 1997).

Secondary sources I have used in preparing this chapter include: N. Daniel, *Islam and the West* (Oxford: One World Press, 1997); Richard Bell, *The Origins of Islam in its Christian Environment* (Edinburgh, T and T Clark, 1953); Geoffrey Parrinder, *Jesus in the Qur'an* (London: Faber, 1965); Jacques Jomier, *The Bible and the Qur'an* (San Francisco: Ignatius Press, 1964); Bernard Lewis, *The World of Islam* (London: Thames and Hudson, 1976); and W. M. Watt, *Muhammed: Prophet and Statesman* (Oxford: Oxford University Press, 1977).

sometimes be of service to humans. The good Djinns can grant favors and wishes to people. Some Moslems say that the bad Djinn shun sunlight, and are responsible for diseases and insanity. Unlike some other metaphysical beings, the Djinn are possessors of free will, and in some traditions, they even have the possibility of being forgiven and redeemed.

Some Islamic thinkers describe three kinds of Djinns. The first are called, *Ghul*, from which is derived the English "ghoul." These are mischievous spirits associated with graveyards. They have the ability to change shape, and dislike the daytime. The second variety of Djinns is called *Sila*. They can appear in any form. The final kind of Djinns is *ifrit*. They are primarily evil spirits that test the moral characters of human beings.

All three kinds of Djinns are associated with magic in Islam. The bad Djinn have a tendency to enter human bodies through five orifices, often going straight to the head to make people mad. Some Islamic accounts attribute sneezing, coughing, and yawning to the Djinns. Al-Hakim agrees with these three types when he writes, "One type flies through the air, another type consists of snakes and dogs. A third is based in one place but travels about.[2]

The Qur'an mentions the Djinn in several places. Sura 15:27 tells us that Allah created Djinn from a "searing wind." Surah 72 is named for the Djinn, and makes a number of observations about their nature. 72:5–6 speak of Allah thinking that men and djinn would never speak a lie about Allah, but some people sought out the help of djinn and this increased their evilness. The Djinn are also mentioned at sura 55:15, 15:27; 7:12; 55:74. The Qur'an's 55:15 speaks of the Djinn being made from fire, as does 15:27 and 7:12. Sura 55:74 suggests that people may be deflowered by Djinns.

In the thirteenth century, a Turkish commentator, Ibn Taymiyyah, wrote an extensive essay on the Djin that included a chapter called "Demonic Vision." Taymiyyah discusses the nature, of the practices, and the incantations employed by the Djinns. He also speaks of their role in divination, possession, and the conjuring of visions in human beings.[3]

Taymiyyah also says that Djinn can take human or animal forms such as cows, scorpions, snakes, or birds. He also reports that the black dog is the Devil of the Djinn and he often appears in this form. Taymiyyah also

---

2. Anonymous, *Le Monde des Djinns* (Paris, 2006) 2. Tahar Gaid, "Djinn," in *Elementary Dictionary of Islam*, edited by T. P. Hughes (London: Allen, 1885) 2:75.

3. Ibid, 5.

tells us that the Devil appears in the form of a black cat. Taymiyyah says that whenever the Djinn take a human or animal form, they are subject to the same physical laws as they remain in these forms for relatively short periods of time.

Ibn Abbas, cousin of Muhammed and revered by both Shiites and Sunnis, also tells us that Djinn were on the earth 2,000 years before humans, and they caused corruption on it and shed blood. Then Allah sent a troop of angels to banish them to islands in the seas. Al-Hakim, an eleventh-century Egyptian commentator suggests: "We cannot ordinarily see the Djinn, unless they take material form, which is usually in an unpleasant or ugly form such as a snake or a black dog, as opposed to angels who take pleasant and handsome forms."[4]

Imam al-Bukhari, ninth-century collector of hadith, tells us that all people are accompanied by a Djinn who tries to incite people to evil. He also tells us that Muhammed is an exception to this practice, because the prophet was only assigned to do the good.[5]

Abu Buhaqi and Al-Tabarani also confirm the three kinds of Djinns. They call the first type, *Amir*, one who lives with people. The second type they call *Shaytan*, those jinni who are wicked. And they call the third kind *Ifrit* because they are stronger and more powerful than Iblis. Buhaqi and Tabarani also tell us that the way of life for the Djinns is just like that of human beings. For example, they are accountable for their actions just as humans are.[6]

Abu Muslim, an eighth-century Persian scholar, tells us that Djinns have *fiqh* (rules) similar to those of humans. Just as Moslems eat the meat of animals slaughtered in the name of Allah, so do the believers among the djinn. In addition, the djinns are allowed to eat the bones of those animals. Muslim also says that humans are not responsible for their evil thoughts, they come from the djinn, and that the term *Shaytan*, Muslim suggests, is also used for disbelieving humans.[7]

Some argue that the good djinns do not bother anyone, but the evil ones do. Allah in the Qur'an speaks of appointing some angels or spirits who protect human beings from unseen spirits (Iblis or the Djinns).

4. Ibid, 7.
5. Ibid, 4.
6. Ibid.
7. Ibid.

These good spirits, sometimes called *hafazah*, only accompany humans when they are pure. The job of the evil djinns is to tease us, and to trick us into sin.

In the Islamic tradition, then, commentators are sometimes divided over whether Iblis is a fallen angel, or the leader of a group of evil spirits. As we shall see later in the chapter, subsequent Islamic thinkers are also sometimes at odds on this issue. Al-Tabari and other hadith collectors suggest that djinns are charged with supervising Paradise. There are also a number of discussions about the djinns that say the good djinns and angels are made of light, while Iblis and the bad djinns are made of fire.

Mary Pat Fisher, in her book, *Living Religions*, discusses the Islamic view of Satan:

> He was originally one of the djinn—immaterial beings of fire whose nature is between that of humans and angels. He proudly refused to bow down before Adam, and therefore was cursed to live by tempting Adam's descendents—all of humanity in other words—to follow him rather than Allah. According to the Qur'an those who fall prey to Satan's devices will ultimately go to hell.[8]

Other traditions present Iblis as one of the terrestrial djinns who was led captive by the good angels to heaven, where later he fell. Iblis is sometimes given the name, *Al-Hakam* before his fall, because Allah had appointed him judge or Lord over the bad djinns. Some say he held this office for a thousand years. Then, because of pride, he provoked the bad djinns. Allah then sent a fire to destroy them, but Iblis fled until the creation of Adam. It is enough now, however, to say that the nature of Iblis is not an entirely clear question. He may be a fallen angel, or he may be the leader, or he may be the leader of the evil djinns.

There are a number of other attributes of Iblis enumerated in the Qur'an. Qur'an 2:33 refers to the known and unknown of the heavens. Some suggest this refers to Iblis who cannot fully be known by humans. 18:50 states explicitly that Iblis is one of the djinns. 15:42 tells us that Iblis will have no power over the righteous, but he will have power over those who fall into error. Qur'an 7:156 suggests that Iblis cannot affect anyone who follows Allah's laws. The Qur'an also suggests those that follow Iblis will be punished by fire. One's bad deeds burn the human personality and keep it from growth.

8. Mary Pat Fisher, *Living Religions* (Englewoof Cliffs, NJ: Prentice Hall, 1994) 311.

The Qur'an 56:79 tells us that Iblis attempts to keep believing Moslems away from the Qur'an; and the final sura in the Qur'an (114) reiterates the points that there is one "who suggests evil thoughts to the hearts of men." Earlier in sura 114, it also tells us: "Say 'I seek refuge with the Lord of men. The king of men The God of men. From the evil of he who breathes temptations into the minds of men.'"[9]

The Qur'an 16:98-100 suggests the Moslem believer should: "Recite the Qur'an and take refuge in Allah from Shaytan the execrable. He does not have power over those who believe and place their trust in the Lord. His power is only over those who have taken him as their patron, and those who ascribe equals to Allah."[10]

The Qur'an 36:60 tells us that Allah commanded humans not to worship Shaytan. The text tells us: "Did I not commit you, O children of Adam, not to worship Satan who is your acknowledged enemy. But to serve Me, who is the straight path."[11]

The Qur'an 35:6 also refers to Satan being our enemy: "Satan is certainly your enemy, so hold him as a foe. He only calls his factions to be residents of Hell. For those who are unbelievers, there is severe punishment; for those who believe and do the right is forgiveness and a great reward."[12]

This passage points to an important difference between Christianity and Islam. The Qur'an in several places discusses with believers the figure of Satan, often calling him an enemy or warning against his temptations. In the Qur'an's discussions of the figure of Job, for example, Job knows he is being inflicted by Iblis, which is a far cry from the Hebrew text.

The Qur'an 8:48 reiterates Iblis' power to tempt: "Satan made their deeds to look alluring to them, and said, 'None will prevail over you this day, for I shall be near at hand.'"[13]

And the Qur'an's 7:200–202 speaks of those who succumb to Iblis' temptation: "If you are instigated by Iblis to do evil, seek refuge in Allah. Those who fear Allah think of Him when assailed by the instigations of

9. Qur'an 114:1–4.

10. Ibid, 16:98.

11. Ibid, 36:60.

12. Ibid, 35:6.

13. Ibid, 8:48.

Shaytan, and lo they begin to understand. Even though their devilish brothers would have them continue in error and would not desist."[14]

The Qur'an 14:22 speaks of the relationship between Iblis and humans. The text tells us:

> When the reckoning is over Shaytan will say, "The promise that was made to you by Allah was indeed a true promise; but I went back on the promise I had made, for I had no power over you except to call you; and you responded to my call. So don't blame me but blame yourselves. I can't help you, and you can't help me. I disavow your having associated me with Allah. The punishment of those who are wicked is painful indeed."[15]

The Qur'an 24:21 speaks explicitly about those who follow Shaytan: "Oh you who believe, do not follow in the footsteps of Satan. For he who follows in the footsteps of Satan will be induced by him to what is shameful and forbidden. But for the grace of Allah and His mercy upon you, none of you would have escaped undefiled."[16]

The Qur'an's suras 15 to 20 mention Iblis four different times. These come at 15:16–42; 16:61–65; 18:50–51; and 20:115–123. Sura 15 discusses the natures of humans and Iblis. It speaks of Iblis' refusal to bow down to Adam, and it contains a rebuke to Iblis by God who is condemned until the Day of Doom. The Qur'an's 16:61-65 speaks of Iblis tempting human beings, making bad actions attractive to them.

Sura 18:50–51 also mentions that Iblis refused to bow down and worship Adam, and suggests that the Djinns are man's enemies. The Qur'an's 20:115–123 also mentions that Iblis was the only angel who refused to bow down to Adam. It also mentions Iblis' tempting of Adam and Eve in the garden.

Finally, Qur'an 22:52–53 tells us more about the nature of Shaytan:

> We have sent no messenger or apostle before you with whose recitations Satan did not tamper. Yet Allah abrogates what Satan interpolates; then He confirms His revelations, for Allah is all knowing and wise. This is in order to make the interpolations of Satan a test for those whose hearts are full of disease and hardened; sinners have gone far in dissent.[17]

14. Ibid, 7:200.
15. Ibid, 14:22.
16. Ibid, 24:21.
17. Ibid, 22:52–53.

IBLIS, CREATION, AND THE END TIMES

In the Qur'an, Iblis appears in two different places in the story of the beginning of the world. The first has to do with when Allah created Adam from clay and had breathed into him the spirit of life. At this point, the Qur'an reports that Allah ordered the angels to bow down to Adam, but Iblis refused to bow down to these mere mortal "created from malleable clay."[18] This scene is recorded at 15:30–33 and 17:61. When Iblis refused, Allah cried, "Then go forth hence, you are accursed (*radjim*). This curse will last until the Day of Doom" (15:33–34).

The Qur'an 15:30–33 describes Iblis' refusal to bow down to Adam: "The angels bowed in homage, all except Iblis. He refused to bow with the adorers. Then the Lord said, 'Oh Iblis, why did you not join those who bowed in homage?' 'How could I bow before a mortal,' he said, "whom you created from fermented clay dried tingling hard?"[19]

At his own request, this tradition suggests, the punishment promised to Iblis is deferred until the Day of Judgment, and he is given the power to lead astray all those who are not faithful servants to Allah. The first of Iblis' deeds was to tempt Adam and Eve in the garden to incite them to disobey Allah, and to eat from the "Tree of Immortality," a significant difference from the Christian account, where the tree in question is the tree of the knowledge of good and evil. Iblis retains his proper name when it is a question of his refusal to bow down to Adam, but when he is the tempter of human beings, then he becomes al-Shaytan, "the Demon."

The revolt of Iblis and the scene in the Garden of Eden as described in the Qur'an has similarities and differences with Christian accounts. In some Christian accounts, the Archangel Michael invites the angels to worship Adam, while that does not appear in Moslem accounts. In Islam, Iblis objected that humans were less and younger than he, thus he and his host were relegated to roaming the earth for his refusal.

In Islam, Allah allows Iblis to tempt human beings until Judgment Day. Iblis is called the "sly whisperer," who whispers evil thoughts into the hearts of men. At the end of time, Iblis will be thrown into the fires of hell, along with his host and the damned. The Qur'an 26:94–95 tells us: "They

---

18. Ibid, 15:30–33.
19. Ibid, 15:30–33.

will be thrown into Hell with those who have gone astray together with the hordes of Iblis."[20]

These verses are reminiscent of Matthew 25:41: "Then shall he say unto them on the left hand, 'Depart from me, you cursed, into everlasting fire, prepared for the devil and his angels.'"[21]

THE SIN OF IBLIS

In general, the Islamic tradition has no hesitation concerning the character of Iblis, the divine curse upon him, and the character of this enemy of Allah and mankind; but there is some disagreement in Islam about the nature of Iblis' sin. Some Moslem traditions say that his sin is pride, while others say it is disobedience. In Islam, the origin of his revolt is generally thought to be his pride. Others say that he was an angel and as such reigned over all the djinns, both on earth and in the lower heavens. It was only after the revolt, this tradition suggests, that Iblis was called by Allah *al-Shaytan al-radjim*.

A third view in Islam has it that the sin of Iblis was jealousy. This position says that the Evil One became jealous of Adam and Eve because of the exalted status they have been given by Allah. In this view, Iblis is jealous of the first humans because they were made of clay, as opposed to the fire and smoke from which the bad angels were made

The question arises, then, of how Iblis could be so blinded by power as to have been confirmed in a perpetual state of disobedience, and how he could justify to himself his poor attitude. The question of why Iblis disobeyed is taken up by a variety of thinkers in the Islamic tradition. In the Sufi tradition it is said that Allah placed Iblis among the unfaithful because he did not submit to the unconditional Will of Allah. The Sufis say he should have preferred the general law, worship Allah alone, to the short-term command to bow down to Adam. Al-Halladj, a tenth-century Persian mystic, scholar and poet, suggests he should have said, "No, I shall worship you alone."[22]

20. Ibid, 26:94–95.

21. Revised Standard Version.

22. Al-Halladj (Abu Mansur al-Hallaj), *Diwan*, translated by Louis Massignon in an edition published in Paris in 1955. Al-Hallaj's poems also have been published by Albin Michel in Paris in 1998. This edition is edited by Sami-Ali. Louis Massignon's *Akhbar Al-Hallaj*, a collection of speeches of Al-Hallaj, was published in Paris by J. Vrin in a 1975 Arabic-French edition; Jacques Keryell's *Garden Given*, is also a treatment of Al-Hallaj. It was published by Saint-Paul Press, in Paris in 1993.

Other Islamic thinkers say that Allah was setting a trap, and Iblis' duty was to evade it by assenting to absolute monotheism. Even more, he preferred to risk incurring Allah's curse to send him to hell, and thus be against Allah, than to follow the edict of Allah to worship him alone. Thus, among the Sufis, Iblis is accorded a certain kind of grandeur, as well as a sympathy for one who was "forced to be disobedient."[23]

Al-Halladj and others, nevertheless, maintain that Iblis' disobedience arose from pride. Indeed, he devoted to the drama of Iblis the very beautiful text, *Ta sin al-azal*, which he composed during his imprisonment in Baghdad in response to the radical Shiite, *Al-Shalmaghan*;[24] but it is significant that among the Sufis, many thinkers advocate a pardoning of Iblis.

IBLIS IN LATER ISLAM

Post-Qur'anic Islamic thinkers, for the most part, concern themselves with the issues discussed above when it comes to the figure of Iblis or Shaytan. Abu Al-Zamakhashari, also called Jar Allah (God's neighbor) was a twelfth-century Moslem scholar. In his *Al-Kashshaf*, (*The Discoverer of Revealed Truths*) Zamakhshari suggests that Iblis is one of the djinns, and that the word angel and djinn refer to the same thing.

This view is contradicted by Al-Baydawi, thirteenth-century Moslem commentator. Baydawi, in his commentary on the Qur'an entitled, *The Secrets of Revelation and Interpretation*, says that Iblis belongs to the angels as far as his hopes were concerned, but that his actions places him among the djinns.[25] Other commentators suggest a class of angels capable of sin, and able to propagate their species as humans and djinns do. When Iblis in the Qur'an declares himself to be "created from fire (*nar*) and not from light (*nur*),"[26] this is because Allah intended that Iblis should utter his own condemnation.

Al-Tabari, a ninth and tenth-century Persian historian and theologian, in his *Annales,* tells us that the djinns are a category of angels who

---

23. Ibid, *Diwan*, p. 93.

24. Ibid, p. 94.

25. Al-Baydawi, *The Secrets of Revelation and Interpretation* (Leipzig, 1846–1848), 1:17. I have also consulted D. S. Margoliouth's *Chrestomathia Beidawiana* (London, 1894), as well as C. Brockelmann's *Geschichte der arabischen Litteratur* (Weimer 1898).

26. Al-Baydawi, *Secrets*, 147.

are charged with the supervision of Paradise (*Al-Djanna*), thus the origins of the name. He agrees that the djinns were made of fire and not light; and Tabari suggests that in the beginning the djinns inhabited the earth, but discord that broke out among them led to bloodshed.[27]

Tabari says that Allah then sent Iblis, who at the time was still called *Azazil* or Al-Harith, accompanied by legions against the fomenters of trouble, who were thrown back into the mountains. Tabari also suggests that the sin of Iblis was his view that he is superior both to Adam and the other angels.

Other post-Qur'anic traditions present Iblis as one of the earthly djinns, who eventually were led captive by avenging angels. The name *Al-Hakam* is also given to Iblis before his fall by some commentators because Allah had appointed him judge over the djinns. In this tradition, he is said to have held this post for 1,000 years, and then he became inflated due to his pride, and eventually invoked disturbances among the bad djinns which also lasted a thousand years. Allah then sent a fire to destroy them, but Iblis took refuge in heaven, this account suggests, and he remained a servant of Allah until the creation of Adam and Eve. This view is held by Ali Al-Masudi (888–957), great Moslem historian and geographer.

A number of other Medieval Islamic commentators tell tales about Iblis. Many of these are conversations involving Isa and Iblis. Ahmad ibn Hanbal, a ninth-century exegete, tells us that Satan asked Isa in Jerusalem, "If you can truly raise people from the dead, then turn this mountain to bread." Satan said, "If you are what you claim to be, jump from this place for the angels will catch you." Isa replied, "Allah ordered me not to put myself to the test, for I do not know whether he will save me or not."[28] This tale is clearly an interpretation of Jesus' temptations in the desert.

Abu Uthman al-Jahiz, a ninth-century collector of hadith, quotes Isa as saying, "The world is Satan's farm, and its people are his plowmen."[29] Similar comments are made by Ahmad ibn Hanbal, who quotes Isa as say-

---

27. Al-Tabari, *The History of Islam* (New York: SUNY Press, 1994) 149. I also have consulted Elma Marin's small section of the *History* of Tabari published in her *The Reign of al-Mutasim*, published in 1951. For more on the life of Tabari, I have consulted Reynold Nicholson's *A Literary History of the Arabs* (London, 1907).

28. Ahmad ibn Hanbal, *Al-Zuhd*, p. 145, number 483.

29. Abu Uithman Amr ibn Bahr, *Al-Bayan wa Al-Tabyin* (Cairo, 1949) 42.

ing, "The greatest sin is love of the world. Women are the ropes of Satan. Wine is the key to every evil."[30]

Almost all Medieval Islamic scholars who describe encounters of Satan with Jesus tell similar tales, where Isa's virtues stand out and Satan's do not. Al-Ghazali, the great twelfth-century Moslem philosopher, suggests that Jesus went out one day and met Shaytan who was carrying honey in one hand and ashes in the other. Jesus said, "Enemy of God, what are you doing with this honey and these ashes?" Shaytan replied, "The honey I put on the lips of backbiters so that they achieve their aim. The ashes I put on the faces of orphans, so that people come to dislike them."[31]

A thirteenth-century Islamic exegete, Sibt ibn Al-Jawzi, conveys the story of Jesus meeting Satan and asking him, "In the name of Allah, the Living and Everlasting, what is it that truly breaks your back?" He answered, "The neighing of horses in the cause of Allah."[32] All the encounters that Medieval Moslem scholars relay about confrontations between Shaytan and Isa have the same characteristics. The virtues of the prophet are shown in their splendor, while the vices of the Evil One are distinctly conveyed. Many of these encounters between Jesus and Iblis are based on narratives from the gospels, but some of them seem to have been created by the interpreter.

THE NATURE OF HEAVEN IN ISLAM

Descriptions of Heaven and Hell throughout the Qur'an are full of images and symbols. Often these descriptions give allegorical renderings of Heaven and Hell. Sometime as part of these allegories the Arabic words, *mathal*, which means "allegory," is used within these descriptions. The Qur'an's 13:35, for example, gives an account of Heaven: "The likeness of Paradise promised the pious and devout of a garden with streams of rippling water, everlasting fruits and shade. This is the recompense of those who keep away from evil; but the recompense of those who deny the truth is Hell."[33]

---

30. Hanbal, *Kitab al-Wara*. Edited by Muhammed Zaghlul. (Beirut: Dar Al-Kitab al Arabi, 1988) 78.

31. Al-Ghazali, *Ihya Ulum al-Din*. (Cairo: Mustafa al-Babi al-Halabi, 1939) 49.

32. Ibn Al-Jawzi, *Al-Adhkiya*. Edited by Usama Al-Rifa. (Damascus: Maktabat Al-Ghazali, 1976) 15.

33. Qur'an 13:35 (author's translation).

A similar description can be seen at 47:15: "The semblance of Paradise promised the pious and devout a garden with streams of water that will not go bad, and rivers of milk whose taste will not undergo a change, and rivers of wine delectable to drinkers, and streams of purified honey, and fruits of every kind in them, and forgiveness of their Lord."[34]

This description is opposed to that of Hell, which is described in the following *ayats* (verses) of sura 47. "Are these like those who will live forever in the Fire, and will be given boiling water to drink which will cut their innards to shreds."[35]

One of the interesting things about these passages is how they are related to people living in a desert. The passages about Paradise promise water and shade for believers, while the lines about Hell promise only more heat. When the Qur'an speaks of Heaven it is always as if it is a garden, when it talks about Hell it is always about intense, everlasting pain.

The Qur'an tells us that the nature of Heaven and Hell is beyond our earthly capacity to understand. The Qur'an 32:17 informs us, "No soul knows what peace and joy lie hidden from them as reward for what they have done."[36] Heaven is most often referred to in the Qur'an as *Al-Jannah*, literally the Garden or Gardens. The Qur'an regularly uses images of Heaven in terms of physical joy or peace: gardens with running water; food without labor; and many sexual partners of the opposite sex. Some exegetes interpret these as metaphorical, along the lines of Hadith that speak of Al-Jannah as a place where no human eye ever has seen nor human ear heard. Al-Bukhari tells us that Al-Jannah has a palace called *Qasab*, which was built for Muhammed's wife, Khadija. He tells us that in this palace there is no fatigue and no noise. Iblis is also mentioned in the Qur'an under the name Shaytan in several other suras, including 2:36; 3:36; 4:117–120; 5:91; 7:200–201; 8:48; 14:22; 15:27; 16:98–100; 22:52–53; 24:21; 35:6; and 36; 60. Most of these passages reflect themes we have seen when the figure is called Iblis; sura 3:36 refers to Shaytan as "the ostracized"; and 5:91 tells us that Shaytan wished to create enmity among human beings, while 8:48 speaks of Shaytan making the fruit of the tree in the garden "alluring to them."

---

34. Ibid., 47:15.
35. Ibid., 47:16.
36. Qur'an 32:17 (author's translation).

Al-Jannah is discussed in seven major suras of the Qur'an: 7, 10, 16, 21, 37, 41, and 51. The Qur'an 7:32-34, 10:3, and 11:7 tell us that the heavens and the Earth were created in "six spans." Sura 16:3 and 51:47 that the heavens were created with reason by the will of Allah. The Qur'an's 41:11–12 tells us that in the beginning the heavens were "made of smoke," and that Allah "created several skies in two spans." The same sura tells us that Allah placed "lamps in the heavens," presumably a reference to the stars.

In several places where Al-Jannah is discussed in the Qur'an, at 2:24–26, 13:35, and 47:15, for examples, the Arabic word *Mathal* is used to describe Paradise. The word is the Arabic equivalent of "allegory." Thus, the Qur'an seems to imply that our understanding of Al-Jannah is a metaphorical one.

The Qur'an's sura 55 tells us that there are two "High Heavens"—one for humans and one for the Djinns. Sura 55 also suggests that there are two "Lower Heavens"—also one for humans and one for Djinns. Water in the High Heaven flows freely (55:50), while the water in the Lower Heaven needs to be pumped (55:56). The High Heaven has all kinds of fruits (55:52), while the Lower Heaven has a limited variety. The people in the High Heaven are joined willingly by their spouses (55:56), while the dwellers of the Lower Heaven must seek out their spouses.

The Lower Heaven is a prize for those who have escaped from Hell (3:185). The Higher Heaven is reserved for those who believed, led a righteous life, and who had developed their souls sufficiently. Al-Jannah is called the Home of Peace in several places in the Qur'an, including 6:127, 10:25, and 35:34. It is a place without sorrow (35:34). The widths of Heaven and Hell are the entire expanse of Heaven and Hell (57:21 and 3:133).

THE NATURE OF HELL IN ISLAM

The Arabic word for Hell is *Jahannam*, sometimes spelled *djahannam*. It is related to the Hebrew *Gehinnom*, as well as the Greek *Gehenna*. In ancient Hebrew culture, *Gehinnom* was a valley south of Jerusalem that was used as a garbage dump. In pre-Israelite times, the Canaanites practiced child sacrifice in the valley to the god Moloch, burning them in an offering to the deity. Consequently, Gehinnom long had had an association with burning fires and distasteful things.[37]

The Arabic word *Djshannam* denotes the idea of depth. Djahannom is sometimes used as a synonym for "fire" (*nar*). Indeed, the word *Nar* is used 129 times in the Qur'an of which 111 are references to Hell fire.

The Qur'an tells us that Djahannom has seven doors (37:71 and 15:43), leading to a fiery crater. At the lowest level of Djahannam is the Tree of Zaqqum (Immortality) and a cauldron of boiling pitch. The level and degree of punishment is both physical and spiritual.

Jahannam is described somewhat ambiguously in the Qur'an and later Islam. In some accounts, Hell seems to be a fantastic monster that Allah can summon at will. In another description, Jahannam is a crater of concentric circles on the underside of the world that all souls must cross in order to enter Paradise by way of a bridge, as narrow as a razor's edge.

A narrative at Qur'an 98:1-8 tells us about the nature of and residents of Hell in Islam. The text tells us: "The unbelievers among the People of the Book and the pagans shall burn in the fire of Hell. They are the vilest of creatures."[38]

The Qur'an 22:19–23 also tells us what happens to unbelievers:

> Garments of fire have been prepared for nonbelievers. Scalding water shall be poured on their heads, melting their skin and that which is in their belly. They shall be lashed with rods of iron. Whenever they are in their anguish and try to escape, they will be dragged back, and will be told, "Taste the torment of the great fire."[39]

The Qur'an 18:28–30 also describes the torment of unbelievers:

> For the wrong doers We have prepared a fire which will encompass them like the walls of a pavilion. When they cry out for help, they will be showered with water as hot as molten brass, which will burn their faces. Evil shall be their drink, and dismal their resting place.[40]

---

37. For more on the Valley, Ge-Hinnom, see 2 Chronicles 28:3 and 3:6, as well as Jeremiah 32:35. The valley also appears in various prophetic oracles at Jer 7:31 and 19:6, as well as Isaiah 66:24.

38. Qur'an 98:6 (author's translation).

39. Ibid, 22:19–23.

40. Ibid, 18:29.

Qur'an 70:15–16 speaks of "the fire of Hell will pluck out of his being right to the skull." The Qur'an 43:74 also speaks of the torment of Hell, where the text tells us, "The unbelievers shall endure forever the torments of Hell. The punishment will never be lightened, they shall be speechless with despair."[41] The Qur'an 76:1–5 tells us more about Hell. "For the unbelievers We have prepared chains and fetters and a blazing fire," and Qur'an 8:73 tells us that the residents of Hell give comfort to each other.[42]

There is also a tradition in Islam, as we have indicated earlier, that the tree from which Adam and Eve were not to eat is the Tree of Immortality, which is discussed at Qur'an 44:40–49:

> The fruit of the Zaqqum tree shall be the unbelievers' fruit. Like dregs of oil, like scalding water, it will simmer in their bellies. A voice will cry, "Seize him, and drag him into the depths of Hell. Then pour out scalding water over his head saying 'Taste this, illustrious and honorable men. This is the punishment which you have doubted.'"[43]

This tradition of the residents of Hell having denied the torments of Hell while on earth is repeated throughout the Qur'an. Sura 52 speaks of "the fire which you have denied."[44] The Qur'an also suggests that the residents of Hell are made of different stuff than the believers, when it says, "We have created the unbelievers out of base metals." The Qur'an also speaks of a poll tax (*a jiziya*), which can only be paid with the hands of humility; and the Qur'an tells believers to smite the necks and finger tips of non-believers.[45]

A hadith from Al-Tirmidhi tells us that the "awnings of Hell have four thick walls, each wall a distance of forty years. Darimi says that "the entrance to Hell is dominated by 99 dragons over the unbelievers in the grave."[46] Darimi adds, "They constantly bite them and sting them until shall come the hour of resurrection. These dragons are so poisonous that

---

41. Ibid, 43:74.
42. Ibid, 76:4–5 and 8:73.
43. Ibid, 44:43–49.
44. Ibid, 52:14.
45. Ibid.
46. The edition of Tirmidhi's Hadith I have used in this chapter is that of M. Hussain, *Shamail Tirmidhi* (London: Kazi, 1994) 99.

if one of them exhales on the Earth, no grass will grow."[47] The ninth-century Sunni commentator, Al-Tirmidhi made a similar remark, but the number of dragons was 70.[48]

Al-Muwatta, an early collector of hadith, relates a conversation of Abu Hurayra, seventh-century Sunni exegete, in which the scholars asks, "Do you think that Hell is red like this fire of yours? It is blacker than tar."[49]

Other passages in the Qur'an describe images of Hell. Qur'an 56:52–56 speaks of the "Tree of Zaqqum," what many Moslems believe is the inner circle of Hell. The Qur'an 44:40–49 also writes of the Tree of Zaqqum. It tells us: "The fruit of the Zaqqum tree shall be the unbeliever's fruit."[50]

The Qur'an's 37:62–64 also gives us a description of the inner most portion of Islam's Hell: "Is this better or the Tree of Zaqqum, which We have reserved as punishment for evil-doers? It is the tree that grows at the bottom of Hell."[51]

The Zaqqum is a thorned tree that grows in Jahannam. It is said to have bitter, thorned fruit which the damned are compelled to eat so to intensify their torment. In some post-Qur'anic traditions, the fruit is said to be shaped like devil's heads. The fruit of the Zaqqum Tree is said to be served with boiling water.

If one drop from the Zaqqum Tree were to land on earth, the people of this planet and all the food here would be destroyed. Other food in Hell is described in the Qur'an (18:29; 14:16–17; 38:57–58; and 55:44) that describes the residents of Hell floating in hot, boiling water.

The Qur'an also has a sustained attack on non-believers and what happens to them in Hell. Passages at 47:4; 5:51; 5:64; and 9:73 all speak of non-believers going to Hell. The Qur'an 9:73 is a representative passage:

---

47. Ibid., 100.

48. Ibid., 101.

49. The edition of Abu Hrurayra I have used in this chapter is that of W. A. Graham, *Divine Word and Prophetic Word in Early Islam* (Berlin: de Gruyter, 1977). I have also consulted a number of secondary sources of Hurayra, including: Eerik Dickinson, *The Development of Early Sunnite Hadith Criticism* (Leiden: Brill, 2001); Ibn 'Abd Al-Salam, *The Belief of the People of Truth* (London: ISCA, 1999); F. E. Peters, *Judaism, Christianity, and Islam: The Classical Texts of Their Interpretation*, vol. 3 (Princeton: Princeton University Press, 1990); and G. R. Hawting, *Approaches to the Qur'an* (London: Routledge, 1993).

50. Qur'an, 56:52–56 and 44:40–49 (author's translation).

51. Qur'an 37:62–64 (author's translation).

"Make war on the un-believers and hypocrites, and deal vigorously with them. Hell shall be their home, and evil fate."[52]

The Qur'an 9:5 goes even farther on how to treat non-believers: "When the sacred months have passed, kill the non-believers wherever you find them, and take them captive, and besiege them and prepare for ambush. But if they repent and establish their worship, and pay what is due, then leave them free."[53]

The Qur'an 5:64 talks specifically about Jews, where it tells us, "The Jews say God's hand is chained. May their own hands be chained. May they be cursed for what they say."[54] The Qur'an 5:51 suggests that Moslems should not make friends with Jews or Christians. The text tells us: "Believers, take neither Jews nor Christians for your friends. They are friends with one another. Whoever of you seek friendship shall become one of their number. Allah does not guide the wrong-doers."[55]

The Qur'an 31:3 also speaks of the treatment of non-believers in Hell:

> Burn the non-believers in a blazing fire. Further, make him march in a chain, where the length is 70 cubits. This was he who would not believe in Allah the Most High and would not encourage the feeding of the indignant. So he has no friends here today, nor has he any food, except the corruption from the washing of wounds.[56]

The Qur'an also makes several references to a poll tax upon the entrance of Hell. This tax is known as *Jiziyah* and can be seen at 9:29, for example. Finally, the Qur'an tells us that Allah sometimes uses thunderbolts in punishing the inhabitants of Hell.

HELL IN THE QUR'AN

There are hundreds of references to Hell in the Qur'an. The Qur'an 3:12 and 13:18 call Hell a wretched place, where one neither lives nor dies (14:17). A perpetual fire is kindled there by Allah (104:6–9). Among the chief occupants of Hell are polytheist and wrong-doers (3:192). Hell can

---

52. Ibid., 9:73.
53. Ibid., 9:5.
54. Ibid., 5:64.
55. Ibid., 5:51.
56. Ibid., 31:37.

never be filled (50:30), and it has enormous depth (15:43–44). There are degrees or ranks in Hell (6:132).

The Qur'an also tells us that the food in Hell are men and stones (66:6); it also suggests that when Hell sees particular people from afar, they will hear Hell raging (25:12). The fire of Hell will be refueled on the Day of Resurrection (81:12–13). The Qur'an tells us that Shaytan beckons people to the penalty of blazing fire (35:6). Anyone who calls people to a false belief system is a grave offense (40:41); and the worst residents of Hell will lose their families and all companionship on the Day of Resurrection.

The Qur'an also informs us that when the occupants of Hell eat the food there they will choke because of its foulness (73:12–13). The Qur'an also makes several references to what the people in Hell eat and drink. This passage from sura 14 is representative of these passages: "Before him is Hell, and he will get putrid liquid to drink. He will sip it, but he will not be able to gulp it down. Death will crowd in upon him from every side, but die he will not. A terrible torment trails him."[57]

The intensity of the suffering of people in Hell is described at various places in the Qur'an. Among these are at 3:91; 5:36; 70:11–16; and 4:145.

The Qur'an 27:90 tells us that evil-doers will be thrown face-first into Hell. The Qur'an's 23:104 informs us that the faces on the people in Hell will be burned into a permanent grin. Several references to the residents of Hell having blackened faces can be found in the Qur'an 3:106 and 10:27, for examples.

The Qur'an also makes several references to the use of chains in Hell (76:4; 73:12–13; 34:33; 69:30–32; and 40:71). The Qur'an also suggests several times that the people in Hell will come to realize their wrong-doings (67:10; 23:106–108; and 32:12–14), but this will be to no avail.

In short, the image of Hell in Islam, particularly in the Qur'an is even more bleak than what we find in Christianity. The residents of Jahannam are in constant pain. They have no sense of hope, and they will never be relieved of their suffering. The only companionship for the residents of Hell will be the existence of other non-believers. They cannot comfort each other, nor can they help themselves.

57. Ibid., 14:16–17.

HELL IN POST-QUR'ANIC ISLAM

Many of the principal collectors and writers of Hadith have made observations about Djahannam. Al-Bukhari, the most known of all Sunni scholars, tells us that Hell is affected by the seasons:

> In very hot weather, you must delay the Zuhr (a ritual prayer), until it becomes a bit cooler because of the severity of the heat is from the raging Hell-fire. The Hell-fire complained to the Lord saying, "My parts are destroying each other." So Allah allowed it to take two breathes, one in winter and the other in summer. The breath in the summer is at the time you feel the most heat, and the breath in winter is when you feel the most cold.[58]

Bukhari also tells this story about Hell:

> A slave of Allah may utter a word which pleases Allah without giving it much importance, and because of that Allah will raise him to degrees of reward; but a slave of Allah may utter a careless word which displeases Allah without thinking of its gravity and because of that he will be thrown into Hell-Fire.[59]

Al-Djahiz (776–868), who some call the father of Islamic Existentialism, did the fullest treatment of fire and Hell-fire among post-Qur'anic thinkers. Al-Djahiz spoke of both religious and non-religious fires. Included among the varieties of fires mentioned by Djahiz is one he calls "*Nar al-ihtiyal*," the "fire of guile" or "the trickster's fire." Djahiz suggests that this fire is used by Iblis in his temptations of humans.

Al-Tirmidhi tells a hadith where Allah sends Gabriel (Jibril) to Paradise and says, "Take a look at it, see what I have prepared for its inhabitants." When he returns, he tells Allah that all will want to enter it. Then Allah sent Gabriel to Hell to look around. Gabriel found that Hell was in layers, one above the other. When Gabriel returns to Allah, he tells Him that no one will enter it. So Allah orders that Hell shall be encompassed by lusts. Then Allah sends Gabriel back to Hell. The angel returns saying, "No one will ever escape from it."[60]

---

58. The edition of Al-Bukhari's hadith I have used in this chapter, is that of Muhammed ibn Ishmail Bukhari, *Imam Bukhari's Book of Muslim Morals and Manners* (London: Al-Saadawi Publications, 1997) 34.

59. Ibid., 36.

60. *Forty Hadith Quidsi* (Aldahieh, Kuwait: Revival of Islamic Heritage Society, 1999.) Hadith number 38.

Another question for debate among post-Qur'anic commentators is how many levels of Hell there are, as well as what are their natures. Abu Jafar al Khazin (900–971) astronomer, mathematician, and philosopher, suggests that Hell is a series of concentric circles, of increasing depth. He says that the higher regions are reserved for Moslems who have committed "grave sins" of which they have not repented and whom Allah has decided to punish for a while.

Ibn Arabi, thirteenth-century Spanish scholar, who is known as Muhyi id-Din (the reviver of religion) also developed a description of the geography of Hell. Asin Palacios in 1943 reproduced a diagram of Arabi's circles of Hell. Al-Baghawi, a twelfth-century Sunni scholar took a much more literal reading of the nature of Hell, perhaps the most traditional and uncritical view of Hell in all of Islamic literature. He describes Hell as a fantastic animal, which he describes with great hyperbole. He says that at the resurrection Hell will be drawn along by 70,000 angels, and that the width between these guardian angels is a distance of a seventy year march. This kind of description of Hell is repeated in Al-Sharani's *Mukhtasar*, where the mouth of the animal is the mouth of Hell.[61]

Al-Tirmidhi was asked about what things would allow a believer to enter Paradise. He answered, "Be careful about one's obligations to Allah and one's good behavior. Then Timidhi was asked, "What are the things which will lead a person to Hell?" His answer was "His mouth and his genitals."[62]

Some post-Qur'anic Islamic traditions describe, in sometimes minute detail, the various levels of Hell. One tradition says there are seven, and their names are: Jaheem, Jahanam, Sa'ir, Ladha, Hawiyah, and Hutama. The most severe level is said to be Hutama, where Islamic hypocrites pretend to believe while inwardly deny the faith. Other Moslem accounts say that Hutama is for liars and slanderers. Sa'ir is a circle of Hell preserved for non-Muslims. Saqar is a division of Hell which is reserved for sorcerers and diviners who have blackened skin. Whoever enters Saqar will be completely burnt. Ladha is the level of Hell reserved for Jews, while Hawiyah is the compartment for Christians. The shallowest level of the Islamic Hell is Jaheem, or Jaheim. It is the section of Hell reserved for

---

61. Al-Djahiz, "The Examination of Trade," in *Historians Arab* (1946) 10–11.

62. This comment comes from a rare manuscript owned by Bouwman Book Shop in London. It is Ms. Arab 146. It is a rare, eighteenth-century Sufi manuscript.

Moslems who ignore Allah's commands. Jahanam is a deeper circle of Islamic Hell, reserved for idol worshippers.

In one hadith from Sahih Bukhari narrated by Abdullah ibn Abbas, he tells us:

> Then I saw the Hell fire, and I have never before seen such a horrible sight as this. And I saw that the majority of inhabitants were women. The people asked, "Oh Allah, what is the reason for this?" He replied, "because of their ungratefulness." Then the people asked, "Do you disbelieve in Allah?" He replied, "They are not thankful to their husbands and are grateful for the favors done to them. Even if you do good to one of them all your life, when she sees some harshness from you, she will say, "I have never seen any good from you."[63]

Bukhari suggests that most of the inhabitants of Hell will be women, and the principal reason shall be their ungratefulness.

In the next chapter, which is the penultimate chapter of this study, we shall explore and discuss one final New Testament image in the Islamic tradition—the idea of the Djaal, the Arabic word for the Anti-Christ. As we have seen in previous chapters, much of this material is familiar, while at the same time there are some fundamental differences from the traditional Christian idea of the Anti-Christ.[64]

CONCLUSIONS

In this chapter, we have attempted to describe and discuss the various Islamic views on Shaytan (Satan), also called Iblis, as well as various Islamic perspectives on Jahannam, the Arabic word for Hell. In the opening section of this chapter, we have explored the nature of, as well as the role played, by Iblis in the Qur'an. As we have seen, one of the principal questions about the nature of Iblis is whether he is fallen angel or the ruler of the Djinns, the evil spirits in Islam.

---

63. Sahih Bukhari, *Hadith* #4:464.

64. For more on the figure of Iblis in Islam, see Jeffry Burton Russell, *Lucifer: The Devil in the Middle Ages* (Ithaca: Cornell University Press, 1986); Muhammed Ali Asadi, *Islam and Christianity: Conflict or Conciliation?* (London: Writers Club Press, 2002); William Richard Wood Stephens, *Christianity and Islam: Four Lectures* (London: Adamant Media Corporation, 2005); and Isya Joseph, *Devil Worship: The Sacred Books and Traditions of the Yezidiz* (London: Kessinger, 1997).

In a second section of this chapter, we have explored the role that Shaytan is said to have played in regard to the creation story, as well as his role in the end of time. We have discussed at length the Islamic view that Iblis refused to bow down to Adam, and we also pointed out in the following section, that there is some disagreement in Islam about whether the sin of Iblis was pride, disobedience, or jealousy.

As we have seen, the disagreements over Iblis' sin and his nature continued in much post-Qur'anic theological debate and commentary. Some writers of hadith think Iblis is an angel, while others maintain he is the leader of the Djinns. We also have shown that much of post-Qur'anic debate about Iblis and Jahanam has been about the nature of Hell and its occupants. Indeed, post-Qur'anic exegetes in Islam often have gone to extraordinary lengths to describe Hell and its residents. More than anything else, one fundamental difference between Islam and Christianity is that Islam had divided Hell into circles and degrees of sins long before Dante Alighieri.

10

The Anti-Christ in Islamic Thought

Given the connections, especially the shared apocalyptic mentality, between Islam and both Judaism and Christianity, it is not surprising to find an Anti-Christ-like figure called the *Dajjal* in the new monotheistic religion that came out of the Arabian desert in the seventh century.

—Bernard McGinn, *Anti-Christ*

Also to while away the time of waiting, I explored a little island named Cassel, which belonged to King Mihrage, and which was supposed to be inhabited by a spirit named Dajjal. Indeed, the sailors assured me that often at night the playing of timbals could be heard upon it.

—*The Arabian Night*, Sinbad's First Voyage

He who recites three verses at the beginning of the Al-Kahf will be protected from the trial of Djaal.

—Al-Tirmidhi

INTRODUCTION

THE NAME FOR THE Anti-Christ in Islam is the *Dajjal*. The word comes from the Arabic verb "to deceive," "to cheat," or "to smear with tar." The word Dajjal does not appear in the *Qur'an*. But it is to be found in all the major collections of *hadith*.

Zeki Saritoprak, a contemporary American scholar, gives a good introduction to the figure of al-Dajjal:

There are many figures that represent evil in the Islamic tradition. Among them are Satan, Iblis, Taghut, Pharaoh, and Ad-Dajjal. However, the only figure with eschatological significance is

Ad-Dajjal. Ad-Dajjal occupies an important place in the body of *Hadith* and manuals of Islamic theology. Very few English words, however, have been written on the subject.[1]

Saritoprak continues his analysis:

His full name is Al-Masih Ad-Dajjal, literally the pseudo-messiah or the opposite of Al-Misih (Isa, or Jesus the messiah or true messiah.) The term Al-Dajjal originally comes from the Syriac language and is used in Arabic. According to some Arabic lexicons, al-Misih means the one who has no eyebrows and a single eye on one side of his face. This characteristic is found in all descriptions of Ad-Dajjal, the pseudo-messiah.[2]

Our principal goal in this chapter is to describe and discuss these major hadith on the figure of Dajjal. In Islam, there are three different aspects to Dijjal. The first is Dajjal, the individual. The second is Dajjal as a world-wide social and cultural phenomenon. The third aspect of Dajjal is as an unseen force, an agent of destruction at the end of the world. Most Islamic scholars believe that Dajjal will not appear until his support system is in place throughout the world.

AD-DAJJAL IN THE QUR'AN

Although the figure of Ad-Dajjal does not explicitly appear in the Qur'an, scholars have debated for centuries whether or not there are any indirect references to him. Zeki Saritoprak points to this debate:

Strictly speaking, the word Ad-Dajjal does not appear in the Qur'an. However, some scholars believe that he is mentioned by character traits. The Qur'anic verses that mention Jesus indirectly make reference to Ad-Dajjal, the Antichrist.[3]

Saritoprak goes on to cite a number of *ayats* from the Qur'an, where the Antichrist may be mentioned indirectly. Among these are 96:6, 2:56–57, 4:51, 60:76, 5:36, and 16:36. The Qur'an's 96:4–7 tells us: "Who taught

---

1. Zeki Saritoprak, "The Legend of Al-Dajjal (Antichrist): The Personification of Evil in the Islamic Tradition," *The Muslim World* 93 (2003) 291 [291–307].

2. Ibid.

3. Ibid., 292.

man by the pen, taught man what he did not know? And yet, man is rebellious, for he thinks he is sufficient in himself."[4]

Saritoprak comments on the passage when he writes: "Here 'man' refers to Ad-Dajjal, the Antichrist of the Muslim world who will 'attack the people of prayer and attack mosques rebelliously."[5]

Saritoprak goes on to cite the Qur'an's 17:4 as another indirect mention of the Antichrist. The text speaks of someone who will "work corruption on the earth twice and will become great tyrants."[6] Modern Egyptian scholar Muhammed Awad believes that this *ayat* refers to the emergence of the Antichrist.[7] A number of the verses in the Qur'an that deal with the struggles of Moses against the Pharaoh are also cited as indirect references to the Antichrist, Al Dajjal. Chief among these are 2:56–57, 4:51, 5:36, 16:36, 39:37, and 60:76. The Qur'an's 16:36 serves an illustrative example. The text tells us:

> To every community We have sent an apostle, saying, "Worship God and keep away from all other deities. Thus some were guided by God and ruin was justified for some. Travel over the earth and see what befell those who accused the apostles of lies.[8]

Whenever the Qur'an speaks of lies, lairs, deceivers, and persuaders, these passages traditionally have often been seen as indirect references to Ad-Dajjal.

PROTECTION FROM THE DAJJAL

The prophet Mohammed told his followers to recite the first and last ten verses of sura Al-Kahf ("the Cave" in the *Qur'an*, as protection from the Dajjal). Mohammed Marmaduke Pickthall offers this translation of the opening ten verses of The Cave, Surah 18:

1.   Praise be Allah Who hath revealed the Scripture until His slave, and hath not placed therein any crookedness.

4. Ibid.

5. Ibid.

6. Ibid.

7. Muhammed Awad, *Masih al-dalalah Ua' al-Fitnah fi Akhir al-Zamajn* (Cairo, 1989) 53.

8. Qur'an 16:36 (author's translation).

2. But hath made it straight, to give warning of strong punishment from Him, and to bring unto the believers who do good words the news that theirs will be fair reward.

3. Wherein they will abide forever.

4. And to warn those who say "Allah has chosen a son."

5. A thing wherein they have no knowledge, nor had their fathers, Dreadful is the words that come out of their mouths. They speak naught a lie.

6. Yet it may be, if they believe not in this statement, that thou (Mohammed) will torment thy soul with grief over the footsteps.

7. Lo! We have placed all that is on their earth as an ornament thereof that We may try them, "Which is best in conduct?"

8. And lo! We shall make all that is thereon a barren mound.

9. Or deem though that the People of the Cave and the Inscription are a wonder among our portents.

10. When the young man fled for refuge to the Cave and said, "Our Lord! Give us mercy from Thy presence, and shape for us right conduct in our plight.[9]

The closing ten verses of Surah 18 are rendered this way by Pickthall:

101. Those whose eyes were hoodwinked from My reminder and could not bear to listen.

102. Do the disbelievers reckon that they can choose My bondmen as protecting friends beside Me? Lo! We have prepared hell as a welcome for the disbelievers.

103. Shall We inform you who will be the greatest losers by their work?

---

9. Qur'an 18:1–10, translated by Mohammed Marmaduke Pickthall. (New York: Kazi, 1996.) Unless otherwise stated, all other Arabic translations are those of the author. For primary sources in this chapter, I have used notes 2 through 10. For secondary sources, I have used the following: Yahya ibn Sharaf, *Forty Ahadith* (London: Islamic Text Society, 1997); Bernard McGinn, *Anti-Christ*, 111–13; the article by A. Abel on the Dajjal in *The Encyclopedia of Islam* (Leiden: Brill, 1965) 2:76–77; David J. Halparin, "The Ibn Sayyad Tradition and the Legend of the Al-Dajjal," *Journal of the American Oriental Society* 96 (1976) 213–25; Gustave E. Von Grunebaum, *Medieval Islam* (Chicago: University of Chicago Press, 1953); and Richard Martin, *Islam: A Cultural Perspective* (Englewood Cliffs: Prentice Hall, 1982).

104.   Those whose effort goes astray in the life of the world, and yet they reckon that they do good work.

105.   Those are they who believe in the revelations of their Lord and in the meeting with Him. Therefore, their work are vain, and on the Day of Resurrection, We assign no weight to them.

106.   That is their reward: hell, because they disbelieved, and made a Jest of Our revelations and Our messages.

107.   Lo! Those who believe and do good works, theirs are the Gardens of Paradise for welcome.

108.   Wherein they will abide, with no desire to be removed from there.

109.   Say, "Though the sea became ink for the Words of my Lord. Verily the sea would be used up before the words of my Lord were exhausted, even though We brought the like thereof to help."

110.   Say, "I am only a mortal like you. My Lord inspires me that your God is only One God. And whoever hopes for a meeting with his Lord, let him do righteous work, and make none sharer of the worship due unto his Lord."[10]

In the opening ten verses of the Cave, Mohammed makes a distinction between those who go straight, and those who are crooked. In the closing ten verses, Mohammed points out that Allah has prepared hell for disbelievers. Indeed, their works will be in vain on the Day of Resurrection. These words were clearly designed as a warning against those who choose to follow Dajjal. Al-Tirmidhi agrees with this tradition of reading the Cave as protection from the Dajjal: "Allah's messenger said, 'He who recites three verses at the beginning of the Al-Kahf will be protected from the trial of Dajjal.'"[11]

10. Qur'an 18:101–110. I have used a number of translations of the *Qur'an* for this chapter, including Yusef Ali, *The Koran* (Washington: American International Printing, 1946); A. J. Arberry, *The Koran Interpreted* (London: Allen and Unwin, 1955); Richard Bell, *The Qur'an Translated with a Critical Rearrangement of the Surahs* 2 volumes (Edinburgh: T. & T. Clark, 1937–1939); and T. B. Irving, *The Qur'an* (Brattleboro, VT: Amana, 1985).

11. John O'Kane, *The Concept of Sainthood in Early Islamic Mysticism: Two Works by Hakim Al-Tirmidhi* (London: Routledge, 1996) 178.

THE NATURE AND END OF DAJJAL

The *Oxford Dictionary of Islam*, edited by John Esposito, gives this account of the *Djaal*:

> Known as Dajjal (the deceiver). Supposed to appear during the age of injustice preceding the end of the world, causing corruption and oppression to sweep over the earth for a period of either forty days or forty years. Appearance is one of the sure signs of the last days. Will deceive many by false teachings and miracles, bringing with him food and water to tempt those who have been suffering. Not mentioned in the Qur'an, but prominent in hadith and later Islamic literature.[12]

Esposito points to a number of features in the Islamic view of Anti-Christ. He will appear at the end of time; he will perform miracles and wonders to convert people to his cause; he will reign over the earth for a specified period of time; and, he will bring food and water to tempt people to follow him. All of these elements, as we shall see in this chapter, contribute to a very complex view of the Islam Anti-Christ—the Dajjal.

In Islamic tradition, the Dajjal will come along with the appearance of the Imam Mahdi (the messiah), who will rally the faithful to oppose Dajjal. Eventually, Isa (the Arabic name for Jesus) will return from heaven and slay the Dajjal. Many Moslem interpreters say this will occur near the Gate of Ludd (the ancient city of Lydda). The defeat of Dajjal and his followers will be followed by a Golden Age for Islam, in which there are only true believers and Jews and Christians have converted to Islam. This scene is very similar to the Christian apocalyptic vision in which Jesus returns to earth and defeats the Anti-Christ and his followers. In the meantime, no one is advised to combat Dajjal because his killing will be accomplished by Jesus.

Moslem literature tells of false messiahs (*mesihu 'd-dajjal*), who will overrun the earth for forty days and leave only Mecca and Medina unharmed. After this reign of forty days or forty years, he will be destroyed by the Mahdi, Jesus. In the *Hadith* Dajjal is described as a plump, one-eyed man, with a ruddy face, and the letters KFR on his forehead. These letters are the root of the Arabic word for "unbelief."

---

12. "Anti-Christ," in *The Oxford Dictionary of Islam*, edited by John L. Esposito (Oxford: Oxford University Press, 2003) 1:21–22.

Tradition suggests that Dajjal will arrive during a time of tribulation. He will work false miracles, and most people will be deceived by him. Tradition also suggests that Dajjal will appear in the East, possibly near Khorasan, or in the West, somewhere in the East Indies. This Eastern view suggests the Dajjal lives on an island, from which sounds of dancing and the playing of timbals can be heard. An alternative Islamic version is possibly connected to the Greek myth of Prometheus. In this version of the tale, Dajjal is bound to a rock on an island in the sea, and is fed by demons. Some Moslem traditions suggest that Dajjal is of enormous size, and travels at the speed of the clouds. They suggest that the distance between Dajjal's ears is 40 arms spans. The deepest parts of the sea reach up to his ankles.[13]

This Eastern view is proposed by Tamim Al-Dari, an early Christian convert to Islam. McGinn talks about him "meeting the Dajjal chained to a monastery on an island in the sea, and the monster predicted he would soon be loosed upon the earth."[14]

Other Moslem traditions on the Dajjal tell us that "The time between the great war and the conquest of the city of Constantinople will be six years, and the Dajjal will come forth in the seventh." Mu'adh ibn Jabal, a young boy in Medina when Mohammed began his teachings, concurs: "The prophet said, 'The greatest war, the conquest of Constantinople, and the coming forth of the Dajjal will take place within a period of seven months.'"[15]

These many references to a relationship between the Dajjal and the conquering of the city of Constantinople by Moslem warriors are most likely related to Islamic attempts to conquer the city, sieges between 673 and 678, and 717 and 718.

Hudhayfah ibn al-Yaman, a seventh-century companion of Mohammed, and one of the earliest converts to Islam, tells us that:

> The Dajjal will come accompanied by a river of fire. He who falls into this fire will certainly receive his reward, and have his load taken off him, but he who falls into this river will have his load retained and his reward taken off him. I then asked, "What will come next?" He said, "The last hour will come."[16]

13. Ahmad Thomson, *Dajjal, the Anti-Christ* (London: Ta-Ha Publishers, 1997) 17.

14. Bernard McGinn, *Anti-Christ*, 112.

15. Ibid.

16. N. K. Singh, *The Prophet Mohammed and his Companions* (Delhi: Global Vision, 1996) 137.

Anas ibn Malik, another well known eighth-century *sahabi* (companion) of the prophet Mohammed, tells us that the Dajjal will be followed by 70,000 Jews of Isfahan wearing Persian shawls.[17]

Amr ibn al-A'as, a contemporary of Mohammed's and an Arab military commander who led the forces to conquer Egypt, writes of signs of the coming of the Dajjal:

> I committed to memory a hadith from Allah's apostle Mohammed, and I did not forget it after Allah's apostle Mohammed said, "The first sign (out of the signs of the appearance of Dajjal) would be the appearance of the sun from the West. The appearance of the beast before the people at noontime, and whichever happens first, the other will occur immediately.[18]

But a tradition from Abu Hairara, the seventh-century narrator of hadith most often quoted by Sunni Moslems contradicts this account: "Allah's messenger Mohammed said, 'Dajjal will come from the Eastern side with the intention of attacking Medina until he will get down behind Uhud. Then the angels will turn his face toward Syria and there he will perish.'"[19]

Uhud was a seventh-century city near Medina. It was the site of a famous battle on March 23, 625 between armies from Mecca and Medina. Tradition has it that the battle was won by the Meccans, though Walt W. Montgomery's *Mohammed at Medina* came to the opposite conclusion.

The Dajjal is often associated with Medina in various Moslem traditions. A hadith from Bukhari and narrated by Abu Said, a fourteenth-century ruler of the state of Ilkhanate, tells us:

> One day Allah's apostle Mohammed narrated to us a long story about Ad-Dajjal and among the things he narrated to us was "Dajjal will come, and he will be forbidden to enter the mountain pass of Medina. He will encamp in one of the salt areas neighboring Medina, and there will appear to him a man who will be the best or one of the best of the people. He will say, 'I testify that you are Ad-Dajjal whose story Allah's apostle has told us. Ad Dajjal will say to his audience, 'Look if I kill this man and then give him life, will you have any doubt about my claim?' They will reply, 'No.'

17. Eerik Dickenson, *The Development of Early Sunnite Hadith Criticism* (London: Brill, 2001) 97.

18. Thomson, *Dajjal, the Anti-Christ*, 21.

19. Ibid.

Then Ad Dajjal will kill that man and then will make him alive. The man will say, 'Now I recognize you more than ever!' Ad-Dajjal will then try to kill him again, but he will not be given the power to do so."[20]

Other hadith of Bukhari also refer to this tradition. "Allah's apostle Mohammed said, 'There are angels at the mountain passes of Medina, so that neither plague nor Ad-Dajjal can enter it.'" And: "The prophet Mohammed said, 'Ad-Dajjal will come and encamp at a place close to Medina. Then Medina will shake three times, and then every *kafir* (disbeliever) and hypocrite will go out of Medina towards him.'"[21]

These stories are most likely related to two traditions from Christianity. First, that the Anti-Christ will have power enough to bring forth miracles and wonders. And second, at the end of time, the Anti-Christ will be the ruler of liars, hypocrites, and non-believers.

DAJJAL WITH ONE EYE

Among Islamic hadith there are many accounts that Dajjal has only one eye. Bukhari, narrated by Abdullah ibn Umar, a prominent seventh-century authority in hadith and the law, tells us:

Allah's apostle Mohammed stood up amongst the people and then praised and glorified Allah as He deserved and then He mentioned Ad-Dajjal and said, "I warn you of him, and there was no prophet but warned his followers of him; but I will tell you something about him which no prophet has told his followers. "Ad-Dajjal has one eye, while Allah does not."[22]

Ibn Umar, one of the earliest of Islamic scholars, tells us that "Allah is not one eyed, while Maseeh ad-Djaal is blind in his right eye. If you still have any doubts about him [the Djaal], then remember your Sustainer is not one eyed."[23] Abu Dawood agrees that the "Djaal will be blind in the right eye."[24]

---

20. Charles F. Horne, *The Sacred Books and Early Literature of the East: Medieval Arabic, Moorish and Turkish* (London: Kessinger, 1997) 131.

21. Ibid., 132.

22. Thomson, *Dajjal, the Anti-Christ*, 27.

23. Ibn Umar, *Figh-us-Sunnah*, 2:135.

24. Ibid, 136.

In another hadith by Bukhari, narrated by Abdullah ibn Umar, they repeat the same claim, "While Al-Masih Ad-Dajjal is blind in the right eye, and his eye looks like a protruding grape."[25] This same tradition is repeated in hadith by Abu Hairara and ibn 'Abbas. It can also be found in another hadith of Bukhari, narrated by Malik ibn Anas, one of the most highly respected scholars of *fiqh*, the study of Islamic law. Malik ibn Anas' traditional dates are 715–796. He tells us: "The Prophet Mohammed said, 'No prophet was sent but that he warned His followers against the one-eyed liar (Ad-Dajjal). Beware! He is blind in one eye, and your Lord is not so. And there will be written between his eyes the word *kafir*."[26]

This tradition of the Dajjal being one-eyed is also found in a hadith by Ubadah ibn Saamit who writes, "If you still have any doubts regarding him (Dajjal) then remember your Sustainer is not one-eyed." A hadith narrated by Hadhrat Huzaifah confirms this view of the one-eyed Dajjal. He tells us: "Dajjal will be blind in his right eye. He will have thick hair on his body and he will also have Paradise and Hell with him. Though his Paradise will appear as *Jannah* (Heaven), in reality it will be Hell, and likewise, though his Hell will appear like Jahannam, in reality it will be Paradise."[27]

It is not entirely clear how this tradition that Dajjal is blind in one eye arose, but not all Moslem scholars see it as physical blindness. One contrary view says this:

> The word "one-eyed" is not to be taken literally. Allah says in the holy *Qur'an* "Whoever is blind in this world will be blind in the hereafter." (17.72) Blindness here evidently means spiritual blindness. Thus, the word under discussion will mean that Dajjal will have no spiritual sight, although his worldly sight will be very sharp; and along with it, he will discover such subtle methods resulting in such wonderful performances, that he will almost appear as one claiming Divinity. But he shall have no spiritual vision whatsoever, as is the case of people of America and Europe today, who have carried the physical side of life to perfection.[28]

---

25. Ibid., 25.

26. O'Kane, 179.

27. Hadhrat Huzaifah, in *Al-Nawawi's Forty Hadith* edited by Yahya ibn Sharaf-al-Nawawi and Ezzeddin Ibrahim (London: Islamic Text Society, 1997) 121.

28. Ibid., 180.

Whether or not the blindness of Dajjal is physical or spiritual is not clear; but what is clear is those who believe it refers to spiritual blindness also believe that the Dajjal will be able to execute "wonderful performances" in the final days. Another thing that is clear is that Dajjal is associated with Gog and Magog in some Islamic traditions.

The *Qur'an* refers to Gog and Magog in two places. The first reference is at 18:94, the second at 21:96. We will look at these two sections of the *Qur'an*, and their relationship to the legend of Dajjal, in the next section of this chapter.

DAJJAL, GOG AND MAGOG

The *Qur'an* refers to Gog and Magog (*Yajooj and Majooj*) twice. The first comes near the end of the Cave, Surah 18. Rashad Khalifa's translation of 18:93–99 goes like this:

> 18.93 When he reached the valley between two palisades, he found people whose language was barely understandable.
>
> 18.94 They said, "Dhul-Qarnain, Gog and Magog are corruptors of the Earth. Can we pay you to erect a barrier between us and them?"
>
> 18.95 He said, "My Lord has given me great bounties. If you cooperate with me, I will build a dam between you and them."
>
> 18.96 "Bring me masses of iron." Once he filled the gap between the two Palisades, he said, "Blow! Once it is hot, help me pour tar on top of it."
>
> 18.97 Thus, they could not climb it, nor could they bore holes in it.
>
> 18.98 He said, "This is mercy from my Lord. When the prophecy of my Lord comes to pass, He will cause the dam to crumble. The prophecy of my Lord is truth."
>
> 18.99 At that time, we will let them invade with one another, then the horn will be blown and we will summon them all together.[29]

Dhul Qarnain, ("the one with two horns") is to be identified with the beasts in Daniel and Revelation. It also refers to the Dajjal, the Moslem version of the Anti-Christ. In Islam, it is the Dajjal that builds the wall. Dajjal constructed the wall out of iron, and then poured molten cop-

---

29. Thomson, *Dajjal, the Anti-Christ*, 58.

per over it, making it difficult to climb or dig under it. Various Islamic scholars locate this wall in various places. Some say it is in the Caucasus Mountains, at Dariel Pass. One Moslem scholar, mufti Ebrahim Desai, the Dear Abby of the Moslem world, calls it "the land of ice."[30]

This same tradition suggests that Gog and Magog attempt every evening to break through the wall, but when it gets late they say, "it's late, we'll finish tomorrow." The next day, when they wake up, they see that all the work they had done the night before had become undone while they slept. This scenario repeats itself, until the day when they finally say, "*in sha Allah*," meaning "by the will of Allah." Then they were able to break through and escape.

The other mention of Gog and Magog in the *Qur'an* comes in Surah 21, verse 96. Khalifa's renders the passage this way:

> 21.95 It is forbidden for any community we have annihilated to return.

> 21.96 Not until Gog and Magog reappear, will they then return—they will come from every direction.

> 21.97 That is when the inevitable prophecy will come to pass, and the disbelievers will stare in horror, "Woe to us, we have been oblivious. Indeed, we have been wicked."[31]

In Islam, the reappearance of Gog and Magog is a sign that Doomsday is near. The age of Dajjal will be instituted, and he will be defeated by the Second Coming of Jesus.

Other Islamic hadith have it that "Gog and Magog are the progeny of Adam,"[32] and "Verily I have created some of My servants whom no one can destroy but Myself."[33] In the same hadith, it is expressly stated that Gog and Magog are the progeny of Adam, which may be connected to another story that Gog and Magog will drink up all the water in the world: "They will drink the water of the world so much so that when some

---

30. Ibid., 111.

31. Qur'an 21:95–97.

32. S. S. Hasan, *Christian Versus Muslims in Modern Egypt* (Oxford: Oxford University Press, 2003) 19.

33. Thomson, *Dajjal, the Anti-Christ*, 18–19.

of them (the inhabitants of Gog and Magog) will pass by a stream, and they will drink all that is in it and leave it dry."[34]

Another hadith has it that the advance guards of Gog and Magog will cross the Gulf of Tiberius, and they will drink the whole mass of water in it. In the hadith of Tamim Dari, Dajjal also asks Tamim Dari about the Gulf of Tiberius, "Tell me about the Gulf of Tiberius, is there any water in it?"[35]

SIGNS OF THE COMING OF THE DAJJAL

In a hadith by Bukhari and narrated by Abu Hairara, we can find eleven signs of the arrival of the Dajjal. Bukhari tells us:

> The hour will not be established until:

1. Two big groups fight each other, whereupon, there will be a great number of casualties on both sides and they will be following one and the same religious doctrine.

2. About 30 Dajjals (liars) will appear, and each one will claim that he is Allah's apostle.

3. Until religious knowledge is taken away the death of religious scholars.

4. Earthquakes will increase in number.

5. Time will pass quickly.

6. Afflictions will appear.

7. Al-Harj (killing) will increase.

8. Until wealth will be in abundance—so abundant that a wealthy person will worry lest nobody should accept Zakat, and whenever he will present it to someone, that person (to whom it is offered) will say, "I am not in need of it."

9. Until people compete with each other in constructing high buildings.

10. Until someone passing by a grave of someone will say, "Would that I were in his place."

11. Until the sun rises in the West.[36]

34. Ibid.
35. Ibid.
36. Ibid.

Bukhari completes this hadith this way:

> So when the sun will rise and the people will see it (rising in the West) they will all believe (embrace Islam); but that will be the time when, as Allah said "No good will it do to a soul to believe then, if it believed not before, nor earned good (by deeds of righteousness) through its faith. And the hour will be established while two men spreading a garment in front of them but they will not be able to sell it, nor fold it up; and the Hour will be established when a man has milk in his she-camel and has taken away the milk but he will not be able to drink it; water (his animals) in it; and the Hour will be established when a person has raised a morsel (of food) to his mouth, but he will not be able to eat it.[37]

It should be clear that the mentions of plagues, pestilences, earthquakes, etc. are directly related to prophecies in Daniel and Revelation. Many of the other signs outlines by Bukhari are unusual or impossible events, suggesting that the end of time will only be brought about by the actions of some powerful figure.

Another tradition of Jabir bin Samurah, narrated by Nafi'bin Utbah, also enumerates signs of the coming of Dajjal, Mohammed tells Jabir: "You will invade the Arabian Peninsula and Allah will grant it to you. Then you will conquer Persia and Allah will grant it to you. Then you will invade Ar-Rum and Allah will grant it to you. Then you invade the Dajjal, and Allah will grant him to you. We do not believe that the Dajjal will appear until Ar-Rum is conquered."[38]

The land of Ar-Rum is Europe. Mohammed suggests that Islam will conquer Rome, after they have conquered the city of Constantinople. In a hadith from Abdullah bin Amir bin Al-Aas, narrated by Imam Ahmad, concurs: "While we were around the Messenger of Allah, we ask, 'Which of these two cities will be conquered first?' Constantinople or Romiyah (Rome). He said, 'The city of Heraclitus will first be conquered.' He meant Constantinople."[39]

Another hadith from An-Nuwas ibn Sam'an tells us of a conversation about the Dajjal between Mohammed and his followers. He tells us:

37. Ibid., 27–28.
38. Ibid., 30.
39. Ibid., 31.

One morning the Prophet spoke about the Dajjal. Sometimes he describes him as insignificant, and sometimes he describes him as so dangerous that we thought he was in a clump of date-palms nearby. When we went to him later, he noticed the fear in our faces and asked, "What is the matter with you?"

We said, "O Messenger of Allah, this morning you spoke of Dajjal; Sometimes you describe him as insignificant and sometimes you describe him as so dangerous that we thought he was in a clump of date-palms nearby.

The Prophet said, "I fear for you in other matters besides the Dajjal. If he appears while I am among you, I will contend with him on your behalf. But if he appears while I am not among you, then each man must contend with him on his own behalf, and Allah will take care of every Muslim on my behalf.[40]

In this same hadith, Mohammed goes on to describe the Dajjal: "The Dajjal will be a young man, with short, curly hair, and one eye floating. I would liken him to Abdul Uzza ibn Qatan. Whoever amongst you lives to see him should recite the opening *ayat* (verses) of Sura al-Kahf. He will appear on the way between Syria and Iraq, and will create disaster left and right. O Servant of Allah adhere to the Path of Truth."[41]

Mohammed's disciples respond by asking how quickly he will be upon the earth. Mohammed answers:

Like a cloud driven by the wind. He will come to the people and call them to a false religion, and they will believe in him and respond to him. He will issue a command to the sky, and it will rain; and to the earth, and it will produce crops. After grazing on these crops, their animals will return with their utters full and their flanks stretched. Then he will come to another people and call them to his fake religion, but they will reject his call. He will depart from them; they will suffer famine and will possess nothing in the form of wealth. Then he will pass through a wasteland and will say, "Bring forth your treasures," and the treasures will come forth, like swarms of bees. Then he will call a man brimming with youth; he will strike him with a sword and cut him in two, then place the pieces at the distance between an archer and his target. Then he will call him, and young man will come running and laughing.[42]

---

40. Ibid., 32–33.
41. Ibid.
42. Ibid., 33–34.

Mohammed continues:

> At that point Allah will send the Messiah, Son of Mary, and he will descend to a white minaret in the East of Damascus, wearing two garments dyed with saffron, placing his hands on the wings of two angels. When he lowers his head, beads of perspiration will fall from it. Every *kafir* (non-believer) who smells this fragrance will die, and his breath will reach as far as he can see. He will search for the Dajjal until he finds him at the Gate of Ludd (biblical Lydda), now known as Lod, where he will kill him.
>
> Then a people that Allah has protected will come to Jesus, the son of Mary, and he will wipe their faces, and tell them of their status in Paradise. At that time Allah will reveal to Jesus, "I have brought forth some of My servants whom on one will be able to fight. Take my servants safely to at-Tur."[43]

Nuwas Samas also sees a role for Gog and Magog for the End Times:

> Then Allah will send Gog and Magog, and they will swarm down from every slope. The first of them will pass by the Lake of Tiberius, and will drink some of its water; the last of them will pass by and say, "There used to be water here." Jesus, the Prophet of Allah and his companions will be besieged until a bull's head will be dearer to them than 100 dinars are to you now."
>
> Then Jesus and his Companions will pray to Allah, and He will send insects who will bite the people of Gog and Magog on their necks, so that in the morning they will all die as one. Then Jesus and his Companions will come down and will not find any nook or cranny on earth which is free from their putrid stench. Jesus and his Companions will again pray to Allah, Who will send a bird like the necks of camels; they will seize the bodies of Gog and Magog, and throw them wherever Allah wishes.
>
> At that time, Allah will send a pleasant wind which will soothe them even under their arm pits, and will take the soul of every Muslim. Only the most wicked people will be left. They will fornicate like asses. Then the Last Hour will come upon them.[44]

Another hadith from Ibn Mas'ud also discusses the role of Jesus in the End Times. Mas'ud was a seventh-century Moslem scholar who had administrative and diplomatic duties under Caliphs Umar ibn al-Khat-

---

43. Ibid.
44. Ibid., 37.

tab and Uthman ibn Affan. Mas'us is also one of the four people whom Mohammed said one should learn the *Qur'an*. Mas'ud's hadith tells us:

> The Prophet said, "On the Night of the Isla (the Night Journey), I met my Father Abraham, Moses, and Jesus, and they discussed the Last Hour. The matter was first referred to Abraham and Moses, and both said, "I have no knowledge of it."
>
> Then it was referred to by Jesus who said, "No one knows about its timing except Allah; what my Lord told me was that the Dajjal will appear, and when he sees me he will begin to melt like lead. Allah will destroy him when he sees me. The Moslems will fight against the *Kafirun*, and even the trees and rocks will say, "O Muslim, there is a *kafir* hiding behind me. Come kill him!" Allah will destroy the *Kafirun*, and the people will return to their own lands.[45]

Ibn Mas'ud, through a narration by Ahmad ibn Hanbul, the ninth-century founder of the Hanibal School of *Figh* (Law) completes the narrative:

> Then Gog and Magog will appear from all directions, eating and drinking everything they find. The people will complain to me, so I will pray to Allah, and He will destroy them, so that the earth will be filled with their stench. Allah will send rain which will wash their bodies into the sea.
>
> My Lord has told me that when that happens, the Last Hour will be very close, like a pregnant woman whose time is due, but her family does not know exactly when she will deliver.[46]

OTHER AHADITH ON THE DAJJAL

Other Ahadith regarding Dajjal inform us that he will emerge between Shaam (Syria) and Iraq, and he will be known when he is in Isfahan (a city in Persia) at a place called Yahudea (Judea). The Jews of Isfahan will be Dajjal's main followers. Dajjal will also have a great number of women followers. He will charm them with his greatest attributes.[47]

Other Ahidith claim the Dajjal will appear with both fire and water, but in reality the fire will be cold, and what appears to be cold water will in

45. Ibid., 37–38.
46. Ibid.
47. Ibid., 42–43.

fact be a blazing fire. He will travel at great speeds, and his means of travel will be a great mule. He will send down rain to those who believe in him, and cause famine and drought to those who do not.[48]

Some ahadith suggest that hidden riches will spill forth at the command of Dajjal. He will stay on earth for a period of 40 days, and the length of the first day shall be a year. The second day will be equal to a month; the third day to a week; the remaining days will be normal. Some say the Dajjal will have a thick fingernail in his left eye. He will claim to be both a prophet, and to be God.[49]

Other important Ahadith tell us that Dajjal has other names, including "the Sick Man of Humanity."[50] He will be the embodiment of all that denotes unbelief. When the Mahdi (the Messiah) and Dajjal meet, at the end of time, all human beings will have a choice to follow one or the other. Those who follow the Mahdi will enter Paradise at the end of time. Those who follow the Dajjal will experience the torments and fires of hell.

THE DAJJAL IN LATER ISLAM

The figure of the Dajjal also appears in the number of imperial prophecies in some late sixteenth-century Ottoman traditions. The sources of this tradition go all the way back to the Old Testament prophet, Ezekiel, who foretold of a great military power "in the latter times" that would mount an invasion against Israel. The invasion was to be led by Gog (what some interpreted as Russia) together with Persia (modern day Iran).

Ezekiel speaks of a people from the extreme north known as Gog: "I will turn you around, put hooks into your jaws, and lead you out. . . . In the latter years, you will come into the land of those brought back from the sword, and gathered from many people on the mountains of Israel, which had long been desolate. They were brought out of the nations, and now all of them dwell safely."[51]

This prophecy has been used by various Islamic prognosticators between the 16th and 19th centuries. All of them tie the events of Ezekiel to the Ottoman Empire and the coming of the end of the world. One good example is Bahaullah, in the Bahai tradition, who predicted that Sultan

48. Ibid.
49. Ibid., 45.
50. Ibid., 47–48.
51. Ezekiel 38:4a and 8b (author's translation).

Abdul Aziz will lose control of the Ottoman Empire. Bahaullah mentions two signs of the end times. He writes: "We have appointed two signs for the coming of the End Times. The first is the development of a single language, and the adoption of a common script. The second sign is the emergence of a Divine philosophy, which will include the discovery of radical approaches to the study of nature."[52]

Many Islamic scholars see this prophecy, and others like it in the Ottoman Empire in the sixteenth to nineteenth centuries, to refer to the coming of the Dajjal, who will convert Moslems to his false religion, and will possess powers over nature not normally associated with human beings. Other Islamic prophecies tie the Ezekiel quote to Mehmed II (reigned 1451–140), who recaptured the city of Consantinople in 1451 at the age of nineteen. There had been twelve previous attempts by Muslim armies to conquer the city, and in the course of those attempts a considerable body of prophetic literature arose that promised the Byzantine Empire would fall to Islam, just before the end of the world, and the coming of the Dajjal. Often these prophecies liken the fall of Rome with the fall of Constantinople and the End Times.

More recently, in 1838 a Millerite leader named Josiah Litch, on the basis of his understanding of Revelation 9:15 that the Ottoman Empire would fall on August 11, 1840. A scholar named Ellen White gave a glowing endorsement of Litch's prediction in her book, *The Great Controversy*: "In the year 1840, another remarkable fulfillment of prophecy excited widespread interest. Two years before, Josiah Litch, one of the leading ministers preaching the Second Advent, published an exposition of Revelation nine, predicting the fall of the Ottoman Empire."[53]

Some who knew of Litch's prophecy also knew of the many Islamic predictions of the fall of the Ottoman Empire, the coming of Dajjal and the drawing of the End Times. One of the great ironies of Litch's prediction is that Russia already had defeated the Ottoman Empire in 1829, when they signed a treaty to protect the Turks.

52. Bahaullah, *Tablets of Bahaullah Revealed after the Kitab-i-Aqdas* (Wilamette, IL: Bahai Publishing Trust, 1994) 97.

53. Ellen G. White, *The Great Controversy* (Mountain View, CA: Pacific Press Publishing Assocation, 1950) 335.

SOURCES FOR THE DJAAL

It should be clear from the discussion in this chapter that principal sources for the idea of the Djaal are the Old and New Testaments. From the Old Testament, Islamic traditions have adopted the idea of the beast, the war of Gog and Magog, and the resurrection at the end of time in chapter 12 of Daniel.

It should be just as clear that Islam adopted many aspects of the Christian idea of the Anti-Christ in its own explications of the End Times. Among apocalyptic New Testament ideas that Islam adopted in its development of the idea of the Djaal were: that the Djaal will have powers beyond normal human abilities; that he will use these powers to perform miracles and to bring beings to his movement; that he will be full of lies and deceit; and that the Djaal will be defeated by Jesus and the Messiah at the end of time. Like the New Testament's Anti-Christ, the Djaal will call people to a false religion. Among the physical powers the Djaal will possess in Islam is the ability to get time to travel quickly, the ability to bring fast changes in the weather, the ability to bring new diseases to human beings, and the ability to have the sun rise in the West.

Other Christian ideas on the Anti-Christ adopted by Islam is the claim that the followers of the Djaal will have a physical mark. In the New Testament, it is the number 666. In Islam, it will be the letters K F R written between the eyes on the foreheads of nonbelievers.

The Islamic traditions also concur with the idea that the Djaal will have some sort of physical disability. Often the descriptions refer to him having one eye, but in all accounts of the Djaal something is unusual about the body of the Anti-Christ, like the various descriptions of the beasts in Daniel and Revelation. Finally, like traditions in the Old and New Testaments, in Islam the Djaal will only come in a time of tribulation that will be preceded by earthquakes, famine, war, and destruction.

ISLAM AS THE ANTI-CHRIST

When the Moslem armies broke out of the Arabian Peninsula and began to spread throughout North Africa and much of the Middle East, many Christian thinkers began to associate Islamic faith with the Anti-Christ and the End Times. Many events in Spain and Portugal in the seventh and eighth century were interpreted that way.

Many Christians in the seventh and eighth centuries began to see Islam, not as another faith, but as a personification of the last of the great heretics. Like many Christian thinkers before them, whom regularly identified the Anti-Christ with various contemporary heretics, Christians in the seventh and eighth centuries began to do the same thing. The rise of Islam came to be seen as another sign of the end of the world.

From this period on, the restraining force of 2 Thessalonians 2:6 began to be identified with the Moslem armies, changing the early Christian view that it was the Roman Empire. By the time of Paulus Alvarus in the ninth century, he argues that Mohammed was not only a heretic, he was also a precursor to the Christian Anti-Christ. Alvarus believed there was no truth outside the Christian tradition, thus people must choose either Christ or Anti-Christ. Alvarus suggests that the fourth beast found in the Book of Daniel describes the Anti-Christ. Alvarus says Mohammed rejected the divinity of Christ and therefore represented the Anti-Christ.[54]

Alvarus took his analysis one step further by rewriting the death of Mohammed, claiming that Islam expected Mohammed to be resurrected at the End of Time. But Alvarus claims that Mohammed's body began to rot, and was eaten by dogs, thus confirming Mohammed as the Anti-Christ.[55]

Around the year 1200, Pope Innocent III called for the Fourth Crusade and suggested that Mohammed was the Anti-Christ. Innocent had intended to recapture the Holy Land. He directed his call toward the knights and nobles of Europe, rather than to kings, for he wished neither Richard I of England, nor Philip II of France, to participate in the Crusade. In order to get the knights and nobles to participate, Innocent repeatedly claimed that Mohammed was the Anti-Christ.

By the fourteenth century, many of the reformers of the Christian Church began to believe that the Pope was the Anti-Christ in the West, and Islam was the Anti-Christ in the East. This view was held by many Protestant thinkers well into the eighteenth century, when it was applied to the Turkish Empire.

During the Reformation, John Calvin, using Revelation 17 and 18, suggests that "Mohamet and the pope are the two horns of Anti-Christ." Martin Luther also believed that the Turks were the small horn that grew

---

54. For more on Alvarus, see Jessica Ferree, "The Approach of Christian Polemicists Against Islam," *Macalester Islam Journal* 1 (2006) 24–28.

55. Ibid., 25.

out of the fourth beast in Daniel 7:8 and 24. Heinrich Bornkamn argues that Luther also connected the Turks with Gog and Magog of Ezekiel 38 and 39: "He [Luther] found them described very accurately in the vision of Ezekiel about Gog. (Ezekiel 38 and 39), the vision which seemed to him particularly confirmed because of its role in the eschatological drama."[56]

Bornkamn continues:

> During his quiet days at Coburg, Luther first started work on a small tract with the translation of Ezekiel 38 and 39 because he was impressed with the danger by the Turks, and wanted to direct the attention of the whole world to this danger. Gog has tasted German blood; he intends to drink his fill of it.
>
> But at the same time, he [Luther] also wanted to uncover the true reason for the Turkish power; our sins "which have awakened God's fury and have hidden his countenance from us, and allow Gog to rage so horribly."[57]

Luther may well have believed, as Calvin did, that Islam and the Turkish Empire of his day, were representations of the Anti-Christ.[58]

MUHAMMED AND ISLAM AS THE ANTI-CHRIST

The *Encyclopedia of Religion*, edited by Mircea Eliade, has an article on the Anti-Christ in its fist volume. The anonymous author of the article points out that "Christian beliefs about the Anti-Christ, especially those originating in Syria, were the sources for Islamic legends regarding a final eschatological foe, called Ad-Dajjal (the deceiver)."[59]

In addition to this notion that the idea of the Dajjal has Christian origins, beginning in the seventh century, and continuing all the way to contemporary theology, various Christian thinkers have claimed that Islam in general, or the prophet Muhammed in particular, is the Anti-Christ.

---

56. Heinrich Bornkamn, *Luther and the Old Testament* (Philadelphia: Fortress, 1969) 68.

57. Ibid.

58. For more on Islam's view of the Anti-Christ, see Joel Richardson, *Anti-Christ: Islam's Awaited Messiah* (Enumclaw, WA: Pleasant Word, 2006); and Robert Livingston, *Christianity and Islam: The Final Clash* (Enumclaw, WA: Pleasant Word, 2004).

59. "Anti-Christ," in *The Encyclopedia of Religion* (New York: Macmillam, 1968) 1:321–22.

John Esposito, the editor of the *Oxford History of Islam*, refers to this phenomenon: "One of the earliest Christians to undertake a serious study of Islam was John of Damascus, a government official during the reign of the Umayyad caliph Abd Al-Malik (reigned 685–705), who left his public post to take up a life of contemplation at a Greek Orthodox monastery."[60] Esposito continues: "Knowledgeable in Arabic, he was well-versed in the main doctrines of Islam, especially those related to Jesus and Christianity. His major theological work contains a section dealing with so-called heresy of the Ismailites (Muslims) and his designation of Muhammed as the Anti-Christ."[61]

This same judgment was arrived at by the eighth-century bishop of Maiuma, a man named Peter. The bishop was sentenced to death because he condemned Islam publicly and he called Muhammed a "false prophet," and "the fore-runner of the Anti-Christ."[62] Daniel J. Sahas, in his book, *John of Damascus on Islam*, points out that this view of Muhammed as the Anti-Christ was held by a number of Christian thinkers before the time of Peter and John of Damascus. Sahas tells us: "This expression ("fore-runner of the Anti-Christ") was not employed for the first time against Islam and Muhammed. It has been used by Emperor Leo III, his son Constantine V, a Patriarch of Constantinople, John VII Grammaticus (836–842) and possibly by some other prominent political and religious leaders."[63]

Esposito, in discussing the eleventh century tells us that when the Fatmid caliph Al-Hakim destroyed the Holy Sepulcher in 1009, he was also spoken of as the Anti-Christ by many Christian scholars of the day.[64] This practice of seeing Muhammed or Islam as the Anti-Christ continued well into the Protestant Reformation and beyond. John Esposito writes of contemporary Protestant thinkers who hold a similar view about Muhammed. Esposito says: "Interfaith efforts have also been hampered by Jewish suspicion of Christian-Muslim collaboration that does not include them, by the reticence of some evangelical Christian participants who see Muslims as the agents of Anti-Christ."[65]

60. John L. Esposito, ed., *The Oxford History of Islam* (Oxford: Oxford University Press, 1971) 1:322.

61. Ibid.

62. Daniel J. Sahas, *John of Damascus on Islam* (Leiden: Brill, 1972) 68.

63. Ibid, 69.

64. Esposito, Esposito, ed., *The Oxford History of Islam*, 1:335.

65. Ibid., 626.

Among a number of contemporary scholars there has been some debate about whether the Al-Dajjal is real or if it is the product of super-stition or mythology. Some contemporary scholars, like Siddiq Hassan Khan who died in 1889, believed that the Djaal will emerge as the figure described in ahadith. A second strain of scholars identify Western civili-zation with the Anti-Christ. Among these scholars is Muhammed Asad, a twentieth-century Moslem Austrian scholars who converted to Islam.

A third group of Moslem scholars identify the Anti-Christ with the Jews. One champion of this idea was Rasid Rida, who suggests that materials about Ad-Dajjal describe a Zionist king and his followers. Still other contemporary Islamic scholars identify the Moslem Anti-Christ as a Devil, or as one of the *Djinn*. In his article, "The Legend of Al-Dajjal (Anti-Christ): The Personification of Evil in the Islamic Tradition," Zeki Saritprak discusses each of these points of view, as well as the view that Al-Dajjal is a mythological creature created by the minds of people who lived in a mythological age.[66]

CONCLUSIONS

In this chapter we have explored the many uses of the concept of the Dajjal, the Arabic word for the Anti-Christ. Like Judaism and Christianity, we have seen that Islam has a number of beliefs about the End Times, and a body of stories about those End Times. Islam has its own version of Apocalyptic Literature. Many of these traditions were borrowed from Judaism and Christianity. Chief among these are a final judgment at the end of time, and a battle between the messiah and the Anti-Christ.

As we have seen, Islam also inherited a number of ideas from the Old Testament, like the coming of the messiah at the end of time, and the idea of Gog and Magog being cities full of nonbelievers. We have also seen in this chapter that Moslem scholars are in agreement with New Testament writers that the Anti-Christ will have powers that go beyond the norm. Powers like controlling the weather, powers of persuasion, and the power to perform miracles are all abilities of the Moslem figure of Dajjal.

We also have explored in this chapter a number of signs that Moslem scholars believe will be evidence that the coming of Dajjal is near. Among

---

66. Zeki Saritoprak, "The Legend of Al-Dajjal (Anti-Christ): The Personification of Evil in the Islamic Tradition," *The Muslim World* 93 (2003) 291–307.

these were rumors of wars, earthquakes, famine and pestilences, not unlike those in Daniel and the Book of Revelation.

We also have seen in this chapter that Islam has an analogue to the mark of 666 from the Book of Revelation. In Islam, the mark contains the letters K F R, the root for the Arabic word for nonbeliever, which will appear on the Dajjal's forehead at the end of time.

Above all, we have seen that the concept of the Dajjal in the Islamic tradition is a moral one. He stands for much that is evil, and that is held by the *Fakirun*, the nonbelievers. We also have seen that Jesus serves a role in the Moslem idea of the End Times. For Islam, Jesus is to be identified with the Messiah, and at the end of time, Jesus will defeat the Dajjal, and bring about judgment for all.

Bernard McGinn sums up his comments on the Anti-Christ in Islam this way:

> The description of Anti-Christ as a one-eyed monster riding on an ass as large as himself and leading the Jews against Islam, appear to have been wide spread in both Sunni and Shiite Islam from the 8th or 9th century CE. Like the Christian accounts (and at least some Jewish ones), Muslim texts also speculate about the miracles that he will or will not be able to perform.[67]

Islam's fascination with the Dajjal is akin to Judaism and Christianity's fascinations with evil matters in their apocalyptic literature. And Islam does not come up short in regard to a wealth of stories, descriptions, and explanations for their version of the Anti-Christ, Ad-Dajjal.[68]

---

67. Bernard McGinn, *The Anti-Christ: Two Thousand Years of the Human Fascination With Evil* (New York: Harpers) 110–11.

68. For more on these texts about the End Times, the Ottoman Empire, and the Dajjal, see Arthur Jeffrey, "The Descent of Jesus in Mohammadan Eschatology," in *The Joy of Study: Papers to Honor Frederick Clifton Grant* , edited by Sherman F. Johnson (New York Macmillan, 1951) 107–26.

11

Some Conclusions

How do you expect them to put their faith to you, when you know that some among them heard the word of Allah and, having understood, perverted it knowingly.

—Qur'an 2:75

It is important for Christians especially to grasp this Qur'anic theology of revelation, because it differs from common Christian theologies.

—C. T. R. Hewer, *Understanding Islam: An Introduction*

Demonstrative truth and Scriptural truth cannot conflict.

—Averroes, "The Decisive Treatise"

INTRODUCTION

THERE ARE TWO PRINCIPAL goals in this eleventh and final chapter. The first of those is to highlight some general conclusions we can derive from chapters one through ten. The second goal is to make some further comments on the relationship of Islam to Christianity, as well as some observations about the role that hermeneutics plays in terms of having a clear understanding of the relationship of both Christianity and Islam to the notion that God speaks through human texts.

As we shall see in this final chapter, what Moslems mean when they say that the Qur'an is the word of Allah is sometimes very different than what Christians mean when they say that the Bible is the word of God. This is particularly true when we comprehend what the Islamic faith, for the most part, means when it speaks of the authority of Scriptures. As we shall see, Christianity and Islam have very different views about the authority of the Scriptures passed down in Judaism and Christianity.

SOME MAJOR CONCLUSIONS FROM
CHAPTERS ONE THROUGH TEN

The most significant conclusions we may draw from the first chapter of this study is that the traditional view of God (Allah) is very similar to the traditional account of the Deity in Judaism and Christianity. Like the other two Religions of the Book, Islam sees Allah as unique, omnipotent, omniscient, and omni-benevolent, as well as the Creator of the Universe out of nothing. In addition to these traditional attributes, Islam refers to Allah having 99 names, many of which are unrelated to ideas in the Judeo-Christian tradition. As we have seen, some of these attributes have negative connotations, ideas not usually associated with God in the West.

We have also explored in the opening chapter the tradition that Islam believes there is a 100th name for Allah, a name unknown to human beings. Some saw this as the genuine name for Allah, while others suggest that the 100th name for Allah is only known by a selective few of His creatures.

The major conclusions we have gleaned from chapter two of this study is that Islam has a completely different view of Abraham/Ibrahim sacrificing his son in chapter 22 of Genesis. For the most part, Judaism and Christianity have thought the identity of the son to be sacrificed is Isaac, while Islam thinks the son in question is Ishmael. This conclusion arises in Islam, for the most part, from the Qur'an's suggestion that Ibrahim sacrifice his "one and only son." Since there was never a time when Isaac was Abraham's one and only son, Islam believes the son in question must have been Ishmael, the product of the prophet's relationship with Hagar.

Two conclusions we have found in chapter three of this study is that in the Islamic faith Moses is often depicted as having a bodily disfigurement, and that he is also shown in Islam to have horns—both in Islamic commentaries of the Qur'an and in Islamic art. In chapter five, we explored the Islamic understandings of a number of other Old Testament partriarchs. For the most part, the Moslem views of Adam, Lot, and others are consistent with those of Judaism and Christianity, with one notable exception. In the Islamic faith, there is no description of King David wishing to acquire Uriah the Hittite's wife through trickery. This story from II

Samuel 11 and 12 is not included in the Qur'an because such a sinful act is unthinkable of prophets in the Islamic faith.

For the most part, Islam holds the view that this story of David must have been included in the Torah after the revelation was complete, for such behavior is unworthy of Islam's prophets. This conclusion, of course, is directly related to Islam's view of exegesis, which we will talk more about at the end of this chapter.

The Islamic view of Ayyub (Job) was the subject matter for chapter six of this study. Islam sees Job as a patient and steadfast prophet much as Judaism and Christianity do; but the Islamic tradition adds features to the Job story that are not to be found in the account of the Hebrew Bible. In Islam, the man from Uz is seen as both the patron saint of skin diseases, and as a man whose sores were healed by kicking the ground and receiving a stream that heals them. We also have seen that in the Moslem faith there is a long tradition of identifying Job's well, his home, and his fields with various places in the Middle East—something not found in Judaism and Christianity's understandings of Job.

In chapter seven of this study, we have explored the Islamic views of Isa (Jesus). Islam sees Isa as a great prophet, and it also understands Jesus to be the Mahdi (the Messiah); but Islam does not believe that Jesus is the son of God, a significant difference between Christianity and Islam, nor does it see Maryam (Mary) as the Mother of God.

In chapter eight, we looked carefully at the roles played by Mary, Joseph, and John the Baptist in Islam. Mary and John the Baptist are both numbered among the greatest of Islamic prophets; Mary is noted for her purity in Islam, but she is not seen as the mother of God. She is seen in Islam, however, as one of the three greatest women who ever lived.

In chapter nine of this study, we have explored the images of Iblis/Shaytan, Heaven, and Hell. We saw that it is not entirely clear in Islam if Iblis is a fallen angel or one of the evil Djinns. We also saw that Islam describes compartments for both Heaven and Hell, and that humans are made of clay, while Djinns are made from smoke. In chapter ten, we have explored the role of the Djaal, the Arabic word for the Anti-Christ. We have seen some significant differences from the Christian view of the figure, including the ideas that the Djaal has only one eye, that he is identified with the armies of Gog and Magog, and that he will fight the Mahdi at the end of time.

SOME FINAL THOUGHTS ON ISLAMIC HERMENEUTICS

In addition to the conclusions mentioned above, we shall also make some further comments on the role of hermeneutics in the Moslem faith. As we have seen, there are some significant discrepancies between Islam and the Judeo-Christian tradition on various Biblical characters. Among these are different views on the son to be sacrificed by Abraham/Ibrahim, the sins of David, the view that Adam and Eve did not sin in the Garden of Eden, and the identity of Jesus as the Son of God.

At the root of the principal differences on these issues are differing points of view about the nature of God revealing himself to human beings. When Moslems say that the Qur'an is the word of God, they are not using it in the same way that modern Western Christians use it when speaking of the Gospels. In Islam, Allah's speech cannot be separated from the speaker. When Allah calls something forth, then that thing is. In the view of most Moslems, the Qur'an, as it was revealed to Muhammed, through the Angel Gabriel is a direct replica of an original Qur'an that resides in Paradise. Thus, there are no errors in the sacred text for Moslems.

If there are discrepancies between what the Bible and the Qur'an have to say about various Biblical figures, then that means that there is something wrong with the Biblical account. In Islam, this discrepancy may be the product of an incomplete original revelation from Allah, or it may be that Allah has supplemented that original revelation with an addendum.

Although the Bible tells us that the son to be sacrificed by Abraham was Isaac, the Qur'an supplemented that revelation by pointing out it was Ishmael. Although II Samuel clearly suggests that David sinned, the Qur'an would say this is impossible. The Hebrew Bible seems to imply that Adam and Eve sinned in the Garden of Eden; but the Qur'an says their actions were the by-product of trickery on the part of Shaytan.

The New Testament implies that Jesus is the Son of God, while the Qur'an denies that claim, as it does that Jesus is part of the Trinity. The New Testament writers clearly describe Mary as the mother of God, while the Qur'an rejects this assertion.

All these differences lead Islam to conclude that the original Biblical revelations discussed above were incomplete. This follows simply from the fact that there are some contradictions between the Bible and the Qur'an.

Since there are no errors in the Qur'an, Islamic scholars argue, there must be some errors in the Bible.

J. Fueck speaks of some of these discrepancies, when he writes:

> Since the Qur'an reflects a rather naïve confusion regarding several facets of biblical history (it is perhaps sufficient here to point out that it confuses Miriam, the mother of Jesus, with the sister of Aaron [sura 19:29 and 66:12].
>
> And identifies Haman as Pharaoh's vizier [sura 28:5 and 7, and 40:38.], and since it further mentions none of the writing prophets, it is clear that Muhammed's knowledge of the prophets was limited.[1]

Various ways of explaining these discrepancies exist in Islamic literature. The most important one is that the Qur'an at 2:75 points out that some have perverted the revelations from Allah. Once Islam accepts this as a given, then all sorts of conclusions may arise in Islam about the authority of the Bible.

There is also a tradition in Islam, like that in Christianity, that the proper interpretation of a Divine revelation is allegorical; but nowhere in the Qur'an is there clear understanding of when we are to comprehend a particular text as literal, and when as allegorical.

This problem first arose in Islam in the tenth to twelfth centuries, when various Moslem philosophers discuss whether the truths of philosophy could contradict the truths of the Qur'an. Averroes, twelfth-century Spanish philosopher, for example, tells us: "All Muslims accept the principle of allegorical interpretation. They only disagree about the extent of its application."[2]

Later, in the same treatise, Averroes makes distinctions among three different kinds of interpretation:

> Texts of Scripture fall in three kinds. [1] Texts which must be taken in their apparent meaning by everyone. [2] Texts which must be taken in their apparent meaning by the lower classes and interpreted allegorically by the demonstrative class. And [3] texts whose

---

1. J. Fueck, "The Originality of the Arabian Prophet," in M. L. Swartz, ed., *Studies in Islam* (New York: Oxford University Press, 1981) 87–88.

2. Averroes, *On the Harmony of Religion and Philosophy,* translated by George F. Hourani (London: Luzac, 1961) 237.

classification under the previous headings is uncertain. Error in this matter by the demonstrative class is excused.[3]

Averroes goes on to describe two different kinds of errors in Scripture. He writes:

> In general, error about Scripture is of two types: either error which is excused to one who is a qualified student of that matter in which the error occurs (as the skillful doctor is excused if he commits an error in the art of medicine and the skillful judge if he gives an erroneous judgment,) but not excused to one who is not qualified in that subject; or error which is not excused to any person whatever, and which is unbelief if it concerns the principles of religion, or heresy if it concerns something subordinate to those principles.[4]

As we can see from these comments, the problem of the discrepancy on truth in the interpreting of Scripture has been an on-going one for the past 1,000 years. Indeed, earlier Moslem philosophers like Avicenna (980–1037) and Al-Ghazali (1058–1111) also wrote a great deal on the problem of Biblical exegesis.

For the last 1,000 years, then, Moslem scholars have traditionally held that the Bible contains errors. These errors are either attributed to carelessness in copying or preservation of manuscripts; or there have been some deliberate changes written into the Bible, changes that later on will be contradicted by Muhammed's revelation of the Qur'an.

One of the major ways that Avicenna, Al-Ghazali, and Averroes resolved this problem is what later will be called the problem of faith and reason was to claim, as Moses Maimonides and Thomas Aquinas did after them, that truth has a double aspect. For Thomas Aquinas, this double truth amounts to a distinction between Natural Truths (truths of Reason) and Revealed Truths (truth gleaned from revelation).

It should be clear from all of this that traditional Islamic interpretations of the Bible are significantly different from two kinds of contemporary Christian exegeses. The first kinds of contemporary Christian exegesis are those very conservative interpreters of Sacred Scripture who say that every jot and tittle of the Bible is true. The second variety of Christian interpretation is the form critical and history of religions approach that arose in Germany in the late nineteenth century. In this second Christian

3. Ibid.
4. Ibid.

approach the truth of a text is best understood in its historical and literal contexts.

Contemporary Islamic scholars reject both of these kinds of Christian exegeses. As we have seen, the major reason for rejecting both is that their conclusions are sometimes in direct contradiction with claims to be found in the Qur'an.

Whatever conclusions we make about exegetical epistemology we make in the Islamic tradition, one point is clear—a truth that cuts to the very heart of contemporary Christian-Islamic relations. There is next to no dialogue about truth and hermeneutics between contemporary Christian and Moslem scholars. This realization perhaps brings us to one valuable area of theological dialogue that we might now engage in.

Among the major goals of this study is a belief that providing information about Islam, as well as how the Muslim faith sees Biblical figures and their places in Islam, is indeed an important thing. Far too little understanding of Islam by non-Moslems is present in the contemporary world. Among other things, this study may serve as a starting point, a point of departure in a dialogue between Muslims, Christians, and Jews. It may also serve as a tool for students in comparative religions courses, as well as introductory courses in Islam for non-Muslims.

Above all, wars and changing geo-political allegiances, as well as contemporary discusses of human rights, all point us in the direction of dialogue—a dialogue that must begin between and among the three great faiths of Abraham. We sincerely hope that this study may contribute to that dialogue.

One of the Mosaic commandments prohibit murder (Exodus 20:13). The Hebrew Bible tells us that murder is wrong because first, it is in obvious conflict with the provision to love one's neighbor (Leviticus 19:17–18, 33–34). And secondly, murder is wrong because people are made in the image of God (Genesis 1:26–27 and 9:6). One might infer from this that no killing of persons is allowed among the ancient Jews, that it would imply strict pacifism and an absolute prohibition against killing. But this is not what the ancient Hebrew concluded. Since many offenses were subject to capital punishment some forms of killing are permitted (see Exodus 21 and 22). We might amend the rule to say all persons have a basic right to not be killed, but they can forfeit that right if they commit certain crimes. This is also consistent with punishing only those guilty of these crimes (Deuteronomy 24:16). This also limits the use of deadly force to the defense of innocents or oneself.

In Islam, we see a similar mixture of values. The Qur'an regularly refers to Allah being compassionate and just. It also says there is no compulsion in the Islamic faith (2:256); that belief in Allah must be freely chosen and not forced. It also urged believers to "argue nicely" with Jews and Christians (16:125 and 29:46).

Some say that Muhammed practiced non-violence early in his career, but soon believed that Allah commanded the use of force, not only defense (22:39–40), but also offensively to expand the territories of Islam.

The Qur'an does have some explicit rules in times of warfare. Women, children, and the elderly are not to be directly attacked, though they could be enslaved. Jihad is not to be indiscriminate, but they were permitted to kill all male soldiers of the enemy, and male civilians if they are not Muslims or have fallen from the faith. Thus, there is no prohibition against noncombatant immunity in Islam.

Ultimately, what Judaism, Christianity, and Islam have in common is a collection of shared values. Among these are the beliefs that God/Allah is compassionate and just. If we truly believe this, we must also consider the possibility that God/Allah does not sanction the killing of innocent people—even if those claims are made in Holy Scripture. We must also begin to have conversations among these three faiths about the nature and possibility of forgiveness, as well as what role remorse should play in the ethics of war and violent struggles. Clearly, all three faiths believe that compassion should temper fury and should restrain us from waging wars of annihilation. This raises perhaps the most important question that may arise in these religious dialogues: Are there times when mercy and compassion are more important than justice?

As of the writing of this conclusion, believers in the Islamic faith amount to 1.3 million people. Most of those Moslems are simply, decent, and good people. Some would like nothing more than to get all troops out of Islamic lands. Our biggest challenge in the twenty-first century is to convince the most violent aspects of the Islamic faith, the Jihadists, that the people of the West are not their enemies.

Appendix

Biblical Figures in Islamic Art

History is a mirror of the past and a lesson for the present.

—Persian Proverb.

Our study of the illustrative cycle shows that the hagiographic literature offered to artists a surprising variety of episodes for illustration. In fact, the range of subjects is far larger than that of other genres.

—Rachel Milstein
Stories of the Prophets

Art is the mirror of a culture and its world view. There is no case to which this statement more directly applies than to the art of the Islamic world. Not only does its art reflect its cultural values, but even more importantly, the way in which its adherents, the Muslims, view the spiritual realm, the universe, life, and the relationship of the parts to the whole.

—Elisabeth Siddiqui
"Islamic Art"

INTRODUCTION

IN THIS APPENDIX WE describe and discuss the development of art in the Islamic faith, concentrating on ways in which Biblical figures have appeared in Islamic painting and the other arts. In the opening section of this appendix, we give a short history of Islamic art from the 7th century to the arising of the Empires in the 16th to 19th centuries. In a second section of this appendix, we talk of Old Testament figures as they have been depicted in Islamic art. In a third section of this appendix, we explore New Testament figures as they appear in Islamic painting. In a concluding section of this appendix, we make a general summary of the ways in which Islam has used Biblical figures, or Biblical prophets, in their aesthetic traditions.

HISTORY OF ISLAMIC ART

The Islamic faith began in the early 7th century and quickly spread throughout the Middle East and North Africa. Before the end of the 8th century, Islam had moved to Byzantium, Persia, Europe, and some parts of Asia. In the first thousand years of Islam, from the revelations of Muhammad to the period of the Empires, Islam flourished. While Europe suffered through the Dark Ages of the 5th to 10th centuries, Muslims in cities like Jerusalem, Damascus, Alexandria, Fez, Tunis, Cairo, and Baghdad, remarkable advances were made in philosophy, science, medicine, literature, and the visual arts. The uniting of so many diverse cultures under one religion had the advantage of quickly disseminating the latest and most important discoveries to all parts of the Moslem realm. Papermaking from China, Arabic numerals from India, classical scientific and philosophical texts from the Greeks, were all shared in the Islamic world.

Under the Abbasid Caliphite, which came after the Umayyads (661–750), the focal point of Moslem political and cultural life shifted eastward from Syria to Iraq where, in 762, the city of Baghdad was established as its new capital. The first two centuries of Abbasid rule saw the emergence and dissemination of a new Moslem style of art. A diverse set of arts flourished during the Abbasid period, including textiles, pottery, architecture, and painting.

Textiles, which were often made with costly materials, such as silver and gold thread and silk, were seen as status items. Islamic textiles were also widely exported to the West. The English words "cotton" and "taffeta," derived from Arabic and Persian respectively, are good examples of Islam's influence on European languages.

The art of pottery was greatly advanced in the Moslem world in the 9th and 10th centuries. The technique known as "luster painting," which is a means of making pottery look like precious metals, was first developed in Iraq. The production of luster pottery was expensive, complicated, and time-consuming, but such objects were also regarded as luxury wares and status symbols.

A city north of Baghdad, called Samarra, replaced the capital for a brief time in the 9th century. The city is particularly important for the development of architecture during the Abbasid period. In the new capital, a new method for carving surfaces, the beveled style, as well as the repetition of geometric forms, and pseudo-vegetative forms, later called "Arabesque," were widely used as wall decorations and on rugs. New styles in metal and wood-working were also popular in the 9th century. Architectural elements were now rendered in stucco and stone buildings in the 9th century. The style soon spread to the rest of the Moslem world, including Egypt.

By the beginning of the 10th century, the Abbasid Empire had begun to crumble, and Abbasid power was now limited to Iraq. New styles of indigenous art began to appear in Egypt, elsewhere in North Africa, in Spain, and in Iran. The new empire was called the Fatimid. It lasted from the 10th to the 12th centuries. The Fatimids developed carved vessels out of rock crystals, a type of transparent, colorless quartz whose surface could be brilliantly polished.

In the Fatimid Period, Old Cairo, known as al-Fustat, became the major center for the production of pottery, glass and metal-work, rock crystal, ivory, and textile factories run by the government. The lusterware techniques were now used on ceramics. Wood carving and new kinds of jewelry were also now quite popular. The Fatimids created new decorative motifs and made greater use of figural forms, both human and animal. Figures were now stylized but lively, with traditional vegetal and geometric forms continuing to be employed.

In the 11th century, the Seljuk Turks briefly ruled over a vast empire that included Iran, the Fertile Crescent and most of Turkey. But by the end of the century, the empire had disintegrated into smaller kingdoms ruled by different branches of the Seljuk Turks. The Ghaznavids, one of the branches, defeated the Byzantine Army in the eastern Anatolia in 1071. This paved the way for the introduction of Islam and Turkish culture into Anatolia. The Seljuk sultanase of Rum (Byzantium) endured until the beginning of the 14th century.

In Central Asia, a branch of the Seljuks established itself in the 11th century. Islam flourished there until the coming of the Mongols in the 13th century. The Seljuks built buildings of majestic proportions and objects of matchless beauty. In their desire to imitate Chinese ceramics, the Seljuk Turks developed the most important innovations in early Medieval

Islamic pottery. They reinvented a technique that combined clay, quartz, and potash, first used by the Egyptians.

The earliest known and distinctive style of Persian painting also dates to the city of Baghdad. The movement was actually referred to as the "Baghdad School." Early painting was used mainly to decorate manuscripts and versions of the Qur'an. By the Mongol Empire, paintings were used to decorate all sorts of books.

ISLAMIC PAINTING AND THE BIBLE

Moslem paintings depicting Biblical legends are quite common in modern Islamic painting. Works about the Bible from the 15th to the 19th century originate in India, Turkey, and particularly in Persia. Paintings from these three areas that depict Bible characters do not differ in their general characteristics from other Persian-Islamic art from the same period. But the pictorial conception of Islamic art of Biblical personages is vastly different from Western European conceptions.

Muslim painting was used primarily for the illustration of manuscripts of the Qur'an. Its objective was to present the most elaborate and attractive illustrations possible. The Moslem painter was not required to imitate nature, or to depict figures as they actually are, nor was he or she concerned with perspective or shadow. Instead the artist attempted to introduce or create the ideal illustration, with rich, colorful depictions that would dazzle and charm the reader/viewer.

The outdoor scenes in Moslem illustration were portrayed against an idealized, uniform background. Stones were grouped together in stylized forms; plants and flowers were painted in clusters; trees and sometimes small rivers or springs were painted the color silver. When the heavens appear, they are usually gold or turquoise in color, with clouds floating above. In contrast, interiors were rarely depicted, or are only schematically represented in excessive ornamental detail.

Brosh and Milstein speak of the use of Biblical stories in Islamic literary works, when they write:

> Biblical stories, called in Arabic, *Isra'iliyaat*, meaning "Israelite Legends," are found in various literary contexts. The most significant of these are the religious works, first and foremost, the Koran, followed by the commentaries the Koran, the *hadith* (oral tradition.) Islamic historiography, and other works which have formed

part of the Islamic historical narrative, especially *Qisas al-Anbiya* (Stories of the Prophets.) These stories are also found in historical manuscripts, mystical writings, and Islamic poetry, particularly Persian and Turkish verse and epic narratives.[1]

Brosh and Milstein continue their analysis:

> The Koran, the Islamic Holy Book which serves as the foundation for all other writings containing stories from the Bible, is devoted primarily to the prophetic revelations and religious ideas of Muhammad. As a consequence of this, and because it is not an historical book, biblical stories appear throughout the Koran in an allusive, segmented, and piecemeal fashion, with little regard for chronology or any other rational order. The only story to be awarded a full chapter of its own is the story of Joseph. Tales from the Bible are used as a means of promoting moral teachings. Moreover, it is not the particular events which are important, but the characters. The creation of the world, for example, becomes the story of Adam and Eve, the story of the flood—the story of Noah, and the exodus from Egypt—the story of Moses.[2]

The Qur'an tells us that Allah sent separate prophets to every nation on earth:

> For every nation there is a Messenger, and when that Messenger is to come
> The matter is decided between them equitably, and then no one is wronged.[3]

The Qur'an does not give a definitive account of the number of these apostles or messengers, but subsequent ahadith have assessed that the number reaches a total of 125,000. The Holy Book of Islam gives the

---

1. Na'ama Brosh and Rachel Milstein, *Biblical Stories in Islamic Painting*. (Jerusalem: The Israel Museum, 1991) p. 11. In preparation of preparing this appendix, we have consulted the following: S. Anderson, "The Whirling and Howling Dervishes," *Muslim World*. Vol. 13, pp. 181–192; T. W. Arnold, *The Old and New Testaments in Muslim Religious Art*. (London, 1932); T.W. Arnold, *Painting in Islam*. (New York: 1965.); E. J. Grube, *Islamic Painting From the 11th to the 18th Century in the Collection of Hans P. Kraus*. (New York: 1972.); D. James, *Islamic Masterpeices of the Chester Beatty Library*. (London, 1981.); A. U. Pope, *A Survey of Persian Art*. (London, 1938.); J. Spenser and Trimingham, *The Sufi Orders in Islam*. (Oxford: Oxford University Press, 1971,); C. A. Storey, *Persian Literature* (London, 1927–1958.); and D. Talbot-Rice, *The Illustrations to the World History of Rashid al-Din*. (Edinburgh, 1976.)

2. Ibid.

3. The Qur'an 10:47 (author's translation).

names of 28 prophets, but some of these are mentioned without any other identifiable details. The first on this list is Adam, and the last is the prophet Muhammad. All of these characters, with the exception of Salih and Hud, are familiar from the Old and New Testaments. Ironically, some of the most revered prophets in ancient Judaism—Isaiah, Jeremiah, and Ezekiel for examples—are not mentioned at all in the Qur'an.

A number of Biblical tales appear in the Qur'an in an altered, or sometimes even confused, rendition. In the story of Moses, for example, Haman is given the role of the Pharaoh's vizier and military leader (40:24.) Miriam, Moses' sister, reappears in the Qur'an as the mother of Jesus (19:28.) This phenomena may be the result of the combination of legends from Jewish, Christian, and other ancient sources, or they may simply be a misunderstanding of these sources.

The random nature of presenting Biblical figures in the Qur'an made it necessary for Qur'anic commentaries to fill in a lot of the gaps. Commentators often expanded the Biblical narratives and sometimes introduce new narrative details, not found in the Biblical accounts.

One of the most important of Qur'anic commentators was the 9th century historian and learned scholar, Al-Tabari who lived most of his life in Baghdad. His commentary on the Qur'an entitled *Jami' al-Bayan fi Tafsir al-Qur'an*, usually abbreviated as the *Tafsir* stands out as the most important of his many works. The text represents the first compendium of traditional commentaries on the Qur'an. The *Tafsir* stood as a model for subsequent interpreters.

Biblical stories constitute a relatively small segment of narratives in the Qur'an and subsequent hadith. Nevertheless, a unique literary genre developed from the *Isra'iliyaat* stories in combination with similar tales from Christianity and other sources. Works of this new genre were given the title *Qisas al-Anbiya*, or "Stories of the Prophets." The *Qisas* tales are based on the Qur'an, but some of them do not have ant references in the Holy Book. The tales of Seth and his descendants, the quarrel between Esau and Jacob, and the stories of Joshua, Jeremiah, and others, also became part of this new genre.

The two most important authors of this new literary genre are Ibrahim al-Tha'labi and Muhammad ibn 'Abd Allah Al-Kisa'i. Another version of the *Qisas* was written by a Persian named Nishupuri. For the most part, these tales deal with the development of monotheism and subsequent believers from the time of Adam to that of Jesus, Mary, and John the Baptist. It also includes the stories of Hud and Sahah who, according to the *Qisas*, lived between the time of Noah and Abraham. Tha'labi also brings in other characters and historical or pseudo-historical events from later periods in Islam as well.

In the late Middle Ages, secular historical works began to appear, with the primary task of immortalizing the authors' patrons—the Turkish rulers. These texts followed the model of Tabari. They often begin with the story of the creation of the world and Adam and Eve, and then generally proceed to several accounts of some prophets. Generally, they give an account of the life and teachings of Muhammad, and go on to tell the history of Islam up to their own times.

The most important of these works is the historical text written by Rashid Al-Din entitled *Jami' al-Tawarikh*, or "The History of the World." Rashid Al-Din was a converted Jew born in Hamdan in the mid-13th century. He was vizier and palace historian for the Mongol ruler, Ghazan Khan. He understood his task as updating the history of the Mongols. When he completed it, he was also commissioned to compose a general history of the world.

Another important figure in this historical genre was Hafiz i-Abru of Heart who lived in the 15th century under Timurid rule. Abru was close to the Persian sultan, Shah Rukh, and completed a first rate history of the Shah's court. Abru also wrote a history of the world called *Majama' al-Tawarikh,* or "The Assembly of Histories," which was actually a synthesis of earlier historical works. A third famous historian was named Luqman, a late 16th century court historian for Sultan Murad III who ruled Ottoman Turkey in the late part of the century. Luqman's most famous work was the *Zubdat al-Tawarikh*, or "Cream of History." It gives an account of what Luqman saw as the historical high lights of the history of the world to his own time.

A final practitioner of this historical genre of writing was the 16th century Sufi author named Mirkhwand, who wrote a work entitled, *Rawdat al-Safa'*, "Ther Garden of Purity." It is a history composed in seven volumes, and it deals primarily with the history of the prophets and rulers prior to the advent of Islam. All of these works were illustrated, with the exception of Tabari, and they greatly influenced the development of subsequent illustrated Biblical and Qur'anic narratives.

OLD TESTAMENT ILLUSTRATIONS IN ISLAMIC ART

There is a great variety of Hebrew Bible illustrated figures in Islam. Among Old Testament figures are Adam and Eve, Abraham and the sacrifice of his son, Joseph and Zulailha, Moses and the Torah, and Jonah and his fish. In Islamic art between the 13th and 16th century, each of these figures is depicted in characteristic scenes, each having several peculiar to them.

It is difficult to find any representations of Adam and Eve before the 16th century. The Qur'an tells us that from the moment of Adam's birth, he was endowed with knowledge that was superior to the angels who were ordered by Allah to prostrate themselves before the first man. Iblis or Shaytan refused to bow down claiming that he was created from fire, while Adam was made from clay. (27:49.) This scene is often found in Islamic art. One example is "The Angels Kneeling Before Adam," in a manuscript entitled *The Stories of the Prophets*, owned by the Topkapi Saray Museum in Istanbul. [H1227, fol. 11a.] Another image of Adam and Eve frequently illustrated in Moslem art is the banishing of the two from Paradise. A fine example of this scene is in a version of the *Stories of the Prophets*, completed around 1575 and owned by the Topkapi Saray Museum in Istanbul. [B250, fol. 36a.]

Two principal scenes from the Qur'anic life of Abraham (Ibrahim) are often depicted in Islamic art. The first of these is Abraham and the Fire. This image was popularized in Islamic painting by the 14th century Persian Schools Milstein, Ruhrdanz and Schmitz describe the scene:

> It depicts Ibrahim's confrontations with Namarud (Nimrod), one of the greatest kings in the history of the world and an archetypical infidel enemy of God, Namrud was said to be the king of Babylon, perhaps the same person as Dahhak, the monstrous usurper of the Persian throne in the Iranian epics. This king, feeling threatened by the monotheistic teaching of Ibrahim, decided to inflict on him an ordeal of a huge fire. But the prophet comes out of the scene unharmed by the blaze.[4]

One example of Ibrahim in the fire can be seen in manuscript own by the Staatsbibliothek in Berlin. [Ms. Diez A, fol. 3.] This is a late 10th century manuscript. Abraham emerges from the fire being greeted by an angel, most likely Jibril (Gabriel.) The most ubiquitous scene of Abraham's

---

4. Rachel Milstein, Karin Ruhrdanz, and Barbara Schmitz, *Stories of the Prophets*. (Costa Mesa: Mazda Press, 1999.) p. 118.

depicted in Islamic art is the prophet and the sacrifice of his son, Ishmael. In most of these images, Ishmael kneels before his father who stands behind the son, a sharp knife usually poised over the father's head. One good example of this genre is a 16th manuscript owned by Columbia University. [Ms. X892.8 Q/Q1.]

Another illustration of the same scene is an image in a manuscript owned by the French National Library in Paris. [Pers. 54.] A third example of Ibrahim about to sacrifice his son in Islamic art is a 15th century manuscript owned by the Topkapi Saray Museum in Istanbul. [E.H. 1430.] In this image, Ishmael kneels in the center of the picture. A flowering tree separates him from his father who holds a knife poised over his head. In an upper register, an angel, probably Jibril, is about to descend to break up the sacrifice.

The figures of the prophet Joseph is depicted in Moslem art in a variety of scenes, including being rescued from the pit; Joseph appearing before the Egyptian ladies who slice off their hands instead of fruit; Joseph reunited with his father Jacob; Joseph enthroned and entertained by the women of the palace; Joseph among the Ishmaelites after being raised from the pit; and many others. One image that incorporates many of these episodes is a 19th century wool carpet from Tehran. In the center of the carpet are four scenes from Joseph's life. Brosh and Milstein describe them this way:

> Joseph and Jacob reunited in Paradise; Joseph being lifted from the
> pit; the court women of Egypt overcome by Joseph's beauty; and
> the meeting between Joseph, Jacob, and the brothers.[5]

Two good depictions of Joseph and the Court Women are in a 19th century Iranian manuscript, and another manuscript completed in Isfahan in the Qajar style, also from the 19th century. The first is owned by Mr. Elghanayan of New York City. The other is a manuscript owned by the British Museum. [Ms. 77.44.1096.] A fine depiction of "Joseph Hosting His Brothers," is a late 18th century Isfahan manuscript. Brosh and Milstein describe the depiction of Joseph this way:

> Joseph sits on a majestic throne surrounded by Egyptian servants.
> In front of him and toward the bottom of the picture are the broth-
> ers donning turbans. The food presented to the guests is depicted

5. Brosh and Milstein, p. 60.

in great detail. Distinguishable items include the 'pilaf" and the "shish-kebob" served on Chinese porcelain trays.[6]

Other images of Joseph include: the appointment of Joseph as Grand Vizier of Egypt; the aged Zulaikha arriving at Joseph's palace; and Joseph appearing in Zulaikha's dream. A 16th century manuscript owned by the Benkaim Collection in Los Angeles, contains an image of Joseph appointed Vizier. The same manuscript has an image of the aged Zulaikha; [Qazvin 1581.] The Benkaim Collection also owns a Mogul style Indian image, completed in Bengal around 1750.

Rachel Milstein points out the importance of the Prophet Yusuf for Sunni Moslems:

> Although not recognized by the Shiites, Yusuf is highly regarded by Sunni Muslims. In general, the Koranic version follows the biblical story, though only the names of Jacob and Joseph are mentioned. Conversely, the Koranic story embraces new motifs, most of which were devised from Jewish sources. Islamic legend introduced further details, designed to emphasize the meaning of the story and accent its moral teachings.[7]

Milstein continues her analysis of these new features:

> Joseph's ordeal is repeated several times in the literature of Islamic commentaries, in which he is described both as a youth who refused to yield to the advances of the Egyptian heroine (later called Zulaikha) and a prisoner who taught the belief of one God (the Koran). The commentators on the Koran, like the Midrash, linked Joseph's disregard for the woman's seduction to her idol worship: "She dragged him from room to room and from chamber to chamber until she stood him upright in his bed. Her idol was placed above her and she took a sheet and covered the idol's face."[8]

Historian Rashid al-Din interprets the story this way:

> Joseph asked Potiphar's wife, "Are you not afraid of God on the Last Day?" But she, who did not believe in God, laughed at him and said: "Today you are our slave and must behave according to our beliefs."[9]

6. Ibid., p. 67.
7. Milstein, p. 32.
8. Ibid.
9. Ibid., pp. 32–33.

Milstein concludes her analysis of the Prophet Joseph:

> The clash between Joseph and Zulaikha is represented in these texts as a confrontation between two religions: the religion of Joseph, prophet of God, and paganism. Seen in context, Joseph was thrown into the pit and sent off to Egypt in order to spread the true religion, which he continued to do even after becoming Grand Vizier.[10]

The figure of Moses has also been popular as the subject of Moslem religious art. Among the most popular scenes of the life and times of Moses in Islamic art are: Moses mother hiding him in the bulrushes; Moses rod changing into a dragon so that it might threaten Pharaoh; and Pharaoh and his army drown in the Red Sea. One fine example of Moses being hidden by his mother is a 17th century Persian manuscript owned by the British Library.[O.S. 3791.0.77]. Two good depictions of Moses staff turning into a dragon are to be seen in a 17th century Iranian text owned by the British Library [591.69.] and an 18th century Isfahan manuscript in the Qajar style. [O.S. 4018.10.77.]

Milstein describes the latter image this way:

> This painting portrays the dramatic moment in which Moses' rod is transformed into a dragon. Those present seem both stunned and terror-stricken, as they fearfully back away from the frightening animal. In order to emphasize the panic, the artist painted overturned chairs strewn across the floor of the room.[11]

Nearly all the images of the Prophet Yunus (Jonah) in Islamic art show the prophet either being swallowed by the fish or being spewed out from the belly of the beast. Similarly, all images of the Prophet Ayyub (Job) depict the holy man in his restored state. Three examples of Yunus and the fish, which are discussed in an earlier chapter, are: "Jonah and the Fish," *Rawdat al-Safa*, owned by the Israel Museum in Jerusalem. [No. 903, fol. 69.]; "Jonah About to Be Thrown into the Sea," from a 17th century Persian religious poem owned by the British Museum. [O.S. 3798.9.80.]; and "Jonah and the Fish," from *The Garden of Purity* an early 17th century work by Mirkhwand, also owned by the British Museum.[903.69.]

10. Ibid., p. 34.

11. Rachel Milstein, *Miniature Painting in Ottoman Baghdad*. (Costa Mesa: Mazda Press, 1990.) p. 15.

Three examples of the Prophet Ayyub, with the angel Jibril and the healing stream are also mentioned in a previous chapter. Among these Islamic Job images are the following:"Job Bathing in the Miraculous Stream," from the *Collected Works* of Sa'di, a late 16th century Iranian artist; "Job Recovering From His Troubles," in a 16th century manuscript owned by the Topkapi Museum in Istanbul. [H1227.]; and the depiction of Ayyub is a 16th century manuscript owned by the New York Public Library. [Ms 46, fol. 109.]

NEW TESTAMENT FIGURES IN ISLAMIC ART

Brosh and Milstein describe the uses and extent of New Testament figures in Moslem illustrations:

> Jesus, like Moses and Muhammad, is considered a prophet who delivered a written law to his nation. Yet compared to the religious personae from the Old Testament, Islamic literature devotes only a modest role to him, possibly because of his divine status in Christian doctrine.[12]

Brosh and Milstein go on to point out that depictions of Jesus in Islam are devoted to "two main episodes, his birth and his execution."[13] In Islamic portrayals of Jesus' death, he is usually depicted as dying by hanging from a rope, rather than being crucified. One fine example of this theme is the 16th century Turkish manuscript owned by the Topkapi Saray Museum in Istanbul. [H1227.] In the center of the image, Isa's 'substitute" hangs from the gallows. Six male figures and one female surround the execution scene. Another fine example of the same theme is "Isa's Substitute Hanging on the Gallows," in which the prophet hangs by a rope around his neck. His hands are tied behind his back, and several men pull the other end of the rope which has been thrown over top of the frame of the gallows. Jesus is surrounded by a dozen or so apostles. In the upper register, six other prophets, or perhaps angels, look down on the scene from the heavens. The manuscript is owned by the Staatsbibliothek in Berlin, and dates from around 1575. [Ms. Diez A, fol. 3.]

Frequently in Moslem art, Jesus is depicted with his mother Maryam. Two good examples of Mary and Jesus are "Mary, the Infant Jesus, and

12. Brosh and Milstein, p. 40.
13. Ibid.

John," from an early 19th century Persian manuscript owned by Mr. Elghanayan of New York City. Rachel Milstein describes the piece:

> In this work, Mary holds Jesus on her lap as John offers him an apple and amuses him. The red rose that Mary grasps is a common feature of paintings of the virgin, symbolizing death to martyrdom. Here the Persian painter depicts only part of Mary's traditional dress: a red frock and a scarf.[14]

The other image, "Mirror Depicting Mary, the Infant Jesus, and Female attendants," is also an early 19th century Iranian image. Mary sits with the baby Jesus on her lap in the center of the image. She is dressed in a red frock, blue cloak, and a scarf. In a lower register four young women attend to the virgin. A third Moslem depiction of the "Annunciation and Flight into Egypt," can be seen in an 18th century Persian pen box, owned by the British Museum. [742.69.] On the cover, Maryam kneels before an altar, while five angels appear to be blessing her. At her side is a vase with a lily, symbolizing the purity that is usually identified with the figure.

On the side of this same pen box, is a scene from the flight into Egypt. Maryam sits atop a donkey, with the baby Isa in her arms. The donkey is being led by Yusuf who holds the reins in his right hand. In his left hand, he holds a walking stick.

Another image on an Iranian pen box depicts Yah Yah (John the Baptist) baptizing his cousin Isa (Jesus.) Jesus stands on a platform by the side of the river, while above, John pours water on the prophet's head. This pen box is also owned by the British Museum and dates from the late 18th or early 20th century. [749.69.]

Another image of the Nativity is in a manuscript owned by the Keir Collection in London. The text is signed by a scribe named Muhammad Zaman. In the image, Mary sits beneath a flowering tree, the baby Jesus swaddled on her lap. A miraculous stream lies at her knees. Occasionally there are depictions in the history of Moslem art of the prophet Muhammad's nativity, though they never seem to involve Muhammad speaking just after birth, or talking with his mother while still in the womb.

Other scenes sometimes depicted in the life of Jesus are: the Annunciation; the Ascension; and Jesus performing miracles. A good example of the Annunciation is an early 17th century Mongol manuscript,

14. Ibid, p. 119.

owned by the Benkaim Collection in Los Angeles. In this image a female angel descends from the clouds to make her announcement, while Mary and Joseph wait below with out-stretched arms. The pair is surrounded by sheep.

A 17th century Iranian manuscript owned by the British Museum contains a depiction of Jesus Performing a Miracle." Jesus is in the center of the image. His right hand passes over a box that sits beneath him on the ground. He is surrounded by ten of the apostles, kneeling and gazing at the action of Jesus. Another miraculous event concerning Jesus sometimes depicted in Islamic art is the illustration of the prophet speaking to a crowd immediately after his birth. One striking version of this theme is Jesus being held by his mother in a field of ripe fruit, while a number of other figures, including the prophet Muhammad, have assembled to listen to the child. One manuscript owned by the Topkapi Saray Museum in Istanbul, depicts the talking Jesus with his mother, while others watch and listen.

Jesus' Ascension is depicted in an early 17th century Indian manuscript done in the Mongol style. The text is owned by the Benkaim Collection in Los Angeles. Rachel Milstein describes the image:

> In the picture, Jesus is standing on a crescent, which is borne by a cloud. He holds a New Testament in one hand and a globe with a cross on it in the other. A halo of light breaks through from a kind of niche behind Jesus; encircling him and before him are two groups of angels, while Seraphs and cherubs hover above.[15]

The Qur'an 18:8–25 contains another lengthy tale from the New Testament. It is generally called "The Seven Sleepers of Ephesus." One fine depiction of the scene is in another 16th century Iranian text, also owned by the Benkaim Collection in Los Angeles. Again, Brosh and Milstein describe the image:

> The story which is told at length in the Koran (18: 8–25) involves seven young Christian men from well respected families who were in the service of Emperor Decius. The young men fled the Emperor's palace in order to avoid serving pagan idols and found shelter in a cave. On their way, a dog followed them. When they

---

15. Ibid, p. 120.

attempted to get rid of it, the dog told them in human speech that he was also a believer in God.[16]

Brosh and Milstein continue their analysis:

> Then they decided to allow the dog to remain with them in the cave. After some time, the young men fall asleep. In the meantime, the Emperor sent his treasurer, a secret believer in Christianity, to pursue the seven and deliver them to the palace. The treasurer returned and reported that all seven had died of starvation. Decius ordered the treasurer to seal up the opening of the cave. According to the Koran, after three hundred years, a Christian king ascended the throne and the seven young men awoke. After they awoke, the seven climbed out of the cave and went to the nearest city. There, another miracle occurred, for they managed to pay for their meal with an outdated coin.[17]

There are a number of Moslem depictions of this scene of the Seven Sleepers of Ephesus. The earliest written texts are found in the writings of 5th and 6th century Syrian writers called the Monophysites. The seven became martyrs in the Orthodox Church, The tale is called "The Shrine of the Seven Sleepers "in a pilgrimage guide by Emperor Theodosius who visited Ephesus in 539 CE.

There was a burial church built in a natural cave on the edge of Mount Pion (Panayir.), to the north of the city of Ephesus in modern Turkey. It is known as the "Seven Sleepers Grotto." After the building of the church, the site became a cemetery, where only the holiest were buried. This Islamic version of the tale is probably why Sura 18 is called "The Cave."

By 16th century India and 17th century Iran, the Holy Family is frequently portrayed in Islamic art. These paintings, which often show Maryam, Isa, and the angels, are often copied from European models, particularly artists from France and Italy. In some cases, the Moslem artist would combine different iconographic scenes in a single painting, perhaps due to a lack of understanding of the Christian sources. Because of this phenomenon, it is sometimes difficult to identify the exact subject matter of these scenes.

In a manuscript owned by the Edinburgh University Library [Ms. Arab 20, fol. 42a.] a man sits in a tower watching Isa riding a donkey

16. Ibid, p. 122.
17. Ibid., p. 41.

and Muhammad riding a camel, according to a prophecy in the Book of Isaiah.

One final New Testament image in Islamic art is an illustration of the Dajjal (the Anti-Christ) entering Jerusalem under the guise of being Isa. This image was originally a part of the dispersed *Fal-nama*, and is now owned by the Collection of Edwin Binney 3rd.[18]

BIBLICAL FIGURES IN SUFI ART

S. A. Nigosian, in his book, *World Religions*, gives us an introduction to the Sufi Movement when he writes:

> The mystical movement in Islam is known as Sufism. The origins of the term *Sufi* is complex, but the word is generally connected to the wearing of an undyed garment made of wool. (Arabic *Suf.*) Initially, Muslims wore such garments as a mark of personal penitence. Later wool garments became the regular uniform of Sufis.[19]

The Sufi Movement emerged with this strict form of asceticism as a reaction to more ritualistic and legalistic tendencies in Islam. Groups of ascetics began to meet together to recite together the Qur'an, and those recitations evolved into a liturgical form with a center of mystical love or union with Allah. Eventually, the Sufis were branded heretics by traditional Muslims. The friction between the legalists and the Sufis culminated in the execution of the Sufi saint al-Hallaj (ca. 857–922) in Baghdad in the early 9th century.

We have seen that Jesus' birth, baptism, and execution have often been the subject of Turkish and Persian religious art. These topics were not treated with prominent emphasis in Sufi literature. Where Islamic mystical painters have devoted much attention, however, is to two other episodes in the life of the prophet. The first of these is the notion of Jesus throwing a stone at Shaytan or Iblis. The other is the tale of the Last Supper. Another scene that appears among the Sufi painters is the ability of Jesus to see the beauty and the good in every object of creation, a level of consciousness that the Sufi mystic would aspire to attain. Mirkhwand's *Rawdat al-Safa'* tells the following tale:

---

18. Brosh and Milstein, p. 127.

19. S. A. Nigosian, *World Religions*. (Boston: Bedford-Saint Martin's Press, 2008.) p. 434.

One day, when Jesus was walking with his students in the bazaar, he saw the cadaver of a dog thrown into the garbage. One after another the students expressed their horror and repugnance. Yet Jesus was able to call their attention to the dead dog's teeth, which glittered like a string of pearls.[20]

This story recurs in a number of illustrations of Persian poetry, especially manuscripts of the *Khamsa* by Nizami Ganjevi, a 12th century Azerbaijanian poet who was the foremost practitioner of the romantic epic in Moslem poetry. Ganjevi is the author of five long poems known collectively as the *Khamsa*, or 'Quintet." It is also known as the *Panj Ganj*, or 'Five Treasures."

Various manuscripts that illustrate Nizami's poems contain illustrations of the Moslem prophets. One of these manuscripts is owned by the Topkapi Saray Museum in Istanbul [R875.] Another is a copy of the *Khamsa*, illustrated in Qazwin in the 1570s. This manuscript is owned by the Pierpont Morgan Library in New York.[M 836.][21]

CONCLUSIONS

In this appendix our major goal was to show that many of the fundamental theological conclusions we have come to in this book are exhibited in the art of Islam. Among these are the special status of Joseph and Jesus; the notion that Jesus was not crucified in the Islamic faith; the fact that the angels were asked to bow down to Adam in Islam, but Shaytan refuses; that Abraham was thrown into a fire by King Nimrod's men, and he does not burn; that Joseph is put on display for the women of the Egyptian Court; that Job's wounds were healed and a miraculous stream that Allah caused to come forth through the actions of the angel Gabriel; and many others.

Like the Qur'an itself, Islamic art sometimes diverges from narratives related in the Biblical materials. For the most part, the Qur'an, as well as the art of Islam, follows the Biblical accounts closely; but Islamic art also makes a number of fundamental statements that are at theological odds with the Old and New Testaments. The judgments we have made throughout this book are, for the most part, the same judgments made by Persian and Turkish artists in the history of Islam.

20. Milstein, p. 40.

21. Ibid., p. 73 and p. 32.

Arabic-English Glossary

Abbasids: The second dynasty of Sunni Islam, based in Baghdad from 750 to 1258 C.E.

Abd: A loving servant of Allah.

Abd: Friend; slave; creature.

Abdallah: Male name for a servant of Allah.

Adhan: The call to prayer before each *salat*.

Ahl al-Bayt: Muhammed's family.

Ahwal: A higher state of being in the Sufi tradition.

Akhira: Survival after death; the afterlife.

Ale Fi'ron: The Pharaoh.

Alim: An Islamic scholar.

Al-Andalus: The Arabic name for Spain.

Amâhah: the trust of the earth given by God to man as having delegated authority over nature

Ansar: The first ground of Islamic followers in Madina (Medina).

Aqiq: A ceremony after the seventh day of birth.

Abkarun: Youths.

Asbab al-nuzul: The occasion of a revelation that appears in the Qur'an.

Ashura: A day of celebration to celebrate the martyrdom of Imam Husayn.

Asrur ut-tanzil wa asrar ut-ta ta'wil: "The secrets of revelation, the secrets of interpretation."

Awra: The allurement of a woman.

Aya: A sign or a verse in the Qur'an.

Ayat Allah: A sign of Allah.

Ayatollah: Literally, "a sign of God." The highest level of religious scholar in Shiite Islam.

Ayyub: Job.

Ba'ya: A bond of faith.

Baainat: Proof.

Banu Israel: The people of Israel.

Baqa: Sunni term for faith in Allah.

Baraka: A blessing from Allah.

Barzakh: Life in the grave between death and resurrection.

Basmala: The Arabic expression, *Bism' Allah al-Rahman al-Ramin.* "In the name of the Merciful and Compassionate."

Batini: An esoteric or hidden interpretation of the Qur'an.

Bohras: A branch of Shiite Moslems.

Al-Baruq: The hound that carried Muhammed on his night journey.

Caliph: Traditional leader of Sunni Islam.

Daff: A drum.

Da'i: Someone who makes *da'wa.*

Da'if: A hadith with a weakness.

Al-Dajaal: The Anti-Christ; the great imposter who will lead the forces of evil in the last days.

Dar al-Har: the areas of mankind as yet subdued to Islam; the house of war, or struggle unto Islamization

Dar al-Islam: the house of Islam, the geographical realm of true domain of Muslim faith and practice; the territory in which Islam is in full devotional, political, and legal actuality

Daud: David.

Da'wa: An invitation for non-Moslems to follow the faith.

Dervish: A Sufi holy-man; a mystic.

Dhikr: A remembrance of Allah in the heart.

Dhimmas: Literally, "protected people"; the status in Islam given to Jews and Christians.

Dhimmi: a non-Muslim subject under Islamic rule, in one of the tolerated minorities: subject to special taxes in lieu of *Zakat*

Din al-fitra: The God-given way of life.

Djinn: Alternative spelling for jinns.

Djuraydj: Carpenter.

Du'a: An informal prayer.

Eid: Alternative spelling of *'Id.*

Fakudh: The daughter of Elizabeth.

Fana: Dying to oneself in Sufi mysticism.

Faqih: An Islamic scholar of law.

Faqir: A Sufi who embraces a life of simplicity and poverty.

Fard: A moral obligation.

Fard-kifiya: An obligation discharged by a group of Moslems.

Fatihah: title of the opening Sura of the Qur'an, being "the Opener" of the book.

Fatima: Daughter of Muhammed.

Fatwa: A learned opinion of law.

Figh: The science of law.

Ghayba: The hidden existence of the twelfth Imam.

Ghul: Ghost.

Ghusl: A ritual bath.

Hadd: A punishment prescribed by the Qur'an.

Hadith: A tradition of Muhammed; something the prophet said, taught, or did.

Hadith qudsi: Sayings from Allah given to Muhammed that were not part of the Qur'an.

Hafiz: Title given to a female who has memorized the Qur'an.

Hajj: The annual pilgrimage to Makka (Mecca).

Al-Hajj: Title given to a male who has completed the hajj.

Al-Hajjah: Title given to a female who has completed the hajj.

Halal: Something compulsory in Islam.

Hamd: Praised.

Al-hamdu li 'llah: "All praise (or thanks) to God."

Hanif: A seeker; a monotheist in search of deeper learning; an idolater.

Haqa'iq: Spiritual truths known only to the few.

Haram: A forbidden action.

Hasan: A beautiful and reliable hadith.

Hasur: Chaste.

Al-Hiwaya: The Abyss; one of the names for Hell.

Hijrah: The emigration of Muhammed and his community from Makka to Madina in 622 A.D., from which the Islamic calendar dates; the definitive crisis of Muhammed's career.

Hud: Virgin; the prophet Heber.

Al-Huda: The guidance of the Qur'an.

Hulul: Indwelling.

Al-Hutama: Literally "that which shatters"; one of the names for Hell.

Ibada: The worshipping of Allah.

Ibara: A literal interpretation of the Qur'an.

Id al-Adha: The festival of sacrifice commemorating Ibrahim's sacrifice of Ishmail.

Id al-Fitr: The festival of fast-breaking, ending Ramadan.

'Idda: A waiting period after divorce in which woman cannot remarry.

Id mubarak: "Happy Ending"; the fast is over.

Ifrit: Evil spirit.

Iftar: The light meal with which Ramadan is broken.

Ihram: Two sheets used by men for clothing on the Hajj.

Ihsan: To live under the watchfulness of Allah.

Ijma: A consensus, or converging, of approval; the means whereby the Muslim community in Sunni Islam serves to identify loyal development in Islamic law and usage.

Ijtihad: An intellectual struggle to solve a problem.

Ilham: Divine inspiration.

Ilm al-Kalam: Theology.

Imam: Infallible leader of Shiite Islam.

Imam: The person who leads the congregation in *salat*.

Imam Khatib: A scholar who addresses the congregation at Friday prayer.

Iman: Faith or belief.

Imram: Father of Mary.

Inabat: A station of the Sufi way.

Infaq: The economic principle of the circulation of wealth.

Injil: The revelation sent to Jesus.

Iqra: Recite.

Ishba: Elizabeth.

Isnad: The chain of transmitters of hadith.

Idras: Enoch.

Ishaq: Isaac.

Isa: Jesus.

Isra: The miraculous journey of Muhammed from Mecca to Jerusalem.

Jahannam: Literally, "the depths"; one of the names for Hell.

Jahiliyyah: the time of ignorance in Arabia, preceding Islam, sometimes over-darkened, the ignorance involves an element of unruliness or uncouthness. Cf. the biblical "forward."

Al-Jahim: Literally "the place for idolaters"; another name for Hell.

Jalut: Goliath.

Al-Janna: A garden; Paradise; Heaven.

Jibril: Arabic name for Gabriel.

Jihad: Struggle on the path of Allah.

Jinn: Spiritual creatures.

Jizya: A tax paid by Christians and Jews in Islamic lands.

Kafir: A non-believer; a liar.

Ka'ba: Building in the center of Mecca said to have been built by Ibrahim and Ishmail.

Kalimah: the word or title given to the *Shahadah*, or confession: "There is no god but God; Muhammed is the apostle of God."

Kasp: acquisition: the view of a leading theologian, Al-Asha'ari, purporting to reconcile Divine disposition with human responsibility, through the formula: "God wills it *in* the will of the doer, who thus acquires the deed."

Khalil Ullah: A friend of Allah.

Kiswa: A black cloth that covers the Ka'ba.

Koran: Another spelling of Qur'an.

Lawh I Ayyub: The tablet of Job.

Lazla: Literally "the Great Furnace." Another name for Hell.

Lut: Lot.

Madhhab: A school of law.

Madras: An Islamic school.

Mahabba: The highest state of being in the Sufi tradition.

Al-Mahdi: The Messiah.

Mahr: A dowry.

Manno-O-Salwa: Mana in the desert.

Maryam: Mary.

Midyan: The Medianites.

Mikael: Michael.

Millat-e-Ibrahim: The religion of Abraham.

Miraj: Muhammed's night journey.

Misih: The Messiah.

Mithrad: A niche built into the qibla.

Minaret: A tower in which Moslems are called to prayer.

Misbah: Prayer beads.

Miswak: Tooth brush.

Mubah: A neutral act that carries neither reward nor punishment.

Muezzin: A person who calls Moslems to prayer.

Mufti: A recognized legal scholar.

Muhtasib: a superintendent, or inspector of ethical behavior, a spiritual accountant in the Muslim community.

Muhyi id-Din: Reviver of religion.

Musa: Moses.

Nabi: Prophet.

Nafs: The soul.

Al-Hajî 'an al-munka: the prohibition of evil, false, and reprehensible behavior.

Al-Nar: Literally, "the Fire." Another name for Hell.

Nasheed: A song of praise.

Nikah: Marriage ceremony.

Namrud: Nimrod.

Nar al-ihtiyal: The fire of guile.

Niyyah: Intention, the conscious focus of purpose that must precede all ritual acts in Islam.

Nuh: Noah.

Qadi: A judge.

Qamis: Shirt.

Qibla: The direction to pray in formal prayer.

Qurba: Sacrifice.

Radjim: Accursed.

Ramadan: Month of fasting.

Rasuliyyah: The apostolate of Muhammed, his dignity and duty both to proclaim and to vindicate the message from God.

Ra'y: Opinion or view (from the verb: to see) held or sponsored as a means to *Ijtihâd* and *Ijmâ* (q.v.); a source, under conditions, of adaptation of law.

Ribat: A Sufi center of spirituality.

Ridda: Apostasy.

Saaee: Effort or struggle.

Sabr: Patience.

Sadum: Sodom.

Sa'ir: Literally, "the blazing inferno." Another name for Hell.

Salam alaykum: Traditional Islamic greeting, "Peace be with you."

Salat: Required five-time daily prayer.

Saleh: Shelah.

Sama: Music.

Saqar: Literally, "scorching fire." Another name for Hell.

Saum: Fasting, particularly during the month of Ramadan: the fourth Pillar of Dîn; lasts the whole lunar month during the daylight hours.

Sayyid: A blood descendant of Muhammed.

Shahadah: Witness or confession, with intention, of *Kalimah* (q.v.). The first pillar of Islam.

Shahid: A martyr.

Shaytan: Another name for Iblis.

Shirk: To associate partners with Allah.

Shukr: Gratitude; to give thanks.

Siddik: The truth.

Sifat: An attribute of Allah.

Sila: Spirit.

Sira: The biography of Muhammed.

Subha: Another name for prayer beads.

Suf: Wool.

Suhuf: Leaves or scrolls.

Sunna: The way of life of Muhammed.

Sunni: The largest brand of Islam.

Sura: A chapter in the Qur'an.

Surah: An alternative spelling of Sura.

Suriya I Sabr: The city of patience.

Tafsir: Explanation or exegesis, of the Qur'an, involving Arabic grammar, study of *asbab-al nuzul* (q.v.) and erudition in tradition, allegory, abrogation, and commentary.

Taqwa: God consciousness.

Tariqh: History.

Tarwiz: A portion of the Qur'an written on parchment and contained in a leather pouch.

Taurat: The Torah.

Tawaf: Walking around the Ka'ba seven times as part of the Hajj.

Tawba: Forgiveness; repentance.

Tawhid: The absolute Oneness of Allah.

Tawil: An allegorical interpretation.

Ulama: A body of scholars.

Ulama: (pl. or *'alim*) doctors of theology or law, learned ones, the custodians of Islamic teachings.

Umayyads: The first dynasty of Sunni Islam, based in Damascus from 661 to 750.

Umma: The world-wide community of Islam.

Ummi: Unlettered, one of the people without Scriptures, or illiterate. See *al-nabî al-ummî*.

Wa laakin shubbiha lahum: "And so it was made to appear to them."

Wahy: Revelation. The receiving of revelation by Muhammed; the state of receptivity in which he received and communicated the Qur'an; revelation and inspiration are not here distinguished.

Wajib: A compulsory act.

Wali: Someone of outstanding piety.

Yaqub: Jacob.

Yah Yah: John the Baptist.

Yusuf: Joseph.

Zabur: The book sent to Daud; the Psalms.

Zahiri: The literalist school of interpretation.

Zakat: Ritual purification.

Zamzam: The miraculous spring discovered by Ishmael and Hagar.

Zaqqum: Forbidden tree in Hell.

Zulayka: Aziz's wife.

Zulm: Wrong-doing, or wrong dealing, the most fundamental Qur'anic term for sin.

Index of Biblical Passages

New Testament

Index of Passages in the Qur'an